Contents

ACKNOWLEDGMENTS 4
THE FLOWERS AT A GLANCE .5
INTRODUCTION 11
Gardening in the North 12
Zones Map 13
Perennial Gardens 16
Getting Started 19
   Light 20
   Soil 21
   Exposure 24
Preparing the Garden 25
   Composting 27
Selecting Perennials 29
Planting Perennials 32
   Bare-root Perennials 34
   Planters 34
Caring for Perennials 37
   Weeding 37
   Mulching 37
   Watering 39
   Fertilizing 40
   Grooming 40

Propagating Perennials 44
   Seeds 45
   Cuttings 49
   Division 54
Problems & Pests 57
   Pests, Diseases & What to Do ..60
   Pest Control Alternatives ...66
About This Guide 68
THE PERENNIALS 69
QUICK REFERENCE CHART ..338
GLOSSARY 344
INDEX 346

Acknowledgments

While researching and writing this book, I was reminded of the many good colleagues, great gardeners, patient industry professionals and wonderful organizations that have taught, corrected, steered and scolded me during my gleeful saunter down the gardening path. It would take a second book to name them all, but a few I'd like to acknowledge: garden writer Lynn Steiner; Mike and Jean Heger, proprietors of Ambergate Gardens, Victoria, Minnesota; the University of Minnesota College of Agricultural, Food and Environmental Sciences; the University of Minnesota Extension Service; and the Minnesota State Horticultural Society.

Special thanks to my coauthor, Don Williamson of Lone Pine Publishing, for his wise and patient indulgence. —Don Engebretson

Don Williamson thanks The Creator.

Both authors gratefully acknowledge the many photographers who provided photographs for this project and the gardeners who allowed them to photograph their private gardens.

The Flowers at a Glance

Pictorial Guide in Alphabetical Order

Ajuga
p. 70

Anemone
p. 74

Artemisia
p. 78

Aster
p. 82

Astilbe
p. 86

Baby's Breath
p. 90

Black-eyed Susan
p. 100

Balloon Flower
p. 94

Bergenia
p. 96

Bleeding Heart
p. 102

Boltonia
p. 106

Brunnera
p. 108

Bugbane
p. 110

Butterfly Weed
p. 112

Campanula
p. 114

Candytuft
p. 118

Cardinal Flower
p. 120

Catmint
p. 124

Chrysanthemum
p. 128

Clematis
p. 132

Columbine
p. 136

Coneflower
p. 140

Coreopsis
p. 142

Cornflower
p. 146

Daylily
p. 148

Delphinium
p. 152

Euphorbia
p. 156

Feverfew
p. 160

Foxglove
p. 166

Gaillardia
p. 170

Flax
p. 162

Foamflower
p. 164

Gas Plant
p. 172

Goat's Beard
p. 178

Goldenrod
p. 182

Globe Flower
p. 174

Globe Thistle
p. 176

Goutweed
p. 184

Hens and Chicks
p. 192

Heuchera
p. 194

Hardy Geranium
p. 186

Hollyhock
p. 198

Hosta
p. 202

Iris
p. 208

Jacob's Ladder
p. 212

Joe-Pye Weed
p. 214

Jupiter's Beard
p. 218

Lady's Mantle
p. 220

Lamb's Ears
p. 224

Lamium
p. 226

Liatris
p. 230

Ligularia
p. 232

Loosestrife
p. 236

Lungwort
p. 240

Lupine
p. 244

Lychnis
p. 248

Mallow
p. 250

Marguerite
p. 254

Meadow Rue
p. 256

Meadowsweet
p. 260

Monarda
p. 264

Monkshood
p. 268

Obedient Plant
p. 272

Oriental Poppy
p. 274

Ox-eye
p. 276

Pachysandra
p. 278

Pasqueflower
p. 280

Penstemon
p. 282

Peony
p. 286

Perennial Salvia
p. 290

Phlox
p. 294

Pincushion Flower
p. 298

Pinks
p. 300

Rose Mallow
p. 304

Russian Sage
p. 306

Shasta Daisy
p. 314

Solomon's Seal
p. 316

Sea Holly
p. 308

Sedum
p. 310

Speedwell
p. 318

Spiderwort
p. 322

Thyme
p. 324

Vinca
p. 330

Turtlehead
p. 328

Wild Ginger
p. 332

Yarrow
p. 334

Introduction

THE CLIMATE OF MINNESOTA AND WISCONSIN, WITH ITS reckless variance in temperature, can cause unusual challenges for gardeners. Up here, spring weather is pure nonsense—occasionally cool, sometimes damp, but just as often warm and dry from Easter on out. In summer, only one word describes the two states: hot. No, wait, two words, 'hot' and 'sticky,' and it's anyone's guess if a sweltering summer will proceed into a reasonably 'normal' fall or instead blister paint off houses from September until Halloween.

Yet our absurd climate offers perennial gardeners in Wisconsin and Minnesota some wonderful advantages. By design, perennials need downtime, which is something the Upper Midwest offers in abundance during winter. This dormancy period signals the end of perennial growth for one season, while providing the rest required for perennials to burst forth with fresh foliage and flowers in spring. Gardeners gain much solace from Minnesota and Wisconsin's seasonal disparity because a lot is possible here. If you yearn to garden in Florida or the Deep South or in Texas or Southern California, you'll have to do without such indispensable perennials as bearded irises, heucheras, peonies, delphiniums, hostas and dozens more. It's simply too hot, for too long, with too brief and mild a winter for many perennials to survive. Gardeners who are new to Minnesota and Wisconsin will enjoy the great variety of perennials they can grow.

Perennials are plants that take three or more years to complete their life cycle. This broad definition includes trees and shrubs. In this book, we use the term to refer to just herbaceous (non-woody) plants that live for three or more years. These perennials generally die back to the ground at the end of the growing season and start fresh with new shoots each spring. Some plants grouped with garden perennials do not die back completely; the sub-shrubs, such as Russian sage, fall into this category. Still others, such as pinks, remain green all winter.

Gardening in the North

GARDENING CONDITIONS IN A REGION ARE INFLUENCED BY TWO main factors: climate and soil. What follows is some important information about these two factors, but additional information is also available from a rich variety of resources around the two states. Individual growers, breeders, societies, schools, publications and public gardens provide information, encouragement and fruitful debate for the gardener. Outstanding garden shows, state and county fairs, public gardens, arboretums and private gardens attract crowds of people all year long. These events and organizations are sources of valuable information and as an added bonus, of inspiration, too.

Climate

'Will it grow here?' is perhaps the most important question that a gardener can ask about a perennial in Minnesota and Wisconsin. To answer that question, find out your United States Department of Agriculture (USDA) zone, which is the established hardiness zone that is based on the average lowest winter temperatures of a region. You can ask at your local nursery or ask a friend who is a more experienced gardener.

Wisconsin includes three hardiness zones: zone 3 in the north; a large area of zone 4 across the central portion of the state; and a balmy strip of zone 5 that runs north to south along the eastern border with Lake Michigan. Proximity to large bodies of water always affects winter low temperatures. The extreme northern tip of Wisconsin along Lake Superior is in zone 4. Yet, 80 miles to the south, the harsher zone 3 begins as the year-round warming effects of the lake dissipate.

Minnesota encompasses three hardiness zones as well. The approximate northern half of the state lies squarely in zone 3 but includes a very small patch of zone 2 around the Red Lake region. Roughly the southern half of Minnesota is assigned to zone 4 (zone map, p. 13).

Don't feel intimidated or limited by either the above information or by other details you'll find on climate zones or perennial hardiness indicators. Hardiness zone divisions are based strictly on the average lowest winter temperatures. A perennial's ability to live through winter is influenced by a mild or harsh winter, the heavy or light snow cover, the soil, the fall care and the overall health of the perennial. More than one perennial listed by the experts as hardy to zone 5 has turned out to like it just fine, thank you, 100 (or 300) miles farther north in zone 4.

Both states benefit from ample annual precipitation. Average annual precipitation averages 30" across Wisconsin, with slightly less in the extreme north and more in the extreme south. As might be expected, Minnesota averages about the same annual precipitation,

Hardiness Zones Maps

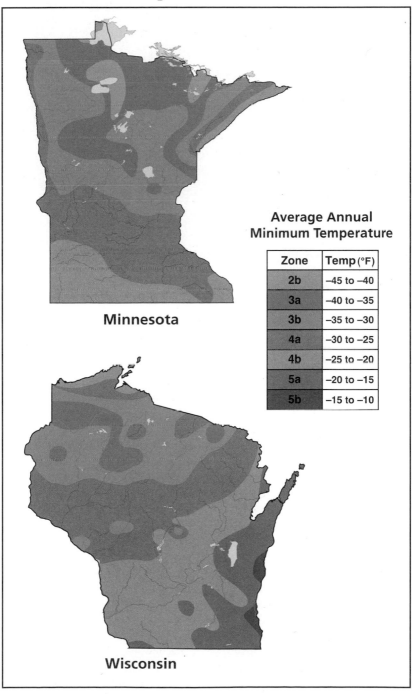

**Average Annual
Minimum Temperature**

Zone	Temp (°F)
2b	−45 to −40
3a	−40 to −35
3b	−35 to −30
4a	−30 to −25
4b	−25 to −20
5a	−20 to −15
5b	−15 to −10

Minnesota

Wisconsin

though it varies more widely across the state. The northwest corner of the state receives the least annual precipitation, just under 20". Precipitation increases in a diagonal line that slides across the state from the northwest to the southeast.

Microclimates & Soil

One exciting, and experimental, part of being a gardener is in the ability to create microclimates: small areas created by the topography in the garden that may be more or less favorable for growing different plants. Microclimates can be created, for example, in the shelter of a nearby building or stand of evergreen trees; in a low, still hollow; at the top of a barren, windswept hill; or by proximity to a large body of water. Microclimates that raise the zone level a notch give gardeners

almost anywhere in Minnesota and Wisconsin the possibility of growing the one perennial that everyone says won't grow here. The challenge of gardening with plants that are borderline hardy is part of the fun of growing perennials.

Of the many factors that affect one's ability to successfully grow a plant, soil type is the most important. Luckily, native soils left after glaciers crossed our region about 14,000 years ago are, in general, very good for all kinds of plants. Our soils are great for farming, as attested by the wide variety and extreme high quality of crops, livestock and dairy products produced by both states.

Soil characteristics vary greatly across Minnesota and Wisconsin. There are hundreds of soil types and distribution patterns. It's important for you to know the soil type of your property. You probably already know if your soil is sandy, heavy clay or predominantly loam. Taking what you have and amending it with organic matter is a step in the right direction. But first, take a step that is too often ignored by gardeners: have your soil tested.

For relatively little cost (about $10), the agricultural departments of the Universities of Minnesota and Wisconsin provide soil-testing services for homeowners. Contact your county university extension service to receive a soil-testing kit and directions on how to take and submit your sample. In usually less than two weeks, you will receive the results, which will give you exact specifications of your soil's pH, macronutrient content and percentage of organic material, in addition to directions on how to alter the soil's characteristics to better grow your perennials and other plants. University soil-testing gives more accurate, comprehensive results and better recommendations than the do-it-yourself soil-testing kits.

Many enthusiastic and creative people, both amateur and professional, are involved in gardening in Minnesota and Wisconsin. Perennials are relatively inexpensive and easy to share with friends and neighbors, and the more varieties you try, the more likely you will be to discover what variety loves to grow in your garden.

Our advice: 'Dig in and just grow for it!'

Perennial Gardens

PERENNIALS CAN BE INCLUDED IN ANY TYPE, SIZE OR STYLE OF garden. From the riot of color in a cottage garden, to the cool, soothing shades of green in a woodland garden, to a welcoming cluster of pots on a front doorstep, perennials open up a world of design possibilities for even the inexperienced gardener.

Perennials can stand alone in a garden or combine with other plants. They form a bridge between the permanent structure provided by trees and shrubs and the season-long, temporary color provided by annuals. Perennials often flower longer and grow to mature size more quickly than shrubs, and in many cases they require less care than annuals.

It is very important when planning your garden to decide what you like. If you enjoy the plants that are in your garden, you will be more likely to take proper care of them.

Visit garden centers to see the range of plants available and to discuss possibilities with the staff. Decide what style of garden you like. Think about the gardens you have most admired in your neighborhood, in books or while visiting friends. Use these ideas as starting points for planning your own garden.

A good perennial garden can be interesting throughout the growing season if you select perennials that bloom at different times all season. Each perennial entry in this book indicates blooming seasons; you will also find the Quick Reference Chart (pp. 338–43) handy when selecting plants that bloom at different times.

Consider the foliage. Leaves can be bold or dainty, coarse or refined; they can be large or small, light or dark; their color can vary from any multitude of greens to yellow, gray, blue, purple, silver, white or brown; and they can be striped, splashed, edged, dotted or mottled. Their surfaces can be shiny, fuzzy, silky, rough or smooth. The famous White Gardens at Sissinghurst, England, did not simply showcase a haphazard collection of white flowers. Rather, they were designed to remove the distraction of color and allow the eye to linger on the foliage, to appreciate its subtle appeal. Flowers may come and go, but a garden planned with careful attention to foliage will always be interesting.

As well, consider the size and shape of the perennials you choose. Use a variety of forms to make your garden more diverse. The size of your garden influences these decisions, but do not limit a small garden to small perennials or a large garden to large perennials. Use a balanced combination of plant sizes that are in scale with their specific location. (See individual entries and Quick Reference Chart, p. 338.)

We tend to focus on color because it is often the first thing we notice in a garden. Choose a variety of flower and foliage colors for your garden and keep in mind that different colors have different effects on our senses. Cool colors, such as blue, purple and green, are soothing and make small spaces seem bigger because they appear to move away

Ligularia anchors this well-designed mixed bed

from the viewer. Warm colors, such as red, orange and yellow, are more stimulating and appear to fill large spaces. White combines well with any color; plants that bloom in white help keep the garden from becoming a blurry, jangled mess. (See individual entries and Quick Reference Chart, p. 338.)

Textures can also create a sense of space. Large leaves are considered bold or coarse in texture. Their visibility from a greater distance makes spaces seem smaller and more shaded. Small leaves, or those that are finely divided, are considered fine in texture. They create a sense of greater space and light. Some gardens have been designed solely on the basis of texture.

Coarse-textured Perennials

- Bergenia
- Black-eyed Susan
- Coneflower
- Hosta
- Lamb's ears
- Ligularia
- Lungwort
- Meadowsweet
- Rose mallow
- Sedum 'Autumn Joy'

Ligularia

Fine-textured Perennials

- Astilbe
- Baby's breath
- Bleeding heart
- Columbine
- Coreopsis
- Hardy geranium
- Meadow rue
- Yarrow

Astilbe

Finally, decide how much time you will have to devote to your garden. With good planning and preparation, you can enjoy a relatively low-maintenance perennial garden. Try to use plants that perform well with little care and those that are generally pest and disease free.

Low-maintenance Perennials

- Aster
- Black-eyed Susan
- Coreopsis
- Daylily
- Euphorbia
- Heuchera
- Hosta
- Monarda*
- Pincushion flower
- Pinks
- Russian sage
- Shasta daisy

may become invasive

Russian sage

Getting Started

ONCE YOU HAVE SOME IDEAS ABOUT WHAT YOU WANT IN YOUR garden, consider the growing conditions. Plants grown in ideal conditions, or conditions as close to ideal as possible, are healthier and less prone to pest and disease problems than plants grown in stressful conditions. Some plants considered high maintenance become low maintenance when grown in the right conditions.

Avoid trying to make your garden match the growing conditions of the plants you like. Instead, choose plants to match your garden conditions. The levels of light, the type of soil and the amount of exposure in your garden provide guidelines that make plant selection easier. In time you will come to know the conditions of your garden.

A sketch of your garden, drawn on graph paper, may help you organize the various points you want to consider as you plan. Knowing your growing conditions can prevent costly mistakes.

Light

There are four categories of light in a garden: full sun, partial shade, light shade and full shade. Available light is affected by buildings, trees, fences and the position of the sun at different times of the day and year. Knowing what light is available in your garden will help you determine where to place your plants.

Full sun locations receive direct sunlight at least six hours per day. An example would be a location along a south-facing wall. Partial shade, or partial sun, locations receive direct sunlight for part of the day (four to six hours) and shade for the rest. An east- or west-facing wall gets only partial sun. Light shade, or dappled shade, locations receive shade most or all of the day, although some sunlight does filter through to ground level. The ground under a small-leaved tree, such as a birch, is often considered to be in light shade. Full shade locations receive no direct sunlight. The north side of a house or under a dense tree canopy is in full shade.

It is important to remember that the intensity of full sun can vary. For example, between buildings in a city, heat can become trapped and magnified, baking all but the most heat-tolerant plants in a concrete oven. Conversely, that shaded, sheltered hollow that protects your plants that hate heat in summer may become a frost trap in winter, killing tender plants that should otherwise survive.

Daylilies in full sun exposure

Perennials for Full Sun
- Artemisia
- Candytuft
- Coreopsis
- Daylily
- Euphorbia
- Mallow
- Marguerite
- Phlox
- Pincushion flower
- Russian sage
- Sedum
- Yarrow

Perennials for Full Shade
- Astilbe
- Bleeding heart
- Goat's beard
- Hosta
- Ligularia
- Lungwort
- Monkshood
- Solomon's seal

Marguerite

Goat's beard

Soil

Plants and the soil they grow in have a unique relationship. Many plant functions go on underground. Soil holds air, water, nutrients, organic matter and a variety of beneficial organisms. Plants depend upon these resources, and the roots use the soil as an anchor to hold the rest of the plant upright. In turn, plants influence soil development by breaking down large clods with their roots and by increasing soil fertility when they die and decompose.

Soil is made up of particles of different sizes. Sand particles are the largest. Sand has lots of air space and doesn't compact easily, which means that water drains quickly out of sandy soil and nutrients are quickly washed away. Clay particles are the smallest, visible only through a microscope. Water penetrates clay very slowly and drains very slowly. Clay holds the most nutrients, but it compacts easily because there is very little room between the particles for air. Silt particles are smaller than sand particles but larger than clay particles. Most soil is made up of a mixture of different particle sizes. These soils are called loams.

If you find nearly impenetrable clay outside your door, it may be a result of the way the foundation of your home was excavated. Many homes in Minnesota and Wisconsin have basements, and the most common method of digging that hole is to leave the subsoil piled nearby. Eventually, the pile is leveled off once the home is built. Topsoil, often only a few inches, is then spread over top, and you are left to cope with the concrete-like subsoil underneath. To improve this type of soil, work as much organic matter as you can find into the top 12–18" of soil. (See Preparing the Garden, p. 25, for more information on organic amendments.)

Particle size is one influence on the drainage properties of your soil; slope is another. Rocky soil on a hillside will probably drain very quickly and should be reserved for those plants that prefer a very well-drained soil. Low-lying areas retain water longer, and some areas may rarely drain at all. Moist areas suit plants that

require a consistent water supply, and areas that stay wet can be used for plants that prefer boggy conditions.

Drainage can be improved in very wet areas by adding organic matter to the soil, by installing some form of drainage tile or by building raised beds. Never add sand to clay soils. Doing so can make your soil as hard as concrete. To turn clay soil into a good growing medium, add copious amounts of organic matter.

Another aspect of soil to consider is its pH—the measure of acidity or alkalinity. A pH of 7 is neutral; higher numbers (up to 14) indicate alkaline conditions, and lower numbers (down to 0) indicate acidic conditions. Soil pH influences nutrient availability for plants. Although

Perennials for Sandy Soil
- Artemisia
- Butterfly weed
- Coreopsis
- Liatris
- Penstemon

Butterfly weed

Perennials for Clay Soil
- Black-eyed Susan
- Foamflower
- Globe flower
- Hardy geranium
- Hosta
- Sedum
- Turtlehead

Turtlehead

some plants prefer acid or alkaline soils, most perennials grow best in a mid-range pH of between 6.0 and 7.0; 90 percent of what we want to grow here prefers a pH of 6.5.

Soil can be made more alkaline by adding horticultural lime. Soil can be made more acidic by adding peat moss, sulfur, alfalfa pellets or chopped oak leaves. Altering the pH of your soil can take a year, often more. If you are trying to grow only one or two plants that require a soil with a different pH from your existing soil, consider growing them in a container or raised bed. There, it will be easier to control and amend the pH as needed.

What to plant alongside streets is a final consideration about soil. The salt that is applied to melt the ice in winter will accumulate in the soil next to the road. Pick plants that are salt tolerant to plant in these locations.

Salt-tolerant Perennials
Catmint
Globe thistle
Hens and chicks
Lamb's ears

Hens and chicks

Perennials for Moist Soil
Anemone
Astilbe
Bleeding heart
Brunnera
Heuchera
Joe-Pye weed
Lady's mantle
Ligularia
Meadowsweet
Monkshood
Rose mallow
Turtlehead

Anemone

Perennials for Dry Soil
Artemisia
Butterfly weed
Coreopsis
Gas plant
Lamb's ears
Pincushion flower
Russian sage
Sedum
Thyme
Yarrow

Pincushion flower

Exposure

Exposure is another important environmental influence in your garden. Wind, heat, cold and rain are some of the elements your garden is exposed to, and some plants are better adapted than others to withstand the potential damage of these forces. Buildings, walls, fences, hills, hedges and trees all influence your garden's exposure.

Wind can cause extensive damage to your plants. Plants become dehydrated in windy locations if they aren't able to draw water out of the soil fast enough to replace the moisture lost through their leaves. Tall, stiff-stemmed perennials can be knocked over or broken by strong winds. Some plants that do not require staking in a sheltered location may need to be staked in a more exposed one.

Use plants that are recommended for exposed locations, or temper the effect of the wind with a hedge or trees. A solid wall creates wind turbulence on the downwind side, while a looser structure, such as a hedge, breaks up the force of the wind and protects a larger area.

Perennials for Exposed Locations

Black-eyed Susan
Candytuft
Columbine
Creeping phlox
Euphorbia
Globe thistle
Penstemon
Sedum (groundcover species)
Yarrow

Sedum

Preparing the Garden

BEFORE YOU PLANT YOUR PERENNIALS, TAKE TIME TO PROPERLY
prepare your flowerbeds. Doing so will save you time and effort later on.
Starting with as few weeds as possible and with well-prepared soil that has
had organic material added will give your plants a good start.

Turning compost into beds

Removing weeds & debris

The first step is to loosen the soil
with a large garden fork and remove
the weeds. Avoid working the soil
when it is very wet or very dry
because you will damage the soil
structure by breaking down the
pockets that hold air and water.

Next, amend the soil with organic
matter.

Organic Soil Amendments

Organic matter is an important
component of soil. All soils benefit
from the addition of organic matter
because it contributes nutrients and
improves the structure of the soil.
Organic matter improves heavy clay
soils by loosening them and allowing
air and water to penetrate. It improves
sandy or light soils by increasing their
ability to retain water, which allows
plants to absorb nutrients before they
are leached away.

Common organic additives
include dried grass clippings, shredded leaves, peat moss, chopped
straw, composted manure, alfalfa
pellets, mushroom compost and garden compost. Alfalfa pellets supply a
range of nutrients, including trace
elements and a plant growth hormone. Composted cow, chicken or
other barnyard manure, available in
bags at most garden centers, are
wonderful products to add to soil.
Composted horse manure is also an
excellent additive, and it is usually
available from stables, often in a
seemingly endless supply. If you have
access to fresh manure, compost it
first and then incorporate it into
your beds the season before planting
(or two week before planting, if you
can't do it the season before).

Work your organic matter into the
soil with a garden fork, spade or

Wooden compost bins

Plastic compost bins

Material for compost

power tiller. If you are adding just one or two plants and do not want to prepare an entire bed, dig holes twice as wide and deep as the rootball of each plant. Add a slow-release organic fertilizer or composted manure mixed with peat moss to the backfill of soil that you spread around the plant. Fresh chicken or barnyard manure can also be used to improve small areas, but it should not be placed in the planting hole. Place only a small amount on top of the soil where it can leach into the soil.

Within a few months, earthworms and other decomposer organisms will break down the organic matter, releasing nutrients for plants. At the same time, the activities of these decomposers will help keep the soil from compacting.

Composting

In forests and meadows, organic debris, such as leaves and other plant bits, breaks down where it falls on the soil surface, and the nutrients are gradually made available to the plants growing there. In the garden, pests and diseases may be a problem, and untidy debris isn't practical. We can easily acquire the same nutrient benefits by composting. Compost is a great regular additive for your perennial garden, and good composting methods will help reduce pest and disease problems.

An active (hot) compost bin

Compost can be made in a pile, in a wooden box or in a purchased composter bin, and the process is not complicated. A pile of kitchen scraps, grass clippings and fall leaves will eventually break down if simply left alone. Such 'passive' or cool composting may take one to two seasons for all the materials to break down.

You can speed up the process and create an 'active,' or hot compost pile by following a few simple guidelines:

Use dry as well as fresh materials, with a higher proportion of dry matter than fresh green matter. Appropriate dry matter includes chopped straw, shredded leaves and sawdust. Green matter may consist of kitchen scraps, grass clippings and pulled weeds. The green matter

Finished compost

breaks down quickly and produces nitrogen, which composting organisms use to break down dry matter. Spread the green materials evenly throughout the pile by layering them between dry materials.

Mix in small amounts of soil from your garden or previously finished compost to introduce beneficial organisms. If the pile seems dry, add some water between the layers. The compost should be moist but not soaking: about as wet as a wrung-out sponge.

Turn the pile over or poke holes in it with a pitchfork every week or two. Air must get into the pile to speed up decomposition. Well-aerated compost piles will generate a lot of heat, reaching temperatures up to 160° F. At this high temperature, weed seeds are destroyed and many damaging soil organisms are killed. Most beneficial organisms, on the other hand, are not killed unless the temperature exceeds 160° F. To monitor the temperature of the compost near the middle of the pile, you will need a thermometer that is attached to a long probe,

similar to a large meat thermometer. Once the temperature drops, turn your compost to stimulate the process to heat up again.

Avoid adding diseased or pest-ridden materials into your compost pile, or they could spread throughout your garden. If you must add questionable material to the pile, place it near the center, where temperatures are the highest.

When you can no longer recognize the matter that you put into the compost bin, and the temperature no longer rises upon turning, your compost is ready to be mixed into your garden beds. The process may take as little as one month, and it will leave you with organic material that is rich in nutrients and beneficial organisms.

Even if you have limited space, you can still make compost using red worms, which are available in any bait shop. The process is simple. Get a large plastic container and drill drainage and air holes. Place shredded, lightly moistened newspaper (avoid glossy newsprint) in the container and bury the worms with cut-up kitchen scraps. Start with about 1 lb. of worms, and they will multiply to fit their space. Your worm composter will not smell if the worms aren't overloaded with too many scraps. The worms will create usable, nutrient-rich compost in as little as six weeks.

Compost worms

Selecting Perennials

PERENNIALS CAN BE PURCHASED OR STARTED FROM SEED.
Purchased plants may begin flowering the same year they are planted, while
plants started from seed may take two to three years to mature. Starting
from seed is more economical if you want large numbers of plants. (See
Propagating Perennials, p. 44, to learn how to start seeds.)

Get your perennials from a rep-
utable source, and check to make
sure the plants are not diseased or
pest-ridden. Garden centers, mail-
order catalogs and even friends and
neighbors are excellent sources of
perennials. A number of garden
societies promote the exchange of
plants and seeds, and many public
gardens sell seeds of rare plants.

Gardening clubs are also a great
source of rare and unusual plants.

Purchased plants come in one of
two main forms. Potted perennials
are already growing in pots. Bare-
root perennials consist of pieces of
root packed in moist peat moss or
sawdust. These roots are typically
dormant, although some of the previous year's growth may be evident

Plant on left is root-bound; plant on right is healthy.

or there may be new growth starting. Sometimes the roots appear to have no evident growth, past or present. Both potted and bare-root perennials are good purchases, and in each case there are things to look for to make sure you are getting a plant of the best quality.

Potted plants come in many sizes, and though a larger plant may appear more mature, a smaller one will suffer less from the shock of being transplanted. Most perennials grow quickly once they are planted in the garden, so the initial size won't matter too much. Select plants that seem to be a good size for the pot they are in. When a plant is tapped lightly out of the pot, the roots should be visible but not winding and twisting around the inside of the pot. Healthy roots will appear almost white.

The leaves should be a healthy color. If they appear to be chewed or damaged, check carefully for diseases or insects. If you find any insects on the plant, don't purchase it unless you are willing to cope with the hitchhikers before you move the plant into the garden.

Once you get your potted plants home, water them if they are dry and keep them in a lightly shaded location until you plant them. Remove any damaged growth and discard it. Plant the perennials into the garden as soon as possible.

Bare-root plants are most commonly sold through mail order, but some are available in garden centers, usually in spring. If you're buying at a garden center, look for roots that are dormant (without top growth). A bare-root plant that has been trying to grow in the stressful conditions of a plastic bag may have too little energy to recover, or it may take longer to establish.

Cut off any damaged parts of the roots with a very sharp knife or garden scissors. Bare-root perennials dehydrate quickly out of soil, so they need to be planted more quickly than potted plants. Soak the roots in lukewarm water for one to two hours to rehydrate them. Do not leave them in water longer than that, or you may encourage root or crown rot. Plant them directly in the garden or into pots with high-quality potting soil until they can be moved to the garden.

It may be difficult to distinguish the top from the bottom of bare-root plants. Usually, there is a tell-tale dip or stub from which the plant grew. If you can't find any distinguishing characteristics, lay the root on its side and the plant will send the roots down and the shoots up.

Root mass of root-bound plant

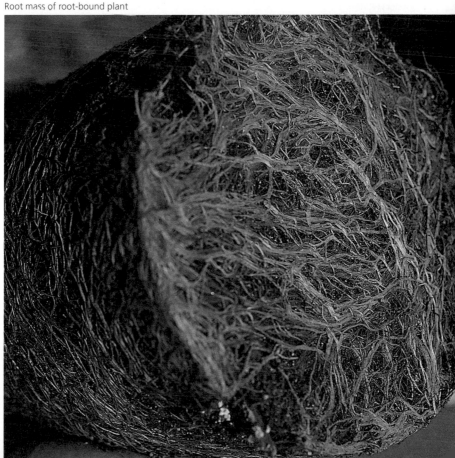

Planting Perennials

ONCE YOU HAVE PLANNED YOUR GARDEN, PREPARED THE SOIL
and purchased your perennials, it's time to plant. If the perennials came with
identification tags, be sure to poke them into the soil next to the new plants.
Next spring, the tags will help you with identification and remind you that
there is indeed a plant in that patch of soil. Most of these tags include information on what care the plant needs. A diagram of your garden is also helpful.

Potted Perennials

Perennials in pots are convenient
because you can arrange them across
the bed before you start to dig. To
prevent the roots from drying out,
do not unpot the plants until immediately before you transplant.

To plant potted perennials, start
by digging a hole about the width
and depth of the pot. Remove the
perennial from the pot. If the pot is
small enough, you can hold your
hand across the top of the pot, letting your fingers straddle the stem
of the plant, and then turn it
upside down. Never pull on the
stem or leaves to get a plant out of
a pot. It is better to cut a difficult
pot off rather than risk damaging
the plant.

If you have taken advantage of an end-of-season sale, you will probably have to deal with root-bound plants. Before planting them, you will need to tease apart the roots if they are winding around the rootball. If there is a solid mat at the bottom of the rootball, remove it, because such roots will not be able to spread out and establish themselves in the soil.

Gently spread out the roots as you plant, teasing a few roots out of the rootball to get the roots growing outward into the soil. The process of cutting into the bottom half of the rootball and spreading the two halves of the mass outward, like a pair of wings, is called 'butterflying,' and it is an effective way to promote fast growth of pot-bound perennials.

Place the plant in the prepared hole. It should be planted at the same level that it was at in the pot, or a little higher, to allow for the soil to settle. If the plant is too low in the ground, it may rot when rain collects around the base. Fill the soil in around the roots and firm it down. Water the plant well as soon as you have planted it and about every three to four days until it has become established. You will need to water more in high heat and wind conditions.

Support plant as you remove pot (above photos)

Fall-planted perennials may be subject to frost heaving if they did not have enough time to establish a good root system. When the ground cools, you may want to mulch plants that were set out in fall, to avoid heaving (see p. 37).

Loosen rootball before planting

Bare-root Perennials

Before planting, bare-root perennials should not be spaced out across the bed unless you previously planted them in temporary pots. Roots dry out quickly. If you want to visualize your spacing, you can poke sticks into the ground or put rocks down to represent the plant locations.

If you have been keeping your bare-root perennials in potting soil, you may find that the roots have not grown enough to knit the soil together and that all the soil falls away from the root when you remove it from the pot. Don't be concerned. Just follow the bare-root planting instructions. If the soil does hold together, plant the root the way you would a potted perennial.

The type of hole you need depends on the types of roots the bare-root perennial has. Plants with fibrous roots need a mound of soil in the center of the planting hole over which the roots can be spread out evenly. The hole should be dug as deep as the longest roots. Mound the soil into the center of the hole up to ground level. Spread the roots out around the mound and cover them with loosened soil.

Plants with a taproot need a hole that is narrow and about as deep as the root is long. Use a trowel to open up a suitable hole, then tuck the root into it and fill it in again with the soil around it. If you can't tell which end is up, plant the root on its side.

Some plants have roots that may appear to be taproots, but the shoot seems to be growing off the side of the root, rather than upwards from one end. These 'roots' are actually modified stems called rhizomes. Many irises, for example, grow from rhizomes. Rhizomes should be planted horizontally in a shallow hole and lightly covered with soil; slightly expose the rhizome surface.

In most cases, you should try to get the crown at or just above soil level and loosen the soil that surrounds the planting hole. Keep the roots thoroughly watered until the plants are well established.

Whether the plants are potted or bare-root, leave them alone for a period of time to let them recover from the stress of planting. In the first month, you will need only to water the plant regularly, weed it and watch for pests. An organic mulch will keep in moisture and control weeds.

If you have prepared your beds properly, you probably won't have to fertilize in the first year. If you do wish to fertilize, wait until your new plants have started healthy new growth, and apply only a weak fertilizer to avoid damaging the sensitive new roots.

Planters

Perennials can also be grown in planters for portable, movable displays. Planters can be used on patios or decks, in gardens with very poor soil or in yards where children and dogs might destroy a traditional perennial bed.

Always use a high-quality potting mix intended for containers. Garden soil can quickly lose its structure and become a solid lump in a container, preventing air, water and roots from penetrating. Perennials will never thrive in containers if planted in soil from the garden. At the very least, mix half garden soil with half peat moss.

Many perennials, such as hostas and daylilies, can grow in the same container without any fresh potting mix for five or six years. Be sure to fertilize and water perennials in planters more often than those growing in the ground. Always check water levels before watering—too much water in the planter causes root rot. Ensure your containers have adequate drainage holes in the bottom or sides.

When designing a planter garden, you can either keep one type of perennial in each planter and display many different planters together, or mix different perennials in large planters together with annuals and bulbs. The latter choice results in a dynamic bouquet of flowers and foliage. Keep the tall upright perennials, such as yarrow, in the center of the planter; the rounded or bushy types, such as coreopsis, around the sides; and low-growing or draping perennials, such as lamium, along the edges. Perennials that have long bloom times or attractive foliage work well in planters.

Choose hardy perennials that are able to tolerate difficult conditions. Planters are exposed to extremes of our variable weather; the perennials will dry out quickly in hot weather and become waterlogged equally quickly after a couple of rainy days. The more invasive perennials often make good choices for planters because they are tough to kill, and their otherwise aggressive spread is kept in check by the container.

Sedum, hens and chicks and other succulents do well in containers.

Heuchera and creeping Jenny in mixed planter

Perennials in planters are more susceptible to winter damage because the exposed sides of the container provide very little insulation for roots against fluctuations in temperature. The container itself may even crack when exposed to a deep freeze. Don't worry—it's not difficult to get planters through a tough winter in great shape. The simplest thing to do is to move the planter to a sheltered spot when winter arrives. Most perennials require some cold in winter in order to flower the following year, so find a spot that is cold but not exposed. An unheated garage or enclosed porch is a good place, and even your garden shed will offer plants more protection than they would get outdoors, open to the elements on all sides.

If you haven't the space or access to these places, consider your basement window wells. These sheltered, below-ground spaces also offer some heat from the windows. Layer straw at the bottom of the well, sit your pots on the straw, then cover them with more straw. Wait until the pots freeze before placing them in the wells, in order to prevent rot and problems with mice. Mice find that the straw makes a comfortable home and the perennial roots a tasty treat, but they can't dig as easily in frozen soil. If mice are a problem, try using Styrofoam insulation under and on top of the pots instead of straw.

The pots themselves can be winterproofed before planting your perennials. Place a layer of Styrofoam insulation, packing 'peanuts' or commercial planter insulation at the bottom of the pot and around the inside before adding soil and plants. Make sure excess water can still drain freely from the container. This technique is particularly useful for high-rise dwellers with balcony or rooftop gardens. This insulation has the added benefit of protecting the roots from overheating in summer.

Planters can also be buried in the garden for winter. Find an open space in a flowerbed or elsewhere on your property, and dig a hole deep enough to allow you to sink the planter up to its rim. This job can be messy, particularly in spring when you dig the planter up. This technique is impractical for large planters, which may require an extensive excavation.

Perennials for Planters

Anemone (tuberous)
Candytuft
Catmint
Daylily
Hosta
Lady's mantle
Lamium
Penstemon
Pincushion flower
Pinks
Sedum
Yarrow

Lady's mantle

Caring for Perennials

MANY PERENNIALS REQUIRE LITTLE CARE, BUT ALL BENEFIT FROM a few maintenance basics. Weeding, mulching, watering, fertilizing and grooming are some of the chores that, when done on a regular basis, keep major work to a minimum.

Weeding

Controlling weeds is one of your most important tasks. Weeds compete with your perennials for light, nutrients and space, and they can also harbor pests and diseases.

Many weed seeds, especially those of annual weeds, need light to germinate. Therefore, try to prevent weeds from germinating by blocking their access to light with a layer of mulch. As your garden matures, some perennials will themselves suppress weeds by blocking the light.

Pull out weeds that do germinate while they are still small—before they have a chance to flower, set seed and start a whole new generation of problems. Weeds can be pulled out by hand or with a hoe. Quickly scuffing across the soil surface with the hoe will pull out small weeds and sever larger ones from their roots.

Mulching

Mulches are an important gardening tool. They prevent weed seeds from germinating by blocking out the light, and small weeds that do pop up in a mulched bed are very easy to pull. Soil temperatures remain more consistent and more moisture is retained under a layer of

Weeding is an important task.

mulch. Mulches prevent soil erosion during heavy rain or strong winds.

Organic mulches include compost, bark chips, shredded leaves, dried grass clippings and numerous shell and husk materials. Organic mulches are desirable because they improve the soil and add nutrients as they break down. Shredded newspaper makes wonderful mulch, though not as attractive as other mulches. Shredding is important for leaves and newspaper because large pieces may keep too much moisture close to the crown of the plant, smothering it. Allow fresh grass clippings to dry for a few days before applying around perennials. A layer of fresh grass clippings will heat up before it dries, and this heat can harm the plants.

Spread a 2–3" layer of mulch over your perennial beds around your plants in spring or early summer, depending on zone. In zones 2 and 3, apply mulch after June 25. In zone 4, apply after June 15. In zone 5, apply after June 1. Doing so gives the sun time to sterilize the garden topsoil, keeping many fungal diseases under control. Keep the area immediately around the crown or stem of each plant clear. Mulch that is too close to plants can trap moisture and prevent good air circulation, encouraging disease. If the layer of mulch disappears into the soil over summer, replenish it.

When frost kills your garden, cut down your perennials to the ground, with the exception of ornamental grasses, and anything that vines or climbs. Or, leave them up and cut down in early spring. However, in spring the plants are floppy and soppy, sometimes covered in fungus, and you're unduly stepping in the bed. Once the ground freezes in late fall, cover the garden with 10–12" of marsh hay or bags of leaves to protect the plants over winter. This fall mulch is particularly important because we can't depend on a steady layer of snow in winter.

Marsh hay is sold in bails and is relatively seedless, minimizing garden contamination via a variety of seeds. The bales will be compacted; pull them apart and fluff over the area. Do not mulch before the ground cools because the trapped heat in the soil will prevent the perennials from entering complete winter dormancy; wait until the top two or three inches of ground have frozen. The goal of winter mulch is not to keep the ground warm, but to keep it frozen, or, at the very least, a constant, cool temperature until spring.

In late winter or early spring, once the weather starts to warm, pull some of the mulch off the plants and see if they have started growing. If they have, pull the mulch back, but keep it nearby in case you need to replace it to protect the tender new

Applying bark chip mulch

growth from a late frost. Once your plants are well on their way and you're no longer worried about frost, remove the protective mulch completely from the bed.

Watering

Watering is another basic of perennial care. Once established, many perennials need little supplemental watering if they have been planted in their preferred conditions and are given a moisture-retaining mulch. Planting perennials with similar water requirements together makes watering easier.

Water infrequently and deeply. Ensure the water penetrates at least 6" into the soil. Plants given a light sprinkle of water every day will develop roots that stay close to the soil surface, making the plants vulnerable to heat and drought. Watering deeply once a week encourages plants to develop a deeper root system. In hot, dry weather, they will be able to seek out the water trapped deep in the ground.

Many perennials grow well with an average of 1" of water per week.

Buy a rain gauge. Install it in the ground or at the top of a fence, and keep it 20' away from trees or any structure. It's fun to keep track of just how much rain fell during that doozy of a thunderstorm, or to know if your plants are getting enough water.

When possible, water first thing in the morning. In the heat of the day, much of the water is lost to evaporation. Late in the day, moisture left on the plant may not dry and will encourage fungal diseases to develop. Always try to water the ground around the plant, not the plant.

Avoid overwatering. Before applying any water, check that the soil is dry by poking your finger into the top 1–2". You can also try rolling a bit of the soil from around the plant into a ball. If the soil forms a ball, it needs no extra water.

Perennials in containers or planters usually need to be watered more frequently than perennials growing in the ground. The smaller the container, the more often the plants will need watering. Containers may need to be watered daily during hot, sunny weather. If the soil in your container dries out, you will have to water several times to make sure the water is absorbed throughout the planting medium. Dig into the soil, and if it is dry at all, water more.

Fertilizing

If you prepare your beds well and add new compost to them each spring, you should not need to add extra fertilizer. If you have a limited amount of compost, you can mix an organic slow-release fertilizer into the soil around your perennials in spring. Some plants, such as rose mallow, are heavy feeders that need additional supplements throughout the growing season.

Many organic and synthetic fertilizers are available at garden centers. Most fertilizer instructions recommend a higher rate than is necessary for good plant growth. Never use more than the recommended quantity because too much fertilizer does more harm than good. Roots can be burned by fertilizer that is applied in high concentrations. Problems are more likely to be caused by synthetic fertilizers because they are more concentrated than organic types.

For perennials it is important to support good root development in the first year or two of growth. Phosphorus is the fertilizer that promotes root growth, so if you lack compost, look for fertilizers high in phosphorus while plants are establishing, providing the results of a soil test noted that your soil requires phosphorus. The typical fertilizer formula is N : P : K (Nitrogen : Phosphorus : Potassium). In the years after the plants establish, nitrogen becomes important for leaf development, and potassium for flower and seed development.

Grooming

Many perennials benefit from grooming. Resilient plants, plentiful blooms and compact growth are the signs of a well-groomed garden. Thinning, trimming, disbudding, deadheading and staking are grooming techniques that can enhance the beauty of a perennial bed. The methods are simple, but you may have to experiment in order to get the right effect in your own garden.

Thinning is done to clump-forming perennials, such as black-eyed Susan and purple coneflower, early in the year, when shoots have just emerged. These plants have stems in a dense clump that allow very little air or light into the center of the plant. Remove half of the shoots when they first emerge to increase air circulation and prevent diseases such as powdery mildew. The increased light encourages compact growth and more flowers. Throughout the growing season, thin any

A well-tended garden

growth that is weak, diseased or growing in the wrong direction.

Pinching or trimming (shearing) perennials is a simple procedure, but timing it correctly and achieving just the right look can be tricky. Early in the year, before the flower buds have appeared, pinch the plant to encourage new side shoots. Remove the tip and some stems of the plant just above a leaf or pair of leaves. You can pinch stem by stem with your fingers, or, if you have a lot of plants, you can trim off the tops with hedge shears to one third of the height you expect the plants to reach. The growth that begins to emerge can be trimmed again. Beautiful layered effects can be achieved by staggering the trimming times by a week or two.

Give plants enough time to set buds and flower. Continual pinching or trimming will encourage very dense growth but also delay flowering. Most spring-flowering plants cannot be pinched back, or they will not flower. Early-summer or mid-summer bloomers should be pinched only once, as early in the season as possible. Late-summer and fall bloomers can be pinched several times but should be left alone past June. Don't pinch a plant if flower buds have formed—it may not have enough energy or time left in the year to develop a new set of buds. Experimenting and keeping detailed notes will improve your pinching skills.

Disbudding is the removal of some flower buds in order to encourage the remaining ones to produce larger flowers. This technique is popular with peony growers

Black-eyed Susan

Perennials to Pinch Early in the Season

Aster
Black-eyed Susan
Catmint
Coneflower
Mallow
Monarda
Rose mallow
Sedum 'Autumn Joy'

and with gardeners who enter plants in fairs or other flower competitions.

Deadheading, the removal of flowers once they are finished blooming, serves several purposes: it keeps plants looking tidy; it prevents the plant from spreading seeds, and therefore seedlings, throughout the garden; it often prolongs blooming; it spurs root growth; and it helps prevent pest and disease problems.

Flowers can be removed by hand or snipped off with hand pruners. Bushy plants with many tiny flowers, and particularly plants with a short bloom period, such as candytuft, can be more aggressively pruned back with garden shears once they have finished flowering. For some plants, such as creeping phlox, shearing will promote new growth and possibly more blooms later in the season.

Deadheading is not necessary for every plant. Some plants have attractive seedheads that can be left in place to provide interest in the garden over winter. Other plants are short-lived, and leaving some of the seedheads in place encourages future generations to replace the old plants. Foxglove is one example of a short-lived perennial that reseeds. In some cases the self-sown seedlings do not possess the attractive features of the parent plant. Deadheading may be required in these cases.

Staking, the use of poles, branches or wires to hold plants erect, can often be avoided by astute thinning and trimming, but a few plants always need support to look their best. Three types of stakes are used for the different growth habits that need support.

Plants that develop tall spikes, such as monkshood and some foxgloves, may require each spike to be staked individually. A strong, narrow pole, such as a bamboo stick, can be pushed into the ground early in the year, and the spike tied to the stake as it grows. Ensure the plant is securely, but not tightly, fastened with plant-friendly ties of a soft,

Flax

Perennials to Shear Back After Blooming
- Candytuft
- Catmint
- Creeping phlox
- Flax
- Hardy geranium
- Marguerite
- Pinks
- Yarrow

stretchable material or plant ties available from garden centers and nurseries. Tomato cages or peony rings may be used if staking each stem is not possible. A forked branch can also be used to support single-stemmed plants.

Many plants, such as peonies, get top heavy as they grow and tend to flop over once they reach a certain height. A wire hoop, sometimes called a peony ring, is the most unobtrusive way to hold up such a plant. When the plant is young, the legs of the peony ring are pushed into the ground around it. As the plant grows, it is supported by the ring. The bushy growth also hides the ring.

Other plants, such as coreopsis, form a floppy tangle of stems. These plants can be given a bit of support with twiggy branches inserted into

Deadheading asters

Meadowsweet

Bleeding heart

Perennials with Interesting Seedheads

Astilbe
Coneflower
Euphorbia
Globe thistle
Meadowsweet
Monarda
Oriental poppy
Pasqueflower
Sedum 'Autumn Joy'

Perennials That Self-Seed

Astilbe
Balloon flower
Bleeding heart (variable seedlings)
Cardinal flower
Columbine
Flax
Foxglove
Jupiter's beard
Lady's mantle
Lanceleaf coreopsis
Mallow
Pinks

the ground around young plants; the plants then grow up into the twigs.

Along with thinning and trimming, there are other steps you can take to reduce the need for staking. First, grow plants in the right conditions. Don't assume a plant will do better in a richer soil than is recommended. Very rich soil causes many plants to produce weak, leggy growth that is prone to falling over. Similarly, a plant that likes full sun will become stretched out and leggy if grown in shade. Second, use other plants for support. Mix in plants that have a stable structure between plants that need support. The weaker plants may still fall over slightly, but only as far as their neighbors will allow. Many plants are available in compact varieties that don't require staking.

Spiral stakes

Propagating Perennials

PROPAGATING YOUR OWN PERENNIALS IS AN INTERESTING AND challenging aspect of gardening that requires time and space and can save you money. Seeds, cuttings and division are three common methods of increasing your perennial population. Each method has advantages and disadvantages.

Shade cloth over cold frame (below)

A cold frame is a wonderful gardening aid regardless of which propagation methods you use. It can be used to protect tender plants over winter, to start vegetable seeds early in spring, to harden plants off before moving them to the garden, to protect fall-germinating seedlings and young cuttings or divisions and to start seeds that need a cold treatment. This mini-greenhouse structure is built so that ground level on the inside of the cold frame is lower than on the outside, so the soil around the outside insulates the plants within. The angled, hinged lid is fitted with glass. The lid lets light in to collect some heat during the day, and it prevents rain from damaging tender plants. If the interior gets too hot, the lid can be raised for ventilation.

Seeds

Starting perennials from seed is a great way to propagate a large number of plants at relatively low cost. You can purchase seeds or collect them from your own or a friend's perennial garden. The work involved is worth it when you see the plants you raised from tiny seedlings finally begin to flower.

Propagating from seed has some limitations. Some cultivars and varieties don't pass on their desirable traits to their offspring. Other perennials have seeds that take a very long time to germinate, if they germinate at all, and may take even longer to grow to flowering size. Many perennials do grow easily from seed, and flower within a year or two of being transplanted into the garden.

Specific propagation information is given for each plant in this book, but there are a few basic rules for starting all seeds. Some seeds can be started directly in the garden (direct sown), but it is easier to control temperature and moisture levels and to provide a sterile environment if you start the seeds indoors. Seeds can be started in pots or, if you need a lot of plants, flats. Use a sterile soil mix intended for starting seeds. The mix will generally need to be kept moist but not soggy. Most seeds germinate in moderately warm temperatures of about 57°–70° F.

Filling cell packs

Using folded paper to plant small seeds

Spray bottle provides gentle mist

Prepared seed tray

Seed-starting supplies are available at garden centers. Many supplies aren't necessary, but some, such as seed-tray dividers, are useful. These dividers, often called plug trays or cell-packs, are made of plastic and prevent the roots of seedlings from tangling and being disturbed during transplanting. Heating coils or pads can also come in handy. Placed under the pots or flats, they keep the soil at a constant temperature.

Fill your pot or seed tray with the soil mix and firm it down slightly—not too firmly or the soil will not drain. Wet the soil before planting your seeds because they may wash into clumps if the soil is watered immediately afterward.

Medium-sized to large seeds can be planted individually and spaced out in pots or trays. If you have divided inserts for your trays, plant one or two seeds per section. Lightly cover medium-sized seeds with soil. Press large seeds into the soil before lightly covering them. Do not cover seeds that need exposure to light to germinate.

Small seeds may have to be sprinkled onto the soil. Fold a sheet of paper in half and place the small seeds in the crease. Gently tap the underside of the fold to bounce or roll the seeds off the paper in a controlled manner. Some seeds are so tiny that they look like dust. These tiny seeds can be mixed with a small quantity of very fine sand and spread on the soil surface. Small and tiny seeds may not need to be covered with any more soil.

Plant only one type of seed in each pot or flat. Each species has a different rate of germination, and the germinated seedlings will require different conditions than the seeds that have yet to germinate.

Water the seeds using a very fine spray if the soil starts to dry out. A hand-held spray bottle will moisten the soil without disturbing the seeds. To keep the environment moist, place pots inside clear plastic bags. Change the bags or turn them inside out once condensation starts to build up and drip. Plastic bags can be held up with stakes or wires poked in around the edges of the pot. Many seed trays come with clear plastic covers that can be placed over the flats to keep moisture in. The plastic can be removed once the seeds have germinated.

The amount and timing of watering is critical to successfully growing perennials from seed. Most germinated seeds and young seedlings will perish if the soil is allowed to dry out. Strive to maintain a consistently moist soil, which may mean watering the seedlings lightly two times a day. As the seedlings get bigger, cut back on the number of times you water, but water a little heavier each time. A handy guideline to follow: when the seedlings have their first true leaves, cut back to watering once a day.

Seeds generally do not require a lot of light in order to germinate, so pots or trays can be kept in any warm, out-of-the-way place. Once the seeds have germinated, place them in a bright location but out of direct sun. Seedlings should be transplanted to individual pots once they have three or four true leaves. True leaves look like the mature leaves. The first one or two leaves are actually part of the seed and are called seed leaves, or cotyledons. Plants in plug trays can be left until neighboring leaves start to touch each other. At this point the plants will be competing for light and should be transplanted to individual pots.

Young seedlings do not need to be fertilized. The seed itself provides all the nutrition the seedling will need. Fertilizer causes seedlings to produce soft, spindly growth that is susceptible to attack by insects and diseases. A fertilizer diluted to one-quarter or one-half strength can be used once seedlings have four or five true leaves. Organic fertilizers have a low potential of burning the new, tiny roots.

All seedlings are susceptible to a problem called damping off, which is caused by soil-borne fungi. An afflicted seedling looks as though someone has pinched the stem at soil level, causing the plant to topple over. The pinched area blackens and the seedling dies. Sterile soil mix, good air circulation and evenly moist soil will help prevent damping

off, as will a ¼" layer of peat moss spread over the seed bed.

Many seeds sprout easily as soon as they are planted. Some, however, have protective devices that prevent them from germinating when conditions are not favorable or from germinating all at once. Some seeds bear thick seed coats; some produce chemicals that prevent germination; and some are programmed for staggered germination. In the wild, such strategies improve the chances of survival, but you will have to lower the defenses of these types of seeds before they will germinate.

Seeds can be tricked into thinking the conditions are right for sprouting. Some thick-coated seeds can be soaked for a day or two in a glass of water, mimicking the beginning of the rainy season, which is when the plant would germinate in its natural environment. The water softens the seed coat and in some cases washes away the chemicals that have been preventing germination. Rose mallow is an example of a plant with seeds that need to be soaked before they will germinate.

Soaking seeds speeds germination

Other thick-coated seeds need to be scratched (scarified) to allow moisture to penetrate the seed coat and prompt germination. In nature, birds scratch the seeds with gravel in their craws and acid in their stomachs. You can mimic this process by nicking the seeds with a knife or file, or by gently rubbing them between two sheets of sandpaper. Leave the scratched seeds in a dry place for a day or so before planting them, to give them a chance to prepare for germination before they are exposed to water. Anemones have seeds that need their thick coats scratched.

Plants from northern climates often have seeds that wait until spring before they germinate. These seeds must be given a cold treatment, which mimics winter, before they will germinate. Yarrows and bergenias are examples of plants with seeds that respond to cold treatment.

One method of cold treatment is to plant the seeds in a pot or tray and place them in the refrigerator for up to two months. Check the container regularly and don't allow the seeds to dry out. This method is fairly simple but not very practical if your refrigerator is crowded.

Oriental poppy

Perennials to Start from Seed

Coreopsis
Foxglove
Hardy geranium species
Lady's mantle
Mallow
Oriental poppy
Phlox
Pincushion flower
Pinks

A less space-consuming method is to mix the seeds with some moistened sand, peat moss or sphagnum moss. Place the mix in a sealable sandwich bag and pop it in the refrigerator for up to two months, again being sure the sand or moss doesn't dry out. The seeds can then be planted into a pot or tray. Spread

Scarifying seeds with sandpaper

Preparing seeds for cold treatment

the seeds and the moist sand or moss onto the prepared surface and press it all down gently.

As noted in certain entries in this book, some plants have seeds that must be planted when freshly ripe. These seeds cannot be stored for long periods of time.

A) Removing lower leaves

Cuttings

Cuttings are an excellent way to propagate varieties and cultivars that you like but that don't come true from seed or don't produce seed. Each cutting will grow into a reproduction (clone) of the parent plant. Cuttings are taken from the stems of some perennials and the roots or rhizomes of others.

B) Dipping in rooting hormone

Stem cuttings are generally taken in spring and early summer. During this time plants produce a flush of fresh, new growth, either before or after flowering. Avoid taking cuttings from plants that are in flower. Plants that are blooming or about to bloom are busy trying to reproduce; plants that are busy growing, by contrast, are full of the right hormones to promote quick root growth. If you do take cuttings from plants that are flowering, be sure to remove the flowers and the buds to divert the plant's energy back into growing roots and leaves.

C) Firming cutting into soil

D) Newly planted cuttings

Because cuttings need to be kept in a warm, humid place to root, they are prone to fungal diseases. Providing proper sanitation (sterile soil mix, clean tools and containers; to sterilize a knife, dip it in denatured alcohol or a 10 percent bleach solution) and encouraging quick rooting will increase the survival rate of your

E) Healthy roots

Campanula

Perennials to Propagate from Stem Cuttings

Aster
Bleeding heart
Campanula
Candytuft
Catmint
Coreopsis
Euphorbia
Penstemon
Perennial salvia
Pinks
Sedum 'Autumn Joy'
Yarrow

that larger cuttings develop more roots and become established more quickly once planted in the garden. You may wish to try different sizes to see what works best for you. Generally, a small cutting is 1–2" long and a large cutting is 4–6" long.

Size of cuttings is partly determined by the number of leaf nodes on the cutting. You will want at least three or four nodes on a cutting. The node is where the leaf joins the stem, and it is from here that the new roots and leaves will grow. The base of the cutting will be just below a node. Strip the leaves gently from the first and second nodes and plant them below the soil surface. Retain the leaves on the top part of the cutting above the soil. Some plants have a lot of space between nodes, so your cutting may be longer than the 1–2" or 4–6" guideline. Other plants have almost no space at all between nodes. Cut these plants according to the length guidelines, and gently remove the leaves from the lower half of the cutting. Plants with closely spaced nodes often root quickly and abundantly.

Always use a sharp, sterile knife to take cuttings. Make cuts straight across the stem. Once you have stripped the leaves, dip the end of the cutting into a rooting-hormone powder intended for softwood cuttings. Sprinkle the powder onto a piece of paper and dip or roll the cutting into it. Discard any extra powder left on the paper to prevent the spread of disease. Tap or blow the extra powder off the cutting. Cuttings caked with rooting hormone are more likely to rot than to

cuttings. Be sure to plant a lot of them to make up for any losses. Dusting with soil sulfur will also help reduce the incidence of fungal disease.

Generally, stem cuttings are more successful and quicker to grow if you include the tip of the stem in the cutting. Debate exists over what length of stem to cut below the tip. Some gardeners claim that smaller cuttings are more likely to root and to root more quickly. Other gardeners claim root, and they don't root any faster than those that are lightly dusted.

Most gardeners plant their cuttings directly into a sterile soil mix. Other gardeners prefer to keep their cuttings in water until they show root growth, and then plant them. If you choose to place cuttings in water, use dark containers instead of clear containers for the best results.

The sooner you plant your cuttings or place them in water, the better. The less water the cuttings lose, the less likely they are to wilt and the more quickly they will root.

Use a sterile soil mix, intended for seeds or cuttings, in pots or trays. You can also root cuttings in sterilized sand, perlite, vermiculite or a combination of the three. Firm the soil down and moisten it before you start planting. Poke a hole in the soil with a pencil or similar object, tuck the cutting in and gently firm the soil around it. Make sure the lowest leaves do not touch the soil. The cuttings should be spaced far enough apart that adjoining leaves do not touch each other.

Cover the pots or trays with plastic to keep in the humidity. The rigid plastic lids that are available for trays may not be high enough to fit over cuttings, in which case you will have to use a plastic bag. Push stakes or wires into the soil around the edge of the pot so that the plastic will be held off the leaves.

Keep the cuttings in a warm place, about 65°–70° F, in bright indirect light. Keep the soil moist. A hand-held mister will gently moisten the soil without disturbing the cuttings. Turn the bag inside out when condensation becomes heavy. A couple of holes poked in the bag will create some ventilation.

Most cuttings require one to four weeks to root. After two weeks, give the cutting a gentle tug. You will feel resistance if roots have formed. If the cutting feels as though it can pull out of the soil, gently push it back down and leave it longer. New growth is also a good sign that your cutting has rooted. Some gardeners simply leave the cuttings alone until they can see roots through the holes in the bottoms of the pots. Uncover the cuttings once they have developed roots.

When the cuttings are showing new leaf growth, apply a foliar feed using a hand-held mister. Plants quickly absorb nutrients through the leaves, and by feeding that way you can avoid stressing the newly formed roots. Your local garden center should have foliar fertilizers and information about applying them.

Once your cuttings have rooted and have had a chance to establish, they can be potted individually. If you rooted several cuttings in one pot or tray, you may find that the roots have tangled together. If gentle pulling doesn't separate them, take the entire clump that is tangled together and try rinsing some of the soil away. Doing so should free enough roots to allow you to separate the plants.

Pot the young plants in sterile potting soil. They can be moved into a sheltered area of the garden or a cold frame and grown in pots until they are mature enough to fend for themselves in the garden. The plants

Mallow

Perennials to Start from Basal Cuttings

  Baby's breath
  Campanula
  Catmint
  Daylily
  Euphorbia
  Hens and chicks
  Lychnis
  Mallow
  Monarda
  Phlox
  Pincushion flower
  Sedum

may need some protection over the first winter. Keep them in the cold frame if they are still in pots, or give them an extra layer of mulch if they have been planted out.

Basal cuttings involve removing the new growth from the main clump of a plant and rooting it in the same manner as stem cuttings. Many plants send up new shoots or plantlets around their bases. Often, the plantlets will already have a few

roots growing. Once separated, these young plants develop quickly and may even grow to flowering size the first summer.

Treat these cuttings in much the same way as you would a stem cutting. Use a sterile knife to cut out the shoot. You may have to cut back some of the top growth of the shoot because the tiny developing roots may not be able to support all of it. Sterile soil mix and humid conditions are preferred. Pot plants individually or place them in soft soil in the garden until new growth appears and roots have developed; then you can transplant to any desired location.

Root cuttings can be taken from some plants. Dandelions are often inadvertently propagated this way: even the smallest piece of root left in the ground can sprout a new plant, foiling attempts to eradicate them. But there are desirable perennials that share this ability.

Cuttings can be taken from the fleshy roots of certain perennials that do not propagate well from stem cuttings. These cuttings should be taken in early or mid-spring when the ground is just starting to warm and the roots are about to break dormancy. At this time, the roots of the perennials are full of nutrients that the plants stored the previous summer and fall, and hormones are initiating growth. You may have to wet the soil around the plant so that you can loosen it enough to get to the roots.

You do not want very young or very old roots. Very young roots are usually white and quite soft; very old roots are tough and woody.

The roots you should use will be tan in color and still fleshy.

To prepare your root, cut out the section you will be using with a sterile knife. Cut the root into pieces 1–2" long. Remove any side roots before planting the sections in pots or planting trays. Roots must be planted in a vertical, not horizontal, position, and they need to be kept in the orientation they were when attached to the parent plant. People use different methods to help them remember which end is up. One trick is to cut straight across the tops and diagonally across the bottoms.

You can use the same type of soil mix as you would for seeds and stem cuttings. Poke the pieces vertically into the soil, leaving a tiny bit of the end poking up out of the soil. Remember to keep the pieces the right way up. Keep the pots or trays in a warm place out of direct sunlight. They will send up new shoots once they have rooted and can be planted in the same manner as stem cuttings (see p. 49).

The main difference between starting root cuttings and starting stem cuttings is that the root cuttings must be kept fairly dry; they can rot very easily. Keep the roots slightly moist but not wet while you are rooting them. Avoid overwatering as they establish.

Rhizome cuttings are the easiest means of propagating plants from underground parts. In addition to true roots, some plants have rhizomes, which are thick, fleshy modified stems that grow horizontally underground. A rhizome sends up new shoots at intervals along its length, and in this way the plant spreads. It is easy to take advantage of this feature.

Dig up a rhizome when the plant is growing vigorously, usually in late spring or early summer. If you look closely at the rhizome, you will see that it appears to be growing in sections. These sections join at places called nodes. It is from these nodes that small, stringy feeder roots extend downwards and new plants sprout upwards. You may even see small plantlets already sprouting. Cut your chunk of rhizome into pieces. Each piece should have at least one of these nodes in it.

Next fill a pot or planting tray to about 1" from the top with perlite,

Perennials to Propagate from Root Cuttings

Bergenia
Black-eyed Susan
Bleeding heart
Bugbane
Columbine
Oriental poppy
Pasqueflower
Phlox
Sedum

Bergenia

Iris

Perennials to Propagate from Rhizomes

Bergenia
Bugbane (with care)
Campanula
Iris
Solomon's seal

vermiculite or seeding soil. Moisten the soil and let the excess water drain away. Lay the rhizome pieces flat on top of the mix, and almost cover them with more of the soil mix. If you leave a small bit of the top exposed to the light, it will encourage the shoots to sprout. The soil does not have to be kept wet; to avoid rot, let your rhizome dry out between waterings.

Once your rhizome cuttings have established, they can be potted individually and grown in the same manner as stem cuttings (see p. 49).

Stolons are very similar to rhizomes except that they grow horizontally on the soil surface. They can be treated in the same way as rhizomes.

Division

Division is perhaps the easiest way to propagate perennials. As most perennials grow, they form larger and larger clumps. Dividing this clump periodically will rejuvenate the plant, keep its size in check and provide you with more plants. If a plant you really want is expensive,

Digging up perennials for division (above & center)

Clump of stems, roots & crowns (below)

consider buying only one, because within a few years you may have more than you can handle.

How often, or whether, a perennial should be divided varies. Some perennials, such as astilbes, need dividing almost every year to keep them vigorous. Other perennials are content to be left alone for a long time, though they can be successfully divided for propagation purposes if desired. Still others should never be divided. They may have a single crown from which the plants grow, or, like peonies, they may simply dislike having their roots disturbed. Perennials that do not like to be divided can often be propagated by basal or stem cuttings.

Each entry in this book gives recommendations for division. In general, watch for several signs that indicate a perennial may need dividing:
- the center of the plant has died out
- the plant is no longer flowering as profusely as it did in previous years
- the plant is encroaching on the growing space of other plants sharing the bed.

Begin by digging up the entire plant clump and knocking any large clods of soil away from the rootball. The clump can then be split into several pieces. A small plant with fibrous roots can be torn into sections by hand. A large plant can be pried apart with a pair of garden forks inserted back to back into the clump. Square-bladed spades made specifically for slicing through root masses are widely available. Plants with thicker tuberous or rhizomatous roots can be cut into sections with a sharp, sterile knife. In all

cases, cut away any old sections that have died out and replant only the newer, more vigorous sections.

Once your clump has been divided into sections, replant one or two of them into the original location. Take the opportunity to work organic matter into the soil before replanting. The other sections can be

Pulling a clump apart

Cutting apart and dividing tuberous perennials

moved to new spots in the garden or potted and given to gardening friends and neighbors.

Get the sections back into the ground as quickly as possible to prevent the exposed roots from drying out. Plan where you are going to plant your divisions and have the spots prepared before you start digging up.

The larger the sections of the division are, the more quickly the plant will reestablish and grow to

Perennials That Should Not Be Divided

- Baby's breath
- Balloon flower
- Butterfly weed
- Euphorbia
- Lady's mantle
- Oriental poppy
- Peony
- Russian sage

Balloon flower

blooming size. For example, a perennial divided into four sections will bloom sooner than the same one divided into eight sections. Very small divisions may benefit from being planted in pots until they are more robust.

Newly planted divisions will need extra care and attention. Water them thoroughly and keep them well watered until they have reestablished. For the first few days after planting, give them shade from direct sunlight. A light covering of burlap or damp newspaper should be sufficient shelter. Divisions that have been planted in pots should be kept in a shaded location.

There is some debate about the best time to divide perennials. Some gardeners prefer to divide perennials while they are dormant, whereas others believe they establish more quickly if divided when they are growing vigorously. You may wish to experiment with dividing at different times of the year to see what works best for you. If you do divide perennials while they are growing, you will need to cut back one-third to one-half of the growth to avoid stressing the roots while they are repairing the damage done to them.

Sometimes if the center of a perennial dies out, it can be rejuvenated without digging up the whole plant. Dig out the center of the plant, ensuring you remove all of the dead and weak growth. Replace the soil you removed with good garden soil mixed with compost, and sprinkle a small amount of alfalfa pellets on top of the mix. The center of the plant should fill in quickly.

Problems & Pests

PERENNIAL GARDENS ARE BOTH AN ASSET AND A LIABILITY WHEN it comes to pests and diseases. Perennial beds often contain a mixture of different plant species. Because many insects and diseases attack only one species of plant, mixed beds make it difficult for pests and diseases to find their preferred hosts and establish a population. At the same time, because the plants are in the same spot for many years, any problems that do develop can become permanent. Yet, if allowed, beneficial insects, birds and other pest-devouring organisms can also develop permanent populations. Plants selected for this book are generally less susceptible to problems. Included are some native plants that have survived the conditions in Minnesota and Wisconsin for millennia.

For many years, pest control meant spraying or dusting, with the goal to eliminate every pest in the landscape. A more moderate approach advocated today is known as IPM (Integrated Pest, or Plant, Management). The goal of IPM is to reduce pest problems to levels of damage acceptable to you.

You must determine what degree of damage is acceptable. Consider whether a pest's damage is localized or covers the entire plant. Will the damage being done kill the plant or is it only affecting the outward appearance? Are there methods of controlling the pest without chemicals? For an interesting overview of IPM, consult the University of Minnesota website at <http://ipm-world.umn.edu/> or the University of Wisconsin website at <http://ipcm.wisc.edu/programs/school/default.htm>.

IPM includes learning about your plants and the conditions they need for healthy growth, what pests might affect your plants, where and when to look for those pests and how to control them. Keep records of pest damage because your observations can reveal patterns useful in spotting recurring problems and in planning your maintenance regime.

An effective, responsible pest management program has four steps. Cultural controls are the most important. Physical controls should be attempted next, followed by biological controls. Resort to chemical controls only when the first three possibilities have been exhausted.

Cultural controls are the gardening techniques you use in the day-to-day care of your garden. Perhaps the best defense against pests and diseases is to grow perennials in the conditions for which they are adapted. It is also very important to keep your soil healthy, with plenty of organic matter.

Other cultural controls are equally simple and straightforward. Choose pest-resistant varieties of perennials. Space your plants so that they have good air circulation in and around them and are not stressed from competing for light, nutrients and space. Remove plants that are decimated by the same pests every year. Dispose of diseased foliage and branches. Prevent the spread of disease by keeping your gardening tools clean and by tidying up fallen leaves and dead plant matter at the end of every growing season.

Physical controls are generally used to combat insect and mammal

Perennials That Attract Beneficial Insects

Ajuga
Aster
Black-eyed Susan
Butterfly weed
Coneflower
Daisies
Feverfew
Goldenrod
Marguerite
Monarda
Speedwell
Thyme
Yarrow

problems. An example of such a control is picking insects off plants by hand; easy if you catch the problem when it is just beginning. Large, slow insects such as Japanese beetles are particularly easy to pick off. Other physical controls include traps, barriers, scarecrows and natural repellents that make a plant taste or smell bad to pests. Garden centers offer a wide array of such devices. Physical control of diseases usually involves removing the infected plant or parts of the plant in order to keep the problem from spreading.

Biological controls make use of populations of natural predators. Such animals as birds, snakes, frogs, spiders, lady beetles and certain bacteria help keep pest populations at a manageable level. Encourage these creatures to take up permanent residence in your garden. A birdbath and birdfeeder will encourage birds to enjoy your yard and feed on a wide variety of insect pests. Many beneficial insects are probably already living in your garden. You can encourage them to stay and multiply by planting appropriate food sources. For example, many beneficial insects eat nectar from flowers.

Another form of biological control is the naturally occurring soil bacterium *Bacillus thuringiensis* var. *kurstaki*, or *B.t.* for short. It breaks down the gut lining of some insect pests. It is available in garden centers.

Chemical controls should be used only as a last resort because they can

Other Plants That Attract Beneficial Insects

Clover
Dandelion
Dill
Fennel
Lavender
Lemon balm
Lovage
Queen Anne's lace

Goldenrod

do more harm than good. These chemical pesticide products can be either organic or synthetic. If you have tried cultural, physical and biological methods and still wish to take further action, call your local county extension office to obtain a list of pesticides recommended for particular diseases or insects. Try to use 'organic' types, available at most garden centers. Organic sprays are no less dangerous than chemical ones, but they will at least break down into harmless compounds, often much sooner than synthetic compounds. Consumers are demanding effective pest products that do not harm the environment, and less toxic, more precisely targeted pesticides are becoming available. See also the environmentally friendly alternatives listed on p. 66.

The main drawback to using any chemical or organic pesticide is that it may also kill the beneficial insects you have been trying to attract. Many people think that because a pesticide is organic, they can use however much they want. An organic spray kills because it contains a lethal toxin. NEVER overuse any pesticide. When using pesticides, follow the manufacturer's instructions carefully and apply in the recommended amounts. A large amount of pesticide is not any more effective in controlling pests than the recommended amount. Note that if a particular pest is not listed on the package, it will not be controlled by that product. Proper and early identification of pests is vital to finding a quick solution.

Pests, Diseases & What to Do

It is the authors' beliefs that any pesticide we apply, whether it's organic or synthetic, disrupts the balance of microorganisms in the soil profile (containers with sterile planting mix excluded), kills many beneficial insects and sets one on the vicious circle of having to use those products to control their problems. The authors would like to see all forms of pesticides used on plants eliminated, or at least severely reduced, and people willing to accept some pest damage.

Anthracnose

Fungus. Yellow or brown spots on leaves; sunken lesions and blisters on stems; can kill plant.
What to Do: Choose resistant plants; keep soil well drained; thin out stems to improve air circulation; avoid handling wet foliage. Remove and destroy infected plant parts; clean up and destroy debris from infected plants at end of growing season. Liquid copper spray can prevent spread to other susceptible plants.

Aphids

Tiny, pear-shaped insects, winged or wingless; green, black, brown, red or gray. Cluster along stems, on buds and on leaves. Suck sap from plants; cause distorted or stunted growth. Sticky honeydew forms on surfaces and encourages sooty mold growth.
What to Do: Squish small colonies by hand; dislodge them with water spray; spray serious infestations with insecticidal soap, horticultural oil or neem oil; encourage predatory insects and birds that feed on aphids.

Aster Yellows

see Viruses

Beetles

Many types and sizes; usually rounded in shape with hard, shell-like outer wings covering membranous inner wings. Some are beneficial, e.g., ladybird beetles ('ladybugs'). Others, e.g., Japanese beetles, flea beetles, blister beetles, leaf skeletonizers and weevils, eat plants. Larvae: see Borers, Grubs. Leave wide range of chewing damage: make small or large holes in or around margins of leaves; consume entire leaves or areas between leaf veins ('skeletonize'); may also chew holes in flowers.
What to Do: Pick beetles off at night and drop them into an old coffee can half filled with soapy water (soap prevents them from floating); spread an old sheet under plants and shake off beetles to collect and dispose of them. Use a hand-held vacuum cleaner to remove them from plant. Parasitic nematodes are effective if the beetle goes through part of its growing cycle in the ground.

Blight

Fungal or bacterial diseases, many types; e.g., leaf blight, snow blight, tip blight. Leaves, stems and flowers blacken, rot and die.
What to Do: Thin stems to improve air

Green aphids

circulation; keep mulch away from base of plants; remove debris from garden at end of growing season. Remove and destroy infected plant parts.

Borers

Larvae of some moths, wasps, beetles; very damaging plant pests. Worm-like; vary in size and get bigger as they bore through plants. Burrow into stems, leaves and/or roots and rhizomes, destroying conducting tissue and weakening stems to cause breakage. Leaves will wilt; may see tunnels in leaves, stems or roots; rhizomes may be hollowed out entirely or in part.

What to Do: May be able to squish borers within leaves. Remove and destroy bored parts; may need to dig up and destroy infected roots and rhizomes.

Budworms

Moth larvae ½"–¾" long; striped; green, yellow-green, tan, dull red. Bore into buds, eat from inside out; may also eat open flowers and new leaf growth. Buds and new leaves appear tattered or riddled with holes.

What to Do: Pick off by hand daily and drop in soapy water. Remove infested plants and

destroy. Can apply preventive spray of *B.t.* on mature plants. Don't replant susceptible varieties.

Bugs (True Bugs)

Small insects, up to ½" long; green, brown, black or brightly colored and patterned. Many beneficial; a few pests, such as lace bugs, pierce plants to suck out sap. Toxins may be injected that deform plants; sunken areas left where pierced; leaves rip as they grow; leaves, buds and new growth may be dwarfed and deformed.

What to Do: Always properly identify bugs before implementing controls. Remove debris and weeds from around plants in fall to destroy overwintering sites. Pick off by hand and drop into soapy water. Use parasitic nematodes if part of bug's growth cycle is in the ground. Spray plants with insecticidal soap or neem oil.

Canker

Swollen or sunken lesions, often on stems, caused by many different bacterial and fungal diseases. Most canker-causing diseases enter through wounds.

What to Do: Maintain plant vigor; avoid causing wounds; control borers and other

tissue-dwelling pests. Prune out and destroy infected plant parts. Sterilize pruning tools before and after use.

Caterpillars

Larvae of butterflies, moths, sawflies. Examples: budworms (see Budworms), cutworms (see Cutworms), leaf rollers, leaf tiers, loopers. Chew foliage and buds; can completely defoliate plant if infestation severe.

What to Do: Removal from plant is best control. Use high-pressure water and soap, or pick caterpillars off by hand. Control biologically using *B.t.*

Caterpillar eating flowers

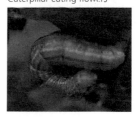

Cutworms

Larvae of some moths. About 1" long, plump, smooth-skinned; curl up when poked or disturbed. Usually affect young plants and seedlings, which may be completely consumed or chewed off at ground level.

What to Do: Pick off by hand. Use old toilet tissue rolls to make

Beneficial predatory ladybird beetle larva (above)

barrier collars around plant bases; push tubes at least halfway into ground.

Damping Off
see p. 47

Galls
Unusual swellings of plant tissues that may be caused by insects, such as *Hemerocallis* gall midge, or by diseases. Can affect leaves, buds, stems, flowers, fruit. Often a specific gall affects a single genus or species.

What to Do: Cut galls out of plant and destroy them. Galls caused by insects usually contain the insect's eggs and juvenile stages. Prevent such galls by controlling insects before they lay eggs; otherwise, try to remove and destroy infected tissue before young insects emerge. Generally, insect galls are more unsightly than damaging to plant. Galls caused by diseases often require

destruction of plant. Avoid placing other plants susceptible to same disease in that location.

Gray Mold (*Botrytis* Blight)
Fungal disease. Leaves, stems and flowers blacken, rot and die.

What to Do: Thin stems to improve air circulation; keep mulch away from base of plant, particularly in spring when plant starts to sprout; remove debris from garden at end of growing season; do not overwater. Remove and destroy any infected plant parts. Use horticultural oil as a preventive measure. Compost tea is also effective.

Grubs
Larvae of different beetles, commonly found below soil level; usually curled in C-shape. Body white or gray; head may be white, gray, brown or reddish. Problematic in lawns; may feed on plant roots. Plant wilts despite regular watering; may pull easily out of ground in severe cases.

What to Do: Toss any grubs found while digging onto a stone path or patio for birds to devour; apply parasitic nematodes.

Leaf Blotch
see Leaf Spot

Leafhoppers & Treehoppers
Small, wedge-shaped insects; can be green, brown, gray or multicolored. Jump around frantically when disturbed. Suck juice from plant leaves, cause distorted growth, carry diseases such as aster yellows.

What to Do: Encourage predators by planting nectar-producing plants. Wash insects off with strong spray of water; spray with insecticidal soap or neem oil.

Leaf Miners
Tiny, stubby larvae of some butterflies and moths; may be yellow or green. Tunnel within leaves, leaving winding trails; tunneled areas lighter in color than rest of leaf. Unsightly rather than health risk to plant.

What to Do: Remove debris from area in fall to destroy overwintering sites; attract parasitic wasps with nectar plants. Remove and destroy infected foliage; can sometimes squish by hand within leaf. Floating row covers prevent eggs from being laid on plant. Bright blue sticky cards, available in most nurseries, attract and trap adult leaf miners.

Leaf Spot

Two common types: one caused by bacteria and the other by fungi. *Bacterial*: small brown or purple speckles grow to encompass entire leaves; leaves may drop. *Fungal*: black, brown or yellow spots; leaves wither; e.g., scab, tar spot, leaf blotch.

What to Do: Bacterial infection more severe; must remove entire plant. For fungal infection, remove and destroy infected plant parts. Sterilize removal tools; avoid wetting foliage or touching wet foliage; remove and destroy debris at end of growing season. Spray plant with liquid copper. Compost tea or a mixture of baking soda and citrus oil also works in most instances.

Mealybugs

Tiny crawling insects related to aphids; appear to be covered with white fuzz or flour. More often found on houseplants than in the garden. Sucking damage stunts and stresses plant. Mealybugs excrete honeydew, promoting sooty mold.

What to Do: Remove by hand from smaller plants; wash off plant with soap and water; wipe off with alcohol-soaked swabs; remove heavily infested leaves;

encourage or introduce natural predators such as mealybug destroyer beetle and parasitic wasps; spray with insecticidal soap. Note: larvae of mealybug destroyer beetle look like very large mealybugs.

Mildew

Two types, both caused by fungus, but with slightly different symptoms. *Downy mildew*: yellow spots on upper sides of leaves and downy fuzz on undersides; fuzz may be yellow, white or gray. *Powdery mildew*: white or gray powdery coating on leaf surfaces that doesn't brush off.

What to Do: Choose resistant cultivars; space plants well; thin stems to encourage air circulation; tidy any debris in fall. Remove and destroy infected leaves or other parts. Spray compost tea or highly diluted fish emulsion (1 tsp. per qt. of water) to control downy and powdery mildew. Control powdery mildew by spraying foliage with mixture of horticultural oil and baking soda in water. Three applications one week apart needed.

Mites

Tiny, eight-legged relatives of spiders. Examples: spider mites, rust

mites, thread-footed mites. Invisible or nearly invisible to naked eye; red, yellow, green or translucent; usually found on undersides of plant leaves. Suck juice out of leaves; may see their fine webs on leaves and stems; may see mites moving on leaf undersides; leaves become discolored and speckled in appearance, then turn brown and shrivel up.

What to Do: Wash off with a strong spray of water daily until all signs of infestation are gone; predatory mites are available through garden centers; apply insecticidal soap, horticultural oil or neem oil.

Nematodes

Tiny worms that give plants disease symptoms. One type infects foliage and stems; the other infects roots. *Foliar*: yellow spots that turn brown on leaves; leaves shrivel and wither; problem starts on lowest leaves and works up plant. *Rootknot*: plant is stunted; may wilt; yellow spots on leaves; roots have tiny bumps or knots.

What to Do: Mulch soil, add organic matter, clean up debris in fall; don't touch wet foliage of infected plants. Can add parasitic nematodes to soil. Remove infected plants in extreme cases.

Rot

Several different fungi or bacteria that affect different parts of plant and can kill plant. *Bacterial soft rot*: enters through wounds; begins as small, water-soaked lesions on roots and leaves. As lesions grow, their surfaces darken but remain unbroken, while underlying tissue becomes soft and mushy. Lesions may ooze if surface broken. *Black rot*: bacterial; enters through pores or small wounds. Begins as V-shaped lesions along leaf margins. Leaf veins turn black and eventually plant dies. *Crown rot (stem rot)*: fungal; affects base of plant, causing stems to blacken and fall over and leaves to yellow and wilt. *Root rot*: fungal; leaves yellow and plant wilts; digging up plant shows roots rotted away.
What to Do: Keep soil well drained; don't damage plant when digging around it; keep mulches away from plant base. Remove infected plants.

Rust

Fungi. Pale spots on upper leaf surfaces; orange, fuzzy or dusty spots on leaf undersides. Examples: blister rust, hollyhock rust, white rust.
What to Do: Choose varieties and cultivars resistant to rust; avoid handling wet leaves; provide plant with good air circulation; use horticultural oil to protect new foliage; clean up garden debris at end of season. Remove and destroy infected plant parts. Do not put infected plants in compost pile.

Scale Insects

Tiny, shelled insects that suck sap, weakening and possibly killing plant or making it vulnerable to other problems. Scale appears as tiny bumps typically along stems or on undersides of foliage. Once female scale insect has pierced plant with mouthpart, it is there for life. Juvenile scale insects are called crawlers.
What to Do: Wipe off with alcohol-soaked swabs; spray with water to dislodge crawlers; prune out heavily infested branches; encourage natural predators and parasites; spray horticultural oil in spring before bud break.

Slugs & Snails

Both mollusks. Snails have a spiral shell, slugs lack shells; both have slimy, smooth skin. Can be up to 8" long; gray, green, black, beige, yellow or spotted. Leave large ragged holes in leaves and silvery slime trails on and around plants.
What to Do: Remove slug habitat, including garden debris or mulches around plant bases. Use slug-repellent mulches. Increase air circulation. Pick off by hand in the evening and squish with boot or drop in can of soapy water. Spread diatomaceous earth (available in garden centers; do not use the kind meant for swimming pool filters) on soil around plants to pierce and dehydrate the soft slug or snail bodies. Commercial slug and snail baits are effective; some new formulations nontoxic to pets and children. Stale beer in a sunken, shallow dish may be effective. Attach strips of copper to wood around raised beds or to small boards inserted around susceptible groups of plants; slugs and snails get shocked if they touch copper surfaces.

Smut

Fungus that affects any above-ground plant parts including leaves, stems and flowers. Forms fleshy white galls that turn black and powdery.

What to Do: Remove and destroy infected plants. Avoid placing same plants in that spot for next few years.

Sooty Mold

Fungus. Thin black film forms on leaf surfaces and reduces amount of light getting to leaf surfaces.

What to Do: Wipe mold off leaf surfaces; control insects such as aphids, mealybugs, whiteflies (honeydew left on leaves encourages mold).

Spider Mites
see Mites

Thrips

Tiny insects, difficult to see; may be visible if you disturb them by blowing gently on an infested flower. Yellow, black or brown with narrow, fringed wings. Suck juice out of plant cells, particularly in flowers and buds, causing gray-mottled petals and leaves, dying buds and distorted, stunted growth.

What to Do: Remove and destroy infected plant parts; encourage native predatory insects with nectar plants; spray severe infestations with insecticidal soap or with horticultural oil. Use blue sticky cards to attract and trap adults.

Viruses

Plant may be stunted and leaves and flowers distorted, streaked or discolored. Examples: aster yellows, mosaic virus, ringspot virus.

What to Do: Viral diseases in plants cannot be treated. Destroy infected plants; control insects such as aphids, leafhoppers and whiteflies that spread disease.

Weevils
see Beetles

Whiteflies

Tiny, white, moth-like insects that flutter up into the air when the plant is disturbed. Live on undersides of leaves and suck juice out, causing yellowed leaves and weakened plants; leave sticky honeydew on leaves, encouraging sooty mold.

What to Do: Usual and most effective remedy is to remove infested plant so insects don't spread to rest of garden. Destroy weeds where insects may live. Attract native predatory beetles and parasitic wasps with nectar plants. Spray severe cases with insecticidal soap. Use yellow sticky cards or make your own sticky trap: mount tin can on stake, wrap can with yellow paper and cover with clear small plastic bag smeared with petroleum jelly; replace bag when full of flies. Plant sweet alyssum in immediate area. Make a spray from old coffee grounds.

Wilt

If watering hasn't helped a wilted plant, one of two wilt fungi may be at fault. *Fusarium* wilt: plant wilts, leaves turn yellow then die; symptoms generally appear first on one part of plant before spreading to other parts. *Verticillium* wilt: plant wilts; leaves curl up at edges; leaves turn yellow then drop off; plant may die.

What to Do: Both wilts difficult to control. Choose resistant plant varieties and cultivars; clean up debris at end of growing season. Destroy infected plants; solarize (sterilize) soil before replanting; contact local garden center for assistance.

Worms
see Caterpillars, Nematodes

Mosaic virus

Pest Control Alternatives

The following common-sense treatments for pests and diseases allow the gardener some measure of control without resorting to harmful chemical fungicides and pesticides.

Ant Control

Mix 3 c. water, 1 c. white sugar and 4 tsp. liquid boric acid in a pot. Bring this mix just to a boil and remove it from the heat source. Let the mix cool. Pour small amounts of the cooled mix into bottlecaps or other very small containers and place them around the ant-infested area. You can also try setting out a mixture of equal parts powdered borax and icing sugar (no water).

Antitranspirants

These products were developed to reduce water transpiration, or loss of water, in plants. The waxy polymers surround fungal spores, preventing the spread of spores to nearby leaves and stems. When applied according to label directions, these products are environmentally friendly.

Baking Soda & Citrus Oil

This mixture treats both leaf spot and powdery mildew. In a spray bottle, mix 4 tsp. baking soda, 1 tbsp. citrus oil and 1 gal. water. Spray the foliage lightly, including the undersides. Do not pour or spray this mix directly onto soil.

Baking Soda & Horticultural Oil

Research has confirmed the effectiveness of this mixture against powdery mildew. In a spray bottle, mix

Slug on leaf

4 tsp. baking soda, 1 tbsp. horticultural oil and 1 gal. water. Spray the foliage lightly, including the undersides. Do not pour or spray this mix directly onto soil.

Coffee Grounds Spray

Boil 2 lbs. used coffee grounds in 3 gal. of water for about 10 minutes. Allow to cool; strain the grounds out. Apply as a spray to reduce problems with whiteflies.

Compost Tea

Mix 1–2 lbs. compost in 5 gal. of water. Let sit for four to seven days. Dilute the mix until it resembles weak tea. Use during normal watering or apply as a foliar spray to prevent or treat fungal diseases.

Fish Emulsion/Seaweed (Kelp)

These products are usually used as foliar nutrient feeds but appear to also work against fungal diseases either by preventing the fungus from spreading to noninfected areas or by changing the growing conditions for the fungus.

Garlic Spray

This spray is an effective, organic means of controlling aphids, leafhoppers, whiteflies and some fungi and nematodes. Soak 6 tbsp. finely minced garlic in 2 tsp. mineral oil for at least 24 hours. Add 1 pt. of water and 1½ tsp. of liquid dish soap. Stir and strain into a glass container for storage. Combine 1–2 tbsp. of this concentrate with 2 c. water to make a spray. Test the spray on a couple of leaves and check after two days for any damage. If no damage, spray infested plants thoroughly, ensuring good coverage of the foliage.

Horticultural Oil

Mix 5 tbsp. horticultural oil per 1 gal. of water and apply as a spray for a variety of insect and fungal problems.

Insecticidal Soap

Mix 1 tsp. of mild dish detergent or pure soap (biodegradable options are available) with 1 qt. of water in a clean spray bottle. Spray the surfaces of insect-infested plants and rinse well within an hour of spraying to avoid foliage discoloration.

Neem Oil

Neem oil is derived from the neem tree (native to India) and is used as an insecticide, miticide and fungicide. It is most effective when used preventively. Apply when conditions are favorable for disease development. Neem is virtually harmless to most beneficial insects and microorganisms.

Sulfur & Lime-Sulfur

These products are good as preventive measures for fungal diseases. You can purchase ready-made products or wettable powders that you mix yourself. Do not spray when the temperature is expected to be 90° F or higher, or you may damage your plants.

About This Guide

THE PERENNIALS IN THIS BOOK ARE ORGANIZED ALPHABETICALLY BY their most familiar common names, which in some cases is the proper botanical name. This system enables those who are familiar only with the common name for a plant to find the plant easily in the book. The botanical name is always listed (in italics). Readers are strongly encouraged to learn these botanical names. Common names are sometimes spread over any number of very different plants. They also change from region to region. The additional common names that appear after the primary reference illustrate this. Only the true botanical name for a plant defines exactly what plant it is, everywhere on the planet. Learning and using the botanical names for plants you grow allows you to discuss, research and purchase plants with supreme confidence.

The illustrated Flowers at a Glance section at the beginning of the book allows you to become familiar with the different flowers quickly, and it will help you find a plant if you're not sure what it's called.

Clearly indicated at the beginning of each entry are height and spread ranges, flower colors, blooming times and hardiness zones. At the back of the book, you will find a Quick Reference Chart that summarizes different features and requirements of the plants.

Each entry gives clear instructions and tips for planting and growing the perennial, and it recommends many of our favorite species and varieties. Note: If height or spread ranges or hardiness zones are not given for a recommended plant, assume these values are the same as the ranges at the beginning of the entry. Keep in mind, too, that many more hybrids, cultivars and varieties are often available. Check with your local greenhouses or garden centers when making your selection.

Pests or diseases commonly associated with a perennial, if any, are also listed for each entry.

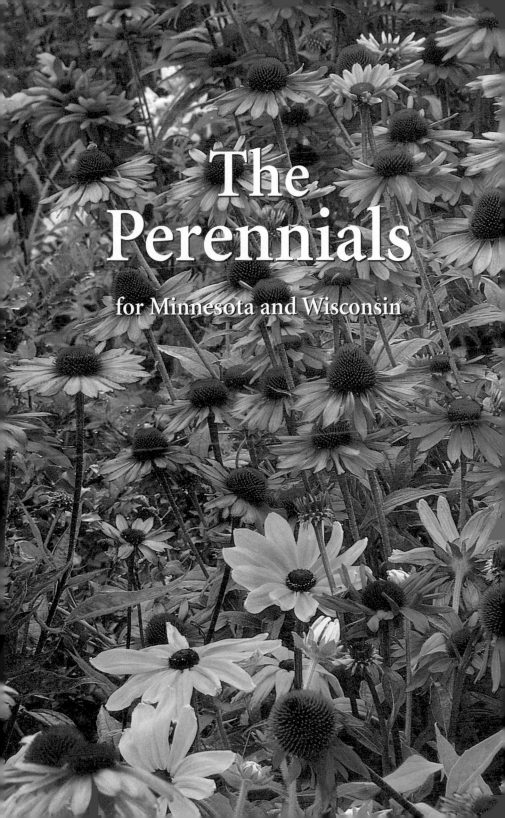

The Perennials

for Minnesota and Wisconsin

Ajuga
Bugleweed
Ajuga

Height: 6–10" **Spread:** 12–24" **Flower color:** blue; plant grown for foliage
Blooms: spring to early summer **Zones:** 3–8

ONCE YOU START GROWING AJUGA, YOU'LL WONDER HOW YOU gardened without it. Whether it is scattered here and there alongside a shady stone path or massed to create a billowy blanket in partial sun, ajuga will quickly become one of your favorite groundcovers. Although pretty in bloom, this plant is grown for its leaves. Credit the nursery industry; new varieties introduced over the past 15 years have created wonderful variations in leaf color that provide striking contrast to the foliage of nearly any plant in near proximity. Try it in combination with astilbe, ferns, hosta and heuchera. It looks good just about everywhere.

Planting

Seeding: Not recommended; foliage often reverts to green in seedlings

Planting out: Spring to fall

Spacing: 12–18"

Growing

Ajugas develop the best leaf color in **partial or light shade,** but they tolerate full sun and full shade. The leaves may become scorched in direct sun. Any **well-drained** soil is suitable. Winter protection, such as a mulch, is recommended if snow cover isn't dependable in your garden. Divide these vigorous plants anytime during the growing season.

Remove any new growth or seedlings that don't show the hybrid leaf coloring.

Tips

Ajugas make excellent groundcovers for difficult sites, such as exposed slopes and dense shade. They are also attractive groundcovers in shrub borders because the ajugas' dense growth will prevent the spread of all but the most tenacious weeds.

A. reptans cultivar

Syrup made from ajuga has been used to cure hangovers.

A. reptans with Achillea filipendulina

A. reptans

A. reptans cultivar

Ajuga reptans *is widely used in homeopathic remedies for throat and mouth irritations.*

A. reptans with Antirrhinum

If you plant ajugas next to a lawn, you may soon be calling them weeds. These plants can easily take over the lawn because they spread readily by stolons (above-ground shoots), and their low growth escapes the lawn-mower blades. The spread of ajugas may be somewhat controlled by the use of bed-edging materials. If an ajuga starts to take over, it is easy to rip out, and the soil it leaves behind will be soft and loose from the penetrating roots. You can use an ajuga in this manner to prepare the soil before you plant anything fussier in a shaded or woodland garden.

If you're not a stickler when it comes to edging beds, plant these aggressive growers in areas bordered by brick or cement. Close spacing and regular watering help these plants spread quickly and fill in, preventing weeds from springing up among the groundcover.

Recommended

A. pyramidalis is a mound-forming plant 6–10" tall and 18–24" wide. Deep blue to pale blue flowers are borne in whorls along the top of the flowering stems from spring to early summer. The flower clusters resemble small pyramids. '**Metallica Crispa**' grows 6" tall and 12–16" wide, with dense, crinkled, iridescent purple-green foliage.

A. reptans is a low, quick-spreading groundcover. It grows about 6" tall and spreads 18–24". '**Braunherz**' ('Bronze Heart') is an excellent, purple-bronze cultivar with bright blue flowers. It remains compact and richly colored all year. **'Burgundy Glow'** has variegated foliage in shades of bronze, green, white and pink. The habit is dense and compact. **'Caitlin's Giant'** has large, bronze leaves. It bears short spikes of bright blue flowers in spring. **'Jungle Beauty'** has large, dark green to purple foliage with red margins and indigo blue flowers held well above the foliage. **'Multicolor'** ('Rainbow,' 'Tricolor') is a vigorous spreader. The bronze leaves are splashed with pink and white. **'Variegata'** is dense and slow growing. The green leaves have silver margins. The best color develops in the shade.

Problems & Pests

Occasional problems with crown rot, leaf spot and root rot can be avoided by providing good air circulation and by ensuring the plant is not standing in water for extended periods.

A. reptans (photos this page)

According to European folk myths, ajugas cause fires if brought into the house.

Anemone
Windflower
Anemone

Height: 1–5' **Spread:** 12–24" **Flower color:** white, pink, purple
Blooms: spring, summer, fall **Zones:** 3–9

IF IT WASN'T FOR THEIR FINICKINESS ABOUT THE CULTURAL
conditions in which they are grown, anemones, a diverse group of plants,
would be far more popular. However, it's worth the little extra effort
required to grow anemones successfully, for each of the species available to
gardeners shares the common trait of attractive dark green foliage and
breathtaking blooms. For beginners, try growing *A. sylvestris* (snowdrop
anemone) in partial shade. It blooms in spring, and its foliage holds its
beauty all season.

Planting
Seeding: Not recommended
Planting out: Spring
Spacing: 4–18"

Growing

Anemones prefer **partial or light shade** but tolerate full sun. The soil should be of **average to high fertility, humus rich** and **moist**. While dormant, anemones should have dry soil. Mulch Japanese anemone the first winter to help it establish. Divide anemones in spring or fall.

Deadhead only to keep a tidy look because removing spent flowers will not extend the bloom.

Tips

Anemones make a beautiful addition to lightly shaded borders, woodland gardens and rock gardens.

Anemones look great when planted in front of red brick or wood siding, particularly natural or unpainted wood.

A. x *hybrida* (photos this page)

A. x hybrida

The name anemone (a-nem-o-nee) comes from the Greek anemos, *'wind,' referring to the windswept mountainside habitat of some species.*

Recommended

A. canadensis (meadow anemone) is a spreading plant with slightly invasive tendencies. It grows 12–24" tall, with an equal spread. The yellow-centered, white flowers are borne in late spring and early summer. To become established, this plant needs regular watering when first planted. (Zones 3–8)

A. x hybrida (Japanese anemone) is an upright, suckering hybrid. It grows 2–5' tall, spreads about 24" and bears pink or white flowers from late summer to early fall. Many cultivars are available. **'Honorine Jobert'** has plentiful white flowers. **'Königin Charlotte'** ('Queen Charlotte') is a vigorous plant with large, semi-double, pink to pale purple flowers. **'Pamina'** has pinkish red, double flowers. **'Whirlwind'** has white, semi-double flowers. (Zones 4–8)

A. sylvestris (snowdrop anemone) grows 12–20" tall and wide and spreads quickly by suckers. It produces slightly drooping, fragrant,

A. canadensis

white flowers with yellow stamens from late spring to early summer. (Zones 4–9)

A. tomentosa is a large, clump-forming plant that spreads by underground shoots. It grows 3–4' tall and spreads 24". The mid-green leaves are very woolly on the under-sides. Clusters of pale pink flowers are borne in late summer to early fall. '**Robustissima**' has gray-green foliage and abundant, soft pink flowers. (Zones 3–8)

Problems & Pests

Rare but possible problems include leaf gall, downy mildew, smut, fungal leaf spot, powdery mildew, rust, nematodes, caterpillars, slugs and flea beetles.

A. x hybrida (photos this page)

Artemisia
Mugwort, Wormwood, Sage
Artemisia

Height: 6"–6' **Spread:** 6–36" **Flower color:** white or yellow, generally inconspicuous; plant grown for foliage **Blooms:** late summer, mid-fall **Zones:** 3–8

I LEARNED TWO THINGS IN MY LAUGHABLE ATTEMPTS AT GROWING artemisia. One, when gardening guides or other gardeners say it needs full sun, they mean full sun—anything less than six hours and the plant grows both poorly *and* horizontally (as it did in my too-shady garden for two seasons). Two, 'Silver Queen,' the cultivar I naively brought home, also has the nerve to be highly invasive. (My problem, not yours.) If any portion of your garden is blessed with full sun, at least one of the less invasive varieties discussed here should be grown; the silver foliage from a perennial that is as easy to grow as artemisia is too striking to exclude.

Planting
Seeding: Not recommended

Planting out: Spring, summer or fall

Spacing: 10–36"

Growing

Artemisias grow best in **full sun**. The soil should be of **average to high fertility** and **well drained**. These plants dislike wet, humid conditions.

Artemisias respond well to pruning in late spring. If you prune before May, the frost may kill any new growth. Whenever artemisias begin to look straggly, they may be cut back hard to encourage new growth and to maintain a neater form. Divide every one or two years when plants appear to be thinning in the centers.

Tips

Artemisias can be used in rock gardens and borders. Their silver gray foliage makes them good backdrop plants to place behind brightly colored flowers, and they are useful for filling in spaces between other plants. Smaller forms may also be used to create knot gardens.

Some species can become invasive. If you want to control horizontal spreading of an artemisia, plant it in a bottomless container. Sunk into the ground, the container is hidden, and it prevents the plant from spreading beyond the container's edges. You can maintain good drainage by removing the bottom of the container.

There are almost 300 species of Artemisia *distributed around the world.*

A. ludoviciana 'Silver Queen'

The genus name may honor either Artemisia, a botanist and medical researcher from 353 BC and the sister of King Mausolus, or Artemis, Goddess of the Hunt and the Moon in Greek mythology.

A. schmidtiana 'Nana'

A. *ludoviciana* 'Valerie Finnis'

A. absinthium *lent its name and its flavor to the liqueur absinthe, which was once popular in France. Absinthe, which contains the wormwood toxin thujone, is illegal to sell in the U.S.*

A. *ludoviciana* with phlox & malva

Recommended

A. absinthium (common wormwood) is a clump-forming, woody-based perennial. It has aromatic, hairy, gray foliage and bears inconspicuous yellow flowers in late summer. It grows 24–36" tall and about 24" wide. '**Lambrook Silver**' has attractive silver gray foliage. (Zones 4–8)

A. lactiflora (white mugwort) is an upright, clump-forming species that is 4–6' tall and 24–36" wide. This species is one of the few artemisias to bear showy flowers; its attractive creamy white blooms appear from late summer to mid-fall. The foliage of this hardy species is dark green or gray-green. '**Guizhou**' is slightly smaller than the species. It has very dark, black-green foliage and dark brown stems that contrast well with the cream-colored flowers. It blooms from late summer to fall. (Zones 4–8)

A. ludoviciana (white sage, silver sage) is an upright, clump-forming species. It grows 2–4' tall and 24" wide. The foliage is silvery white, and the flowers are inconspicuous. The species is not grown as often as the cultivars. '**Silver King**' is compact and very hardy. It has very hairy, silvery white foliage. It grows about 24" tall. '**Silver Queen**' has deeply divided, silvery foliage. It can be invasive. It grows 24–30" tall. '**Valerie Finnis**' is a good choice for hot, dry areas. It has very wide, silvery leaves, is less invasive than the species and combines beautifully with many other perennials. (Zones 4–8)

A. schmidtiana (silvermound) is low, dense and mound-forming. It grows

12–24" tall and spreads 12–18". The foliage is feathery, hairy and silvery gray. **'Nana'** (dwarf silvermound) is very compact, growing 6–10" tall and wide. This cultivar is extremely hardy and can be grown in all parts of Minnesota and Wisconsin. (Zones 3–8)

A. stelleriana grows to 24" tall and spreads by rhizomes. The deeply toothed foliage is covered in dense, white hairs. **'Silver Brocade'** is a low, somewhat spreading cultivar about 6" tall and up to 18" in spread. Its soft, pale gray leaves have rounded lobes. This very hardy cultivar can be grown all over Minnesota and Wisconsin. (Zones 3–8)

Problems & Pests

Rust, downy mildew and other fungal diseases are possible problems for artemisias.

A. lactiflora

A. ludoviciana 'Silver King'

Aster

Aster, Symphyotrichum

Height: 10"–5' **Spread:** 12–36" **Flower color:** red, white, blue, purple, pink
Blooms: late spring, summer, fall **Zones:** 3–9

SHOW ME A GARDEN THAT HAS NO VIBRANT, FRESH BLOOMS IN late summer, and I'll show you a gardener who has not yet discovered the joy of asters. Asters, which are prolific bloomers, range from the low-growing varieties that are outstanding in rock gardens to towering specimens required of the modern cottage garden. I find that shorter asters serve best as single plantings; their foliage doesn't bring much to the party, meaning if you plant three or more together you create a large area that commands little interest until bloom time. The very tall varieties among the New England asters, however, look great in broad swaths.

Planting

Seeding: Not recommended

Planting out: Spring or fall

Spacing: 18–36"

Growing

Asters prefer **full sun**, but they tolerate partial shade. The soil should be **fertile, moist** and **well drained**. Pinch or shear these plants back in early summer to promote dense growth and to reduce disease problems. Mulch in winter to protect plants from temperature fluctuations. Divide every two to three years to maintain vigor and to control spread.

Plant the New England asters to the rear of the bed where their narrow, plain leaves are hidden by other plants.

Tips

Asters can be used in the middle of borders and in cottage gardens. These plants can also be naturalized in wild gardens.

Recommended

Some *Aster* species have recently been reclassified under the genus *Symphyotrichum*. You may see both names at garden centers, but we will stick with *Aster* here.

A. novae-angliae

These old-fashioned flowers were once called starworts because of the many petals that radiate out from the center of the flowerhead.

A. novae-angliae

A. alpinus is an erect, clump-forming plant 10" tall and 18" wide. Solitary, occasionally 3–4 in a cluster, 2" wide, yellow-centered, violet to blue violet flowers are produced in late spring to mid-summer. (Zones 3–8)

A. dumosus (bushy aster) is a mounding plant that grows 15–36" tall and 24–36" wide and produces loose clusters of $1/2$" wide, yellow-centered, lavender, blue or white flowers in late summer to fall. The following cultivars are bushy, mounding plants that grow 12–18" tall and 18–24" wide, with good disease resistance and abundant flowers. **'Wood's Light Blue'** ('Wood's Blue') has light blue flowers. **'Wood's Pink'** has pink flowers. **'Wood's Purple'** bears purple flowers. (Zones 4–9)

A. ericoides (heath aster) is a bushy, well-branched plant, growing 36" tall and 12" wide, that spreads by rhizomes. The $1/2$" wide, yellow-centered, white flowers are borne abundantly in loose clusters from late summer to fall. The flowers are sometimes flushed with pink or blue. The lower leaves of this species

drop early, so plant something to hide the exposed lower stems. (Zones 3–8)

A. x *frikartii* produces abundant and continuous blooms in light to dark shades of purple. These hybrids can be temperamental and may need replanting after several years. They grow up to 24" tall and spread to 18". 'Mönch' is a taller variety, up to 30", with abundant lavender blue flowers. (Zones 4–9)

A. laevis (smooth aster) is a tall, mounding plant that grows 3–3¹/₂' tall and 12–24" wide producing large leaves and narrow, pyramidal clusters of violet to blue flowers with yellow centers. This species and its cultivars are mildew resistant. 'Bluebird' grows 30–36" tall and 24" wide and bears violet blue flowers. (Zones 3–8)

A. lateriflorus (calico aster) is a many-stemmed plant that grows 3–4' tall and 12–18" wide. It produces clusters of very small, reddish pink-centered, white to pale violet flowers from mid-summer to fall. 'Lady in Black' is an upright, spreading plant that grows 3–4' tall and 24–36" wide. It has small, purple black foliage and red-centered, pink-flushed, white flowers. 'Prince' is a well-branched plant growing 24–30" tall and 24–36" wide, with dark purple foliage and red-centered, white flowers. (Zones 3–8)

A. novae-angliae

A. novae-angliae (New England aster) is an upright, spreading, clump-forming perennial that grows to 5' tall and spreads to 24". It bears yellow-centered, purple flowers. 'Alma Potschke' bears bright salmon pink or cherry red flowers. It grows 3–4' tall and spreads 24". 'Hella Lacy' grows 3–4' tall and 24–36" wide bearing bright purple-pink flowers. 'Purple Dome' is dwarf and spreading with dark purple flowers. It grows 18–24" tall and spreads 24–30". This cultivar resists mildew. (Zones 3–8)

Problems & Pests

Powdery mildew, aster wilt, aster yellows, aphids, mites, slugs and nematodes can cause trouble.

Astilbe

Astilbe

Height: 10"–4' **Spread:** 8–36" **Flower color:** white, pink, peach, purple, red
Blooms: late spring, early, mid- or late summer **Zones:** 3–9

INTEREST IN THIS MOST DESIRABLE PERENNIAL HAS
skyrocketed in recent years. A lot of new gardeners are learning an important horticultural lesson from growing it.
Many perennials that are listed as requiring full sun bloom
nicely in partial shade, but plants such as astilbe that prefer
partial shade will usually fry up and die in full sun. You
can't grow it in full sun unless you water it every 35 minutes. Instead, plant astilbe where it receives only a half-
day of sun or dappled shade throughout the day.
Remember to water it about twice as often as most
other perennials. Then stand back and marvel at this
perennial, which has refined, lace-like foliage and
graceful, bedazzling blooms.

Planting

Seeding: Not recommended; seedlings do not come true to type

Planting out: Spring

Spacing: 18–36"

Growing

Astilbes enjoy **light or partial shade** and tolerate full shade, though with reduced flowering in deep shade. The soil should be **fertile, humus rich, acidic, moist** and **well drained**. Astilbes like to grow near water sources, such as ponds and streams, but they dislike standing in water. Provide a mulch in summer to keep the roots cool and moist. Divide every three years in spring or fall to maintain plant vigor.

Tips

Astilbes can be grown near the edges of bog gardens or ponds and in woodland gardens and shaded borders.

The root crown of an astilbe tends to lift out of the soil as the plant grows.

A. x arendsii (photos this page)

In late summer, transplant seedlings found near the parent plant for plumes of color throughout the garden.

A. *x arendsii* (above & next page)
A. *japonica* 'Deutschland'

This problem can be solved by applying a top dressing of rich soil as a mulch when the plant starts lifting or by lifting the entire plant and replanting it deeper into the soil.

Astilbe flowers fade to various shades of brown. Deadheading will not extend the bloom, so the choice is yours whether to remove the spent blossoms. Astilbes self-seed easily, and the flowerheads look interesting and natural in the garden well into fall. Self-seeded plants are unlikely to look like the parent plant.

Recommended

A. x *arendsii* (Arendsii Group, astilbe, false spirea) grows 1½–4' tall and spreads 18–36". Many cultivars are available from this hybrid group, including the following popular selections: '**Bressingham Beauty**' bears bright pink flowers in mid-summer; '**Cattleya**' bears reddish pink flowers in mid-summer; and '**Etna**' grows 24–30" tall and spreads 18–24". It bears dark red flowers in early summer. '**Fanal**' bears red flowers in early summer and has deep bronze foliage. '**Weisse Gloria**' bears creamy white flowers in mid- to late summer.

A. chinensis (Chinese astilbe) is a dense, vigorous perennial that

Astilbes make great cut flowers, and if you leave the plumes in a vase as the water evaporates, you'll have dried flowers to enjoy all winter.

tolerates dry soil better than other astilbe species. It grows about 24" tall and spreads 18". It bears fluffy, white, pink or purple flowers in late summer. 'Pumila' is more commonly found than the species. This plant forms a low groundcover 10" tall and 8" wide. It bears dark pink flowers. 'Veronica Klose' grows 16" tall and bears rose purple flowers. 'Visions' grows 12–18" tall. It has bronze-green foliage and raspberry rose flowers that begin blooming in early summer.

A. japonica (Japanese astilbe) is a compact, clump-forming perennial. The species is rarely grown in favor of the cultivars. 'Avalanche' grows 24–36" tall and has arching clusters of white flowers. 'Deutschland' grows 20" tall and spreads 12". It bears white flowers in late spring. 'Peach Blossom' bears peach pink flowers in early summer. It grows about 20" tall.

A. simplicifolia is a mound-forming plant 16" tall and 12" wide. It bears glossy, deeply cut or lobed foliage and narrow clusters of star-shaped, white flowers that bloom in summer. The hybrid 'Hennie Graafland' grows 16" tall and 12" wide with bronze-green foliage and bears light rose pink flowers in mid- to late summer.

Problems & Pests

A variety of pests, such as whiteflies, black vine weevils and Japanese beetle, can occasionally attack astilbes. Powdery mildew, bacterial leaf spot and fungal leaf spot are also possible problems.

Baby's Breath

Gypsophila

Height: 8–36" **Spread:** 1–4' **Flower color:** white, pink, lilac, pale purple
Blooms: summer, fall **Zones:** 3–7

TOO MANY GARDENERS SET OUT TO GROW BABY'S BREATH, BUT
then have difficulty keeping a healthy specimen around for more than a season or two. Meanwhile, my neighbor across the street tears it out in great
clumps every four years so it doesn't carpet every inch of her garden. The
difference is in ensuring you have proper soil. *Gypsophila* prefers an alkaline
soil (the name is derived from the Greek word meaning 'lime-loving') that
drains well. Test your soil to determine pH. A little lime, worked into the soil
at the base of the plant, is likely required.

Planting

Seeding: Species plants are easy to start from seed. Sow in cold frame in early spring or direct sow in early fall or spring; soil temperature should be 70°–80° F for germination. Cultivars and hybrids may not come true to type.

Planting out: Spring or fall

Spacing: 24"

Growing

Grow these plants in **full sun**. The soil must be **neutral** or **alkaline**, of **average fertility** and very **well drained**. In moist, acidic soil these plants are prone to rotting.

Once the main flowering period passes, they can be cut back to encourage rebloom in fall.

Baby's breath plants develop a large, thick taproot that should not be disturbed once it is established, so do not divide these plants. Rather, propagate them by root cuttings in late winter or by basal cuttings in summer.

G. paniculata

G. paniculata cultivar

Tips

Baby's breath plants, with their cloud-like flower clusters, tie together other plantings in a border. They are effective when planted with plants that have broad leaves.

These plants may require staking if they are not grown among other perennials or annuals.

Recommended

G. paniculata is a mound-forming, open, branched perennial growing 36" tall and 2–4' wide. It bears tiny, white flowers for an extended period in summer. '**Bristol Fairy**' bears pure white, double flowers. '**Perfecta**' ('Fairy Perfect') has large, white, double flowers. '**Pink Fairy**' grows 18–24" tall and wide and bears double, pink flowers that bloom

G. repens

G. paniculata cultivar

until frost. 'Viette's Dwarf' is a smaller plant, 12–16" tall, with pink, double flowers.

G. repens is a low-growing species that reaches up to 8" tall and spreads to form a mat 12–20" wide. This species is more acid tolerant than *G. paniculata* and may be used in rock gardens, on rock walls, on pathway edges or at the front of a border. It bears loose clusters of white, lilac or pale purple flowers for a long period in summer. 'Rosea' has pink flowers arising from deep rose-colored buds.

Problems & Pests

Baby's breath plants attract slugs. Problems with crown gall, bacterial soft rot or crown or stem rot can be avoided with proper drainage.

G. paniculata

Fresh or dried, the sprays of flowers make a wonderful addition to arrangements.

G. repens

Balloon Flower

Platycodon

Height: 24–36" **Spread:** 12–18" **Flower color:** blue, pink, white
Blooms: summer **Zones:** 3–8

ONLY A HANDFUL OF PERENNIALS ARE AS ELEGANT AS BALLOON flower. In bloom, this flower seems to say 'Eat your heart out.' The bloom is unique—what begins as a puffed-out, five-sided, sealed box bursts open to create a cupped, star-shaped flower, often up to eight per stem. Because I can't seem to have enough blue in my garden, I grow and adore the standard blue variety, but the pink- and white-blooming varieties also display arresting elegance. As with all superior perennials, deadheading balloon flower (without cutting the main stem) will greatly prolong the bloom period.

When using these flowers in arrangements, singe the cut ends with a lit match to prevent the milky white sap from running.

Planting

Seeding: Start indoors in late winter or direct sow in spring; plants bloom second year after seeding

Planting out: Spring

Spacing: 12–18"

Growing

Balloon flower grows well in **full sun** or **partial shade.** The soil should be of **average to rich fertility, light, moist** and **well drained.** Balloon flower dislikes wet soil. It sprouts late in the season, so mark its location to avoid accidentally damaging it before it sprouts.

Balloon flower rarely needs dividing. It resents having its roots disturbed and can take a long time to reestablish itself after dividing. Propagate by gently detaching the side shoots that sprout up around the plant. Plants will self-seed, and the seedlings can be moved to new locations.

Tips

Use balloon flower in borders, rock gardens and cottage gardens.

Pinch off spent flowers to improve appearance.

Recommended

P. grandiflorus is an upright, clump-forming perennial; the cultivars tend to be lower and more rounded in habit. The species grows 24–36" tall, spreads 12–18" and bears blue flowers in summer. '**Albus**' bears white flowers, often veined with blue. '**Double Blue**' is a compact plant with purple-blue, double flowers. '**Shell Pink**' has clear, pale pink flowers.

Except for occasional problems with slugs, snails and leaf spot, balloon flower is a relatively trouble-free plant.

'Double Blue' (above)

'Albus' (center)

P. grandiflorus (below)

Bergenia

Bergenia

Height: 12–24" **Spread:** 12–24" or more **Flower color:** red, purple, pink, white **Blooms:** spring **Zones:** 3–8

HERE WE HAVE AN UNUSUAL ASIATIC PERENNIAL VALUED AS MUCH for its evergreen, cabbage-like leaves as its curious bloom habit. Bergenias make wonderful edging plants and are useful as groundcovers. In spring, clusters of small, five-petaled flowers rise out of the broad foliage on reddish, 12–24" stems, for a most unusual display. Though bergenias are hardy to zone 3, flowering is somewhat diminished following harsh winters; you can use a mulch of marsh hay in fall to help alleviate the effects of those conditions.

Planting

Seeding: Seeds may not come true to type. Fresh, ripe seeds should be sown uncovered, either indoors or in the garden. Keep soil temperature at 69°–70° F.

Planting out: Spring

Spacing: 10–20"

Growing

Bergenias grow well in **full sun** or **partial shade.** The soil should be of **average to rich fertility** and **well drained.** A **moist** soil is preferable, especially when plants are grown in full sun, but these plants are somewhat drought tolerant once established. Divide every two to three years when the clump begins to die out in the middle.

Propagating by seed can be somewhat risky; you may not get what you want. A more certain way to get more of the plants you have is to propagate them with root cuttings. Bergenias spread just below the surface by rhizomes, which may be cut off in pieces and grown separately as long as a leaf shoot is attached to the section. Top-dress soil with compost in spring if rhizomes appear to be lifting out of the soil.

Tips

These versatile, low-growing, spreading plants can be used as groundcovers, as edging along borders and pathways, as part of rock gardens and in mass plantings under trees and shrubs.

B. 'Bressingham White'

B. cordifolia

Once flowering is complete, in early spring, bergenias still make a beautiful addition to the garden with their thick, leathery, glossy leaves. A bergenia provides a soothing background for other flowers with its expanse of green. As well, many varieties turn attractive shades of bronze and purple in fall and winter.

Recommended

B. 'Abëndglut' ('Evening Glow') grows about 12" tall and spreads 18–24". The flowers are a deep magenta crimson. The foliage turns red and maroon in winter.

B. 'Bressingham White' grows about 12" tall and has white flowers.

B. cordifolia (heart-leaved bergenia) grows about 24" tall, with an equal or greater spread. Its flowers are deep pink, and the foliage turns bronze or purple in fall and winter. 'Rotblum' grows 18" tall and has bright red flowers. The foliage turns red in winter.

B. cordifolia (photos this page)

B. 'Wintermärchen' ('Winter Fairy Tale') grows 12–18" tall and spreads 18–24". The flowers are rose red, and the dark green leaves are touched with red in winter.

B. 'Winterglut' ('Winter Glow') grows 12–18" tall and wide and produces red flowers in spring and often again in fall. It was developed from *B. c.* 'Rotblum' and has excellent red fall and winter foliage color. This plant comes true from seed.

Problems & Pests

Rare problems with fungal leaf spot, root rot, weevils, slugs, caterpillars and foliar nematodes are possible.

These plants are also called elephant ears, because of the large, leathery leaves, and pigsqueek, for the unusual sound made when a leaf is rubbed briskly between thumb and forefinger.

Black-Eyed Susan

Rudbeckia

Height: 1¹/₂–10' **Spread:** 12–36" **Flower color:** yellow or orange, with brown or green centers **Blooms:** mid-summer to fall **Zones:** 3–9

RUDBECKIA IS ONE OF THE MOST POPULAR PERENNIALS ACROSS the upper Midwest, and varieties that are available in the trade are long-lived and easy to grow. Large, daisy-like flowers appear in abundance from July well into fall, and they make excellent cut flowers. This prairie native looks best when massed across a large area, and it combines wonderfully with tall grasses and other sun-loving plants, such as *Liatris, Echinacea* and *Echinops.*

Planting

Seeding: Start seed in cold frame or indoors in early spring. Soil temperature should be about 61°–64° F.

Planting out: Spring

Spacing: 12–36"

Growing

Black-eyed Susans grow well in **full sun** or **partial shade**. The soil should be of **average fertility** and **well drained**. Fairly heavy clay soils are tolerated. Regular watering is best, but established plants are drought tolerant. Divide in spring or fall every three to five years.

Pinch plants in June to make shorter, bushier stands.

Tips

Use black-eyed Susans in wildflower or naturalistic gardens, in borders and in cottage-style gardens. They are best planted in masses and drifts.

Although deadheading early in the season keeps the plants flowering vigorously, seedheads are often left in place later in the season for winter interest and as food for birds in fall and winter.

R. nitida 'Herbstsonne'

Black-eyed Susan cut flowers are long lasting in arrangements.

Recommended

R. fulgida is an upright, spreading plant. It grows 18–36" tall and spreads 12–24". The orange-yellow flowers have brown centers. **Var. *sullivantii* 'Goldsturm'** bears large, bright golden yellow flowers.

R. laciniata (cutleaf coneflower) forms a large, open clump. It grows 4–10' tall and spreads 24–36". The yellow flowers have green centers. The cultivar **'Goldquelle'** grows 36" tall and has bright yellow, double flowers.

R. nitida is an upright, spreading plant. It grows 3–6' tall and spreads 24–36". The yellow flowers have green centers. **'Herbstsonne'** ('Autumn Sun') has bright golden yellow flowers.

R. subtomentosa (sweet coneflower) is an upright plant that grows about 28" tall and 12" wide with branched stems. The mid-green foliage has soft, gray hairs. Purple-brown to black-centered, yellow to orange flowers are produced in fall.

R. fulgida with echinacea

Problems & Pests

Rare problems with slugs, aphids, rust, smut and leaf spot are possible.

Bleeding Heart

Dicentra

Height: 8"–4' **Spread:** 8–18" **Flower color:** pink, white, red-pink
Blooms: spring, summer, fall **Zones:** 3–9

THE DAINTY, PENDANT, HEART-SHAPED BLOOMS OF *DICENTRA* ARE one of the great joys of the spring garden, particularly when gusts of wind cause the flowers to flutter. The age-old cottage-garden standby *D. spectabilis* remains hard to beat for long-lived, disease-free performance, but newer introductions, such as *D.* 'Luxuriant,' offer longer periods of bloom. All varieties self-seed freely; seedlings are easy to dig and transplant, or put them in pots as presents for friends.

Planting

Seeding: Start freshly ripened seed in cold frame. Plants self-seed in the garden.

Planting out: Spring

Spacing: 18–36"

Growing

Bleeding hearts prefer **light shade** but tolerate partial shade or full shade. The soil should be **humus rich, moist** and **well drained**. Although these plants prefer to remain evenly moist, they tolerate drought quite well, particularly if the weather doesn't get hot. Very dry summer conditions cause the plants to die back, but they revive in fall or the following spring. To prolong the flowering period, bleeding hearts must remain moist while blooming. Constant summer moisture will keep the flowers coming until mid-summer.

Common bleeding heart and fringed bleeding heart rarely need dividing.

D. spectabilis

D. exima

D. spectabilis (photos this page)

Tips

Bleeding hearts can be naturalized in a woodland garden or grown in a border or rock garden. They make excellent early-season specimen plants. They do well near a pond or stream.

Recommended

D. exima (fringed bleeding heart) forms a loose, mounded clump of lacy, fern-like foliage. It grows 15–24" tall and spreads about 18". The pink or white flowers are borne mostly in spring, but they may be produced sporadically over summer. Unless kept well watered, the plant will go dormant during hot, dry weather in summer. 'Snowdrift' is a repeat blooming selection with large, pure white flowers.

D. 'King of Hearts' is a compact plant growing 8–15" tall and 8–12" wide. It produces delicate, soft, blue-green foliage and pink to rose pink, heart-shaped flowers from mid-spring to fall. The repeat blooming of this plant is enhanced by deadheading.

D. **'Luxuriant'** is a low-growing hybrid, with blue-green foliage and red-pink flowers. It grows about 12" tall and spreads about 18". Flowers appear in spring and early summer. After initial flowering, cut the plant down to basal foliage to produce a second wave of bloom from late summer into fall.

D. spectabilis (common bleeding heart) forms a large, elegant mound up to 4' tall and about 18" wide. It blooms in late spring and early summer. The inner petals are white, and the outer petals are pink. This species is likely to die back in the summer heat and prefers light, dappled shade. **'Alba'** has entirely white flowers.

D. exima

Problems & Pests

Slugs, downy mildew, *Verticillium* wilt, viruses, rust and fungal leaf spot can cause occasional problems.

These delicate plants are the perfect addition to a moist woodland garden. Plant them next to a shaded pond or stream.

D. spectabilis 'Alba'

Boltonia

Boltonia

Height: 3–6' **Spread:** up to 4' **Flower color:** white, mauve or pink, with yellow centers **Blooms:** late summer and fall **Zones:** 4–9

THAT BOLTONIA IS A TALL, EASY-TO-GROW, PEST- AND DISEASE-free plant that blooms profusely for four weeks or more is plenty of reason to grow this outstanding perennial. That it lands on the relatively short list of perennials that bring fresh color to the garden late in the season makes it, in my mind, essential. Boltonia, which is sometimes called 'thousand flower aster,' has tiny flowers, but when one stalk kicks out hundreds of them, no matter. If the plants grow too tall for your liking, cut the stems back by one-third in June. 'Pink Beauty' supplies much-needed fresh blooms in August; 'Snowbank,' my favorite variety, bursts forth in September.

Planting

Seeding: Start seeds in cold frame in fall

Planting out: Spring or fall

Spacing: 36"

Growing

Boltonia prefers **full sun** and tolerates partial shade. It prefers soil that is **fertile, humus rich, moist** and **well drained** but adapts to less fertile soils and tolerates some drought. Divide in fall or early spring when the clump is becoming over - grown or seems to be dying out in the middle.

The stout stems rarely require staking. If necessary, circle the plant with a peony hoop or use twiggy branches that are installed while the plant is young. The hoop or twiggy branch will be hidden by the growing branches.

Tips

This large plant can be used in the middle or at the back of a mixed border, in a naturalized or cottage-style garden or near a pond or other water feature. The small, narrow foliage is not particularly showy. Plant boltonia where it is not noticed until it blooms.

A good alternative to Michaelmas daisy, boltonia is less susceptible to powdery mildew.

Recommended

B. asteroides is a large, upright perennial, with narrow, grayish green leaves. It bears lots of white or slightly purple, daisy-like flowers with yellow centers. '**Pink Beauty**' has a looser habit and bears pale pink flowers. '**Snowbank**' has a denser, more compact habit and bears more plentiful white flowers than the species.

Problems & Pests

Boltonia has rare problems with rust, leaf spot and powdery mildew.

B. asteroides (photos this page)

Boltonia is native to the eastern and central United States.

Brunnera
Siberian Bugloss
Brunnera

Height: 12–18" **Spread:** 18–24" **Flower color:** blue
Blooms: spring **Zones:** 3–8

BRUNNERA IS ALWAYS ONE OF THE FIRST WORDS OUT OF MY mouth when someone asks, 'What can I grow here instead of hosta?' Frankly, there are many wonderful shade plants in this book suited perfectly to our northern climate. Brunnera happens to be one of the best. The richly varie-gated foliage of 'Dawson's White' and 'Hadspen Cream' leaps to the eye when tucked into the woodland floor. Clear blue flowers are pro-duced from late April to early June. Brunnera combines effortlessly with *Thalictrum, Polygonatum, Dicentra, Heuchera* and the aforementioned hosta.

Planting

Seeding: Start seeds in cold frame in early fall or indoors in early spring

Planting out: Spring

Spacing: 12–18"

Growing

Brunnera prefers **light shade** but tolerates morning sun with consistent moisture. The soil should be of **average fertility, humus rich, moist** and **well drained**. The species and its cultivars are not drought tolerant. Divide in spring when the center of the clump appears to be dying out.

Cut back faded foliage mid-season to produce a flush of new growth.

Tips

Brunnera makes a great addition to a woodland or shaded garden. Its low, bushy habit makes it useful as a groundcover or as an addition to a shaded border.

Recommended

B. macrophylla forms a mound of soft, heart-shaped leaves and produces loose clusters of blue flowers all spring. **'Dawson's White'** ('Variegata') has large leaves with irregular creamy patches. **'Hadspen Cream'** has leaves with creamy margins. Grow variegated plants in light or full shade to avoid scorched leaves. **'Langtrees'** has blue flowers and large leaves with silver spots.

B. macrophylla

This reliable plant rarely suffers from any problems.

'Dawson's White'

Bugbane
Black Cohosh, Black Snakeroot
Cimicifuga

Height: 2–7' **Spread:** 24" **Flower color:** cream, white, pink
Blooms: late summer to fall **Zones:** 3–8

AS TREES IN MANY AMERICAN NEIGHBORHOODS HAVE MATURED, what were once sunny lots are now in various degrees of shade. Too often, gardeners bemoan this transition, thinking that without full sun, growing tall, commanding perennials is no longer possible. Well, repeat after me: 'sim-ih-siff-YOU-guh'! A true shade perennial, bugbane gives you vertical to the point of vertigo. I grow the towering, dark and wondrous 'Atropurpurea' in the center of a shade bed anchored by a triangular planting of three tall white cedars. When the upward-curling, ivory-colored bottlebrushes of bloom ignite in August, I stand in awe.

Planting

Seeding: Start fresh seed in cold frame in fall; should germinate the following spring

Planting out: Spring

Spacing: 18–24"

Growing

Bugbanes grow best in **partial or light shade**. The soil should be **fertile, humus rich** and **moist**. Plants may require support from a peony hoop. The roots resent being disturbed, so the plants should not be divided. Bugbanes spread by rhizomes, and small pieces of root can be unearthed carefully and replanted if more plants are desired.

Tips

These plants make attractive additions to an open woodland garden, shaded border or pondside planting. They don't compete well with tree roots or other vigorous-rooted plants. They are worth growing close to the house because the late-season flowers are wonderfully fragrant.

Recommended

C. racemosa is a clump-forming perennial 4–7' tall and about 24" in spread. Long-stemmed spikes of fragrant, white flowers are borne from late summer into fall. **'Atropurpurea'** has bronzy purple foliage and bears spikes of creamy white- or pink-tinged flowers.

C. simplex is also a clump-forming perennial. It grows 3–4' tall and spreads about 24". The scented, bottlebrush-like spikes of flowers are borne in fall. **'Brunette'** has dark purple foliage and pink-tinged flowers. **'White Pearl'** bears white flowers on plants 24–36" tall.

Problems & Pests

Occasional problems are possible with rust and with insect damage to the leaves.

C. racemosa

In herbal medicine C. racemosa rhizomes, usually under the name black cohosh, are used to treat menopausal problems, rheumatism and tinnitus (ringing in the ears).

C. simplex 'Brunette'

Butterfly Weed

Asclepias

Height: 1½–6' **Spread:** 12–24" **Flower color:** orange, yellow, white, red, pink, light purple **Blooms:** late spring, summer, early fall **Zones:** 4–9

THIS WONDERFUL MINNESOTA AND WISCONSIN NATIVE IS A welcome addition to gardens where soil is sandy or of poor quality. It's best to plant *Asclepias*, which is easily grown from seed, where it can remain undisturbed for many years—it develops a whopper of a taproot.

Planting

Seeding: Start fresh seed in cold frame in early spring

Planting out: Spring

Spacing: 12–24"

Growing

Butterfly weeds prefer **full sun**. *A. tuberosa* grows in any **well-drained** soil. It prefers **fertile** soil but does very well in sandy, dry soils. It is drought tolerant. *A. incarnata* prefers a **moist** or **boggy**, **fertile** soil. *A. syriaca* grows in most soils but prefers **poor to moderately fertile** soil.

To propagate, remove the plantlets that grow around the base of the plants. The deep taproot makes division very difficult.

Deadhead to encourage a second blooming.

Tips

Use *A. tuberosa* in meadow plantings and borders, on dry banks, in neglected areas and in wildflower, cottage and butterfly gardens. Use *A. incarnata* in moist borders and in bog, pondside or streamside plantings. *A. syriaca* is best used in a native, meadow or wildflower garden where it will not overrun less aggressive plants.

Recommended

A. incarnata (swamp milkweed) grows about 36" tall and spreads up to 12". It bears clusters of pink, white or light purple flowers in late spring or early summer. Although it naturally grows in moist areas, it appreciates a well-drained soil in the garden. 'Cinderella' produces sweetly scented, pink flowers. 'Ice Ballet' bears white flowers.

A. syriaca (common milkweed) is an erect plant with stout stems that can spread relatively quickly by rhizomes. It typically grows 24–36" tall and 12" wide, but it can reach heights of 6'. It produces domed clusters of fragrant, light lavender flowers. The seedpods have a warty appearance.

A. tuberosa (butterfly weed) forms a clump of upright, leafy stems. It grows 18–36" tall and spreads 12–24". It bears clusters of orange flowers in mid-summer to early fall. 'Gay Butterflies' bears orange, yellow or red flowers.

A. tuberosa

Although butterfly weed is a relatively trouble-free plant, aphids and mealybugs can be a problem.

A. incarnata

Campanula
Bellflower
Campanula

Height: 4–36" **Spread:** 12–36" **Flower color:** blue, white, purple
Blooms: summer, early fall **Zones:** 3–7

FEW PERENNIALS OFFER THE WIDE RANGE OF COLORS, BLOOM types, heights and forms, as do the campanulas. Most attention of late has been placed on the species *C. carpatica* and the very attractive varieties 'Blue Clips,' 'White Clips' and 'Bressingham White,' but the older varieties are worth seeking out as well. I have long regarded the blue-flowering *C. glomerata* 'Superba,' which blooms in my garden in mid-June, as one of the two or three most bedazzling perennials available to northern gardeners.

Planting

Seeding: Not recommended because germination can be erratic, but if done, direct sow in spring or fall

Planting out: Spring or fall

Spacing: 12–36"

Growing

Campanulas grow well in **full sun, partial shade** or **light shade**. The soil should be of **average fertility** and **well drained**. Campanulas appreciate a mulch to keep their roots cool and moist in summer and protected in winter, particularly if snow cover is inconsistent. It is important to divide these perennials every few years in early spring or late summer to keep them vigorous and to prevent them from becoming invasive.

C. persicifolia

Campanula can be propagated by basal, new-growth or rhizome cuttings.

C. carpatica

C. persicifolia

Prompt deadheading keeps campanula looking tidy and extends its bloom time.

C. carpatica cultivar

Deadhead to prolong blooming. Use scissors to cut back one-third of the plant at a time, allowing other sections to continue blooming. As the pruned section starts to bud, cut back other sections for continued blooming.

Tips

Low, spreading and trailing campanulas can be used in rock gardens and on rock walls. Upright and mounding campanulas can be used in borders and cottage gardens. You can also edge beds with the low-growing varieties.

Recommended

C. x **'Birch Hybrid'** is low growing, only 4" tall and 20" wide, and bears light blue to mauve flowers in summer.

C. carpatica (Carpathian bellflower, Carpathian harebell) is a spreading, mounding perennial. It grows 10–12" tall, spreads 12–24" and bears blue, white or purple flowers in summer. **'Blue Clips'** is a smaller, compact plant with large, blue flowers. **'Bressingham White'** is a compact plant with large, white flowers. **'Jewel'** is low growing—4–8" tall—and has deep blue flowers. **'White Clips'** is similar to 'Blue Clips,' except it bears white flowers.

C. glomerata (clustered bellflower) forms a clump of upright stems. It grows 12–24" tall, with an equal or greater spread. Clusters of purple, blue or white flowers are borne over most of summer. **'Superba'** is a vigorous plant 24" tall with violet blue to deep purple flowers.

C. persicifolia (peach-leaved bell-flower) is an upright perennial. It grows about 36" tall and spreads about 12". It bears white, blue or purple flowers from early summer to mid-summer.

C. portenschlagiana (Dalmatian bellflower) is a low, spreading, mounding perennial. It grows 6" tall and spreads 20–24". It bears light or deep purple flowers from mid- to late summer.

C. poscharskyana (Serbian bell-flower) is a trailing perennial. It grows 6–12" tall and spreads 24–36". It bears light purple flowers in summer and early fall.

C. rotundifolia (bluebell, harebell) is a variable to erect plant with well-branched stems and heart-shaped to rounded foliage. It grows 6–18" tall and wide and bears sparse clusters of white to dark purple, pendulous, bell-shaped flowers from erect buds in summer.

Problems & Pests

Minor problems with vine weevils, spider mites, aphids, powdery mildew, slugs, rust and fungal leaf spot are possible.

Over 300 species of campanula grow throughout the Northern Hemisphere in habitats ranging from high, rocky crags to boggy meadows.

C. poscharskyana

Candytuft

Iberis

Height: 6–12" **Spread:** 10–36" **Flower color:** white **Blooms:** spring, fall
Zones: 3–9

GROW THIS CHEERY, OLD-FASHIONED FAVORITE AT THE FRONT OF
the bed, where its bright white clusters of flowers dazzle in the sun by day
and glow in the moonlight at night. *Iberis* looks great spilling over the edges
of sidewalks and pathways. Glossy, dark green foliage remains attractive all
season if plants are sheared after flowering. An evergreen, *Iberis* benefits
from a winter mulching of marsh hay.

Planting

Seeding: Direct sow in spring

Planting out: Spring

Spacing: 6–12"

Growing

Candytuft prefers **full sun**. The soil should be of **poor to average fertility, moist, well drained** and **neutral to alkaline**.

In spring, cut away any brown sections resulting from winter damage when the new buds begin to break. As the stems spread outwards, they may root where they touch the ground. These rooted ends may be cut away from the central plant and replanted in new locations.

Candytuft should be sheared back by about one-third once it has finished flowering to promote new, compact growth. Every two or three years it should be sheared back by one-half to two-thirds to discourage the development of too much woody growth and to encourage abundant flowering. Division is rarely required.

I. sempervirens (photos this page)

Tips

Use candytuft as an edging plant, in borders and rock gardens, in the crevices of rock walls and as a companion for spring-blooming bulbs.

Recommended

I. sempervirens is a spreading evergreen that grows 6–12" tall and spreads 16–36". It bears clusters of tiny, white flowers. 'Autumn Snow' bears white flowers in spring and fall. 'Little Gem' is a compact, spring-flowering plant that spreads only 10". 'Snowflake' is a mounding plant that bears large, white flowers in spring.

Problems & Pests

Occasional problems with slugs, caterpillars, damping off, gray mold and fungal leaf spot are possible.

If you arrive home after dusk on a spring night, the white flowers of candytuft will provide a welcoming glow in the moonlight.

Cardinal Flower

Lobelia

Height: 2–5' **Spread:** 12–36" **Flower color:** red, white, blue, purple
Blooms: summer to fall **Zones:** 3–9

ALTHOUGH SOMEWHAT SHORT-LIVED, *LOBELIA* is a majestic addition to the garden. Few late-season bloomers stand out as regally, and with proper care it is sure to delight. The fact that the plant self-seeds freely usually ensures that there are always some blooming specimens about. *Lobelia* looks stunning near water, but it may be used anywhere the tall, erect stems and spires of unusual flowers will be seen. I use the plant sparingly, though in large gardens I have seen pink- and white-blooming varieties massed to great effect.

Planting

Seeding: Direct sow in garden or cold frame in spring, when soil temperature is about 70° F

Planting out: Spring

Spacing: 12–18"

These lovely plants in the bellflower family contain deadly alkaloids and have poisoned people who tried to use them as herbal medicine.

Growing

Cardinal flowers grow well in **full sun, light shade** and **partial shade**. The soil should be **fertile, slightly acidic** and **moist**. Never allow the soil to dry out for extended periods, especially in a sunny garden. Provide a mulch over winter to protect the plants. Divide every two to three years in fall to stimulate growth. To divide, lift the entire plant and remove the new rosettes growing at the plant base. Replant immediately in the garden.

Pinch plants in early summer to produce compact growth. Deadheading may encourage a second set of blooms.

Cardinal flowers self-seed quite easily. Because these plants are short-lived, lasting about four or five years, self-seeding is an easy way to ensure continuing generations of plants. If you remove the spent flower spikes, be sure to allow at least a few of them to remain to spread their seeds. Don't worry too much though—the lower flowers on a spike are likely to set seed before the top flowers are finished opening

L. cardinalis (photos this page)

L. cardinalis
L. siphilitica

Tips

These plants are best used in streamside or pond-side plantings or in bog gardens.

Cardinal flowers may require a more acidic soil than the other plants that grow along a pond. If they do need more acidic soil, plant them in a container of peat-based potting soil and sink into the ground at the edge of the pond.

Recommended

L. cardinalis (cardinal flower) forms an erect clump of bronze-green leaves. It grows 2–4' tall and spreads 12–24". It bears spikes of bright red flowers from summer to fall. **'Alba'** has white flowers and is not as hardy as the species.

L. **'Purple Towers'** grows 3–5' tall and 12–24" wide. It produces rich, dark purple flowers from mid-summer to fall.

L. **'Ruby Slippers'** grows 30–36" tall and 12–36" wide and bears rich, deep maroon to ruby red, velvety flowers from mid-summer to fall.

L. siphilitica (great blue lobelia, blue cardinal flower) forms an erect clump with bright green foliage. It grows 2–4' tall and spreads 12–18". Spikes of deep blue flowers are produced from mid-summer to fall. **Var.** *alba* has white flowers.

Problems & Pests

Rare problems with slugs, rust, smut and leaf spot can occur.

Lobelia *was named after the Flemish botanist Mathias de l'Obel (1538–1616).*

L. cardinalis (photos this page)

Catmint

Nepeta

Height: 10–36" **Spread:** 12–36" **Flower color:** blue, purple, white, pink
Blooms: summer, sometimes again in fall **Zones:** 3–8

CATMINT HAS FINALLY BEGUN TO RECEIVE THE ATTENTION IT
deserves. It is reasonable to say that *N. sibirica* 'Souvenir d'Andre Chaudron'
has become one of the most widely purchased and talked about perennials of
recent years. Catmint leaves, ranging from silver-gray to gray-green, provide
useful foliage contrast with surrounding plants. Yes, some varieties can get a
little floppy, so grow them at the front of the bed, where they will flop for-
ward with conviction, or contain unruly specimens with hoops. For lush
new growth and occasional reblooming, remove supports and shear all varieties back by two-thirds after flowering.

Planting

Seeding: Most popular hybrids and cultivars are sterile and cannot be grown from seed

Planting out: Spring

Spacing: 12–24"

Growing

Catmints grow well in **full sun** or **partial shade**. The soil should be of **average fertility** and **well drained**. The growth tends to be floppy in rich soil. Divide the plants in spring or fall when they begin to look overgrown and dense. Catmints are drought tolerant but look best with regular watering.

Pinch tips in June to delay flowering and make the plants more compact. Once the plants are almost finished blooming, you may cut them back by one-third to one-half to encourage new growth and more blooms in late summer or fall.

N. x faassenii

Catmints have long been cultivated for their reputed medicinal and culinary qualities.

N. x faassenii 'Walker's Low'

Tips

Catmints can be used to edge borders and pathways. They work well in herb gardens and with roses in cottage gardens. Taller varieties make lovely additions to perennial gardens, and dwarf types can be used in rock gardens.

Think twice before growing *N. cataria* (catnip) because cats are attracted to the aromatic foliage of this plant. You may be laying out a welcome mat for the neighborhood cats to come and enjoy your garden. Cats do like the other catmints, but not quite to the same extent.

Recommended

N. x *faassenii* forms a clump of upright and spreading stems. It grows 18–36" tall, with an equal spread, and it bears spikes of blue or purple flowers. This hybrid and its cultivars are sterile and cannot be grown from seed. '**Blue Wonder**' grows 12–15" tall and 12–24" wide with gray-green foliage and abundant, lavender blue flowers. '**Dropmore**' has gray-green foliage and light purple flowers. '**Snowflake**' is low-growing, compact and spreading with white flowers. It grows

N. x *faassenii* cultivar

N. x *faassenii*

12–24" tall and spreads about 18". **'Walker's Low'** has gray-green foliage and bears lavender blue flowers. It grows about 10" tall.

N. grandiflora **'Dawn to Dusk'** is an upright, bushy plant with gray-green foliage. It grows 24–36" tall and 24–30" wide and has pink flowers with rose purple calyces.

N. sibirica **'Souvenir d'Andre Chaudron'** is an upright plant with erect stems that grows 36" tall and 24" wide and spreads by invasive roots. It has gray-green foliage and deep lavender blue flowers.

N. subsessilis grows 18–24" tall and 24" wide with aromatic, gray-green foliage. Deep violet blue flowers with maroon spots bloom for an extended period in summer.

It is no mystery where the name 'catmint' comes from—cats love it! Dried leaves stuffed into cloth toys will amuse your kitty for hours.

Problems & Pests

These plants are pest free, except for an occasional visit from a cat or bout of leaf spot.

N. x faassenii

Chrysanthemum

Fall Garden Mum, Hybrid Garden Mum

Dendranthema

Height: 10"–4' **Spread:** 18–36" **Flower color:** orange, yellow, pink, red, purple, white **Blooms:** late summer and fall **Zones:** 4–9

AS A BOY, I THOUGHT THE ONLY FLOWERS YOU COULD GROW were chrysanthemums. That's because my father grew loads of them, entire beds of them, in every sunny spot in our yard. As an adult I learned of the thousands of additional perennials that can be grown, but I still am certain that you can't have a proper garden without ample use of mums. Kings of the fall color parade, these botanical time bombs lie in wait all season, then delight the senses with masses of bloom from September to frost. Mums offer a wide range of sizes, colors and flower types. Once you grow mums, you will want more and more. My father, age 87, still grows them by the dozens.

Planting

Seeding: Not recommended

Planting out: Spring, summer or fall

Spacing: 18–24"

Growing

Chrysanthemums grow best in **full sun**. The soil should be **fertile, moist** and **well drained**. Divide in spring or fall every two years to keep plants vigorous and to prevent them from thinning out in the center.

Pinch plants back in early summer to encourage bushy growth. In late fall or early winter, you can deadhead the spent blooms, but leave the stems intact to protect the crowns of the plants.

The earlier in the season you can plant chrysanthemums, the better. Early planting improves their chances of surviving winter.

Tips

These plants provide a blaze of color in the late-season garden, often flowering until the first hard frost. Dot or group them in borders or use them as specimen plants near the house or in large planters. Some gardeners purchase chrysanthemums as flowering plants in late summer and put them in the spots where summer annuals have faded.

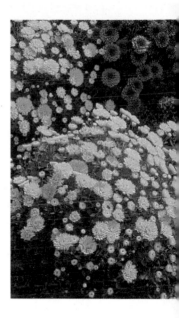

Although the name Chrysanthemum *comes from the Greek and means 'golden flower,' these plants now come in a wide range of bright colors.*

D. Prophet Series 'Stacy'

Recommended

The hybrid plants in this section were formerly classified under *Chrysanthemum* x *morifolium*, but they have all been moved to *Dendranthema* x *grandiflorum*. Rumor has it that they may switch back to *Chrysanthemum*. Regardless, these plants generally grow 18–36" tall and wide.

D. 'Mei-Kyo' is a mound-forming plant 18–24" tall and wide. It produces pale pink to deep lavender rose, double flowers with yellow centers.

D. **Morden Series** was developed in Canada and is reliably hardy to Zone 4. Plants come in a wide variety of colors and grow about 24" tall.

D. **My Favorite Series** is a new introduction, and it is heralded as a series of truly perennial mums and prolific flower producers. The plants grow to about 24" tall and spread about 4'. 'Autumn Red' has red flowers.

D. **Prophet Series** is popular and commonly available. Plants grow about 24" tall and spread 24–36". Flowers come in all colors. 'Christine' has deep salmon pink, double flowers with yellow centers. 'Raquel' has bright red, double flowers with yellow centers. 'Stacy' has yellow-centered flowers with pink petals that have white bases.

D. Prophet Series 'Christine'

D. **Rubellum Group** cultivars are mound-forming hybrids growing 36" tall and 24" wide with flowers in shades of red, orange and pink. '**Clara Curtis**' grows 18–30" tall and wide and bears single, pink flowers with raised yellow centers. '**Mary Stoker**' has soft orange, single flowers.

D. weyrichii is a mat-forming plant that spreads by rhizomes. It grows 12" tall and 18" wide. The sometimes branched stems are purple-green. Pink or white flowers with yellow centers bloom in late summer to fall. '**Pink Bomb**' grows to 10" tall and has pink flowers. '**White Bomb**' bears pink-tinged, white flowers.

Problems & Pests

Aphids can be a true menace to these plants. Insecticidal soap can be used to treat the problem, but it should be washed off within an hour because it discolors the foliage when the sun hits it. Also watch for spider mites, whiteflies, leaf miners, leaf spot, powdery mildew, rust, aster yellows, blight, borers and rot, though these problems are not as common.

D. Prophet Series 'Raquel'

Clematis

Clematis

Height: 1½–30' **Spread:** 2–4' **Flower color:** blue, purple, pink, yellow, red, white **Blooms:** early to late summer, early fall **Zones:** 3–8

THANK HEAVEN FOR CLEMATIS! WHEN A NORTHERN GARDENER needs a fast-growing climbing vine that covers itself with large, beautiful blooms, no other plant fits the bill better. Non-climbing varieties are rapidly being discovered by gardeners who appreciate the option of growing clematis near the back of the flowerbed without having to provide a trellis or other type of vertical support system. The climbing varieties remain the favorites of gardeners young and old, however, because few plants are as breathtaking in bloom. Be sure to mulch the area around the base of the clematis or grow large-leaved plants in front, so the soil around the clematis roots stays cool.

Planting

Seeding: Indoors or in cold frame, in late summer or fall

Planting out: Spring or fall

Spacing: 2–4'

Growing

Clematis prefers **full sun** but tolerates partial shade. The soil should be **fertile, humus rich, moist** and **well drained**. These plants are quite cold hardy, but they will fare best when protected from the winter wind. The rootball of vining clematis should be planted 2" beneath the surface of the soil. Division of vining clematis plants is difficult and not recommended, but herbaceous clematis may be carefully divided in early spring. Vining clematis can be propagated by taking stem cuttings in summer.

The semi-woody, vine-type clematis plants need to be pruned. Those that bloom in early summer on the previous year's growth should be thinned after the vine blooms by pruning lateral branches back to three or four nodes. Mid- to late-season varieties that bloom on the current year's growth, such as Jackman clematis, should be pruned back to 12" early in spring before the new growth appears. Large mid-season varieties that bloom on year-old wood and then again on new growth should be thinned occasionally after the vine ceases its first round of blooms.

C. tangutica seedheads

Combine two clematis varieties that bloom at the same time to provide a mix of tone and texture.

C. heracleifolia

C. x jackmanii

C. tangutica

Tips

Clematis plants are attractive for most of the growing season. They are useful in borders and as specimen plants. Vine-type clematis need a structure such as a trellis, railing, fence or arbor to support them as they climb; they will not grab onto stone or the exterior wall of a house or garage. They can also be allowed to grow over shrubs, up trees and as groundcovers.

Shade the roots with a mulch or groundcover. Do not shade with a flat rock, which was a common practice in the past, because the rock will absorb heat and defeat the purpose of shading the roots.

Recommended

C. 'Gravetye Beauty' is a vining late-season bloomer about 8' tall. Its small, bright red flowers bloom on new growth.

C. heracleifolia (tube clematis) is a herbaceous plant. It grows up to 36" tall and 4' wide. The tube-shaped flowers are purple-blue. **Var.** *davidiana* has fragrant, larger flowers. Cut these plants back to the ground in early spring. Pinch plants when they are 15" tall to promote upright growth.

C. integrifolia (solitary clematis) grows 18–36" tall and bears flared, bell-shaped, purple flowers. It grows upwards to a point, then falls to the ground and sprawls, spreading to about 4'. Stake in spring to help keep this colorful character upright.

C. x *jackmanii* (Jackman clematis) is a mid- to late-summer bloomer. The twining vines of this hybrid grow about 10' tall. Large, purple flowers appear on side shoots from the previous season's growth and on new growth for most of the summer.

C. recta (ground clematis) is a bit more upright than the other two herbaceous species. It reaches 4' in height and only 24" in width. The fragrant, white flowers are borne in dense clusters. The cultivar 'Purpurea' has red-tinged leaves and white flowers. Cut these plants back after flowering for a flush of new growth.

C. tangutica (virgin's bower) is a vining late-season bloomer that reaches 16' or more in height. Its capacity for spreading makes it a good choice on a chain-link fence, where it will fill in thickly and create a privacy screen. The nodding, yellow flowers of this species are followed by distinctive fuzzy seedheads that persist into winter.

C. terniflora (*C. maximowicziana*) (sweet autumn clematis) is a robust vine that can grow 30' in one season. It produces tiny, creamy white, sweetly scented blooms in abundance from late summer to early fall. Rosy red seedpods will develop and may lead to self-seeding of new plants that can be moved to new locations. The vines are semi-evergreen in warmer areas of the state but die back in northern areas and should be pruned to 10" in spring.

Problems & Pests

Problems with scale insects, whiteflies, aphids, wilt, powdery mildew, rust, leaf spot and stem canker can occur. To avoid wilt, keep mulch from touching the stem. Protect the fragile stems of newly planted clematis from injury; a bruised or damaged stem is an entry point for disease.

C. x jackmanii cultivar

In England, vines are trained onto the outer limbs of trees and over shrubs.

C. integrifolia

Columbine

Aquilegia

Height: 12–36" **Spread:** 12–24" **Flower color:** red, yellow, pink, purple, blue, white; color of spurs often differs from that of petals **Blooms:** spring, summer **Zones:** 2–9

WHAT ADULT RAISED IN MINNESOTA OR WISCONSIN DOESN'T recall pinching off the nectar-filled tips of native columbine and savoring its honey-sweet taste as a child? Wild columbine (*A. canadensis*) is found throughout wooded areas across most of North America, and most hybridized varieties retain their native form and old-fashioned mystique. I'm fond of the McKana hybrids and use them to naturalize my somewhat shady backyard. Nearly all the hybrid varieties are attractive to me, with the exception of *A. vulgaris* 'Nora Barlow,' popular with some, but far too removed in form from my cherished boyhood memories.

Planting

Seeding: Direct sow in spring

Planting out: Spring

Spacing: 18"

Growing

Columbines grow well in **full sun** or **partial shade.** They prefer soil that is **fertile, moist** and **well drained** but adapt well to most soil conditions. These plants self-seed, and young seedlings can be transplanted. Division is not required but can be done to propagate desirable plants. The divided plants may take a while to recover because they dislike having their roots disturbed.

Tips

Use columbines in a rock garden, a formal or casual border or a naturalized or woodland garden.

Columbines self-seed but are in no way invasive. Each year a few new plants may turn up near the parent plant. If you have a variety of

columbines planted near each other, you may even wind up with a new hybrid because these plants crossbreed easily. The wide variety of flower colors is the most interesting result. The new seedlings may not be identical to the parents, and there is some chance they will revert to the original parent species.

A. x hybrida McKana hybrids

A. alpina

*Columbines are short-lived
perennials that seed freely,
establishing themselves in
unexpected, and often charming,
locations. If you wish to keep a
particular form, you must
preserve it carefully through
frequent division or root cuttings.*

A. vulgaris 'Nora Barlow'

Recommended

A. alpina is an erect plant with nodding, blue and white or bright blue flowers. It grows 12–24" tall and 12–15" wide and blooms in early summer.

A. caerulea grows 16–24" tall and 12" wide, bearing light to deep blue flowers, sometimes blue and white bicolored, from mid-spring to early summer.

A. canadensis (wild columbine, Canada columbine) is native to most of eastern North America and is common in woodlands and fields. It grows up to 24" tall, spreads about 12" and bears yellow flowers with red spurs.

A. chrysantha is a bushy, clump-forming plant 24–36" tall and 12–24" wide. Long-spurred, yellow flowers are produced in late spring to summer. This species is somewhat more sun tolerant than most columbines. '**Yellow Queen**' has bright yellow flowers with long, curved spurs.

A. x *hybrida* (*A.* x *cultorum*) (hybrid columbine) forms mounds of delicate foliage and has exceptional flowers. Many groups of hybrids have been developed for their showy flowers in a wide range of colors. When the exact parentage of a columbine is uncertain, it is grouped under this name. '**Double Pleat**' (double pleat hybrids) includes plants that grow 30–32" tall and bear double flowers in combinations of blue and white or pink and white. '**Dragonfly**' (dragonfly hybrids) includes compact plants up to 24" tall and 12" in spread, with a wide range of flower colors. **McKana hybrids** ('McKana Giants') are popular and bear flowers in yellow, pink, red, purple, mauve and white. They grow up to 36" tall.

A. **Songbird Series** includes compact plants with large, non-fading flowers held above the foliage. Plants in this series grow 12–24" tall and 12–16" wide with flowers in bright sky blue, dark blue and white, blue and white, red and white, pure white, pure light yellow, lavender and white and rose and white.

A. vulgaris (European columbine, common columbine) grows about 36" tall and spreads 18". Flowers come in a wide variety of colors, and this species has been used to develop many hybrids and cultivars. 'Nora Barlow' is a popular cultivar with double flowers in white, pink and green-tinged red.

A. x *hybrida* McKana hybrids (photos this page)

Problems & Pests

Mildew and rust can be troublesome during dry weather. Other problems include fungal leaf spot, aphids, caterpillars and leaf miners.

Coneflower
Purple Coneflower, Echinacea
Echinacea

Height: 2–5' **Spread:** up to 18" **Flower color:** purple, white, with orange centers **Blooms:** mid-summer to fall **Zones:** 3–8

THE POPULARITY OF CONEFLOWERS IS EASY TO UNDERSTAND. The large, daisy-like flowers can reach up to 6" across, and they are highly attractive to butterflies. The period of bloom extends beyond that of most perennials. Growing coneflowers is easy—give them lots of sun and any soil that drains well and they'll do fine. Coneflowers are unmatched by any other perennial for scattering throughout large areas, and if you wish to naturalize a sunny portion of garden, they should be considered the anchor plant. Good combination plants include *Monarda, Liatris, Coreopsis, Achillea, Solidago* and *Rudbeckia.*

Planting

Seeding: Direct sow in spring

Planting out: Spring

Spacing: 18"

Growing

Purple coneflower grows well in **full sun** or very **light shade**. Any **well-drained** soil is tolerated, though an **average to rich** soil is preferred. The thick taproot makes this plant drought resistant, but it prefers to have regular watering. Divide every four years or so in spring or fall.

Deadhead early in the season to prolong flowering. Later in the season you may wish to leave the flowerheads in place to self-seed. If you don't want to allow self-seeding, remove all the flowerheads as they fade. Pinch plants back in early summer to encourage bushy growth that is less prone to mildew.

Tips

Use purple coneflower in meadow gardens and informal borders, either in groups or as single specimens. The dry flowerheads make an interesting feature in fall and winter gardens.

Recommended

E. purpurea is an upright plant 5' tall and up to 18" wide, with prickly hairs all over. It bears purple flowers with orangy centers. The cultivars are generally about half the species' height. 'Leuchstern' ('Bright Star') has large, 4" wide, purplered flowers. 'Magnus' bears flowers like those of the species but larger, up to 7" across. 'White Swan' is a compact plant with white flowers.

Problems & Pests

Powdery mildew is the biggest problem. Also possible are leaf miners, bacterial spot and gray mold. Vine weevils may attack the roots.

E. purpurea

Echinacea *was an important medicine for Native Americans, and today it is a popular immunity booster in herbal medicine.*

'Magnus' & 'White Swan'

Coreopsis

Tickseed

Coreopsis

Height: 12–36" **Spread:** 12–18" **Flower color:** yellow, pink **Blooms:** early to late summer **Zones:** 3–9

BRIGHT, CHEERY FLOWERS, RELIABLE HARDINESS AND A RELATIVELY long season of bloom have kept *Coreopsis* popular with northern gardeners for generations. I must be honest; I wasn't particularly impressed with *C. verticillata* 'Moonbeam' when it became so wildly popular in the '90s, but I find *C. grandiflora* 'Early Sunrise' a welcome addition to any sunny proceeding. Some years, when deadheaded weekly, this plant has bloomed nearly the entire season in my garden. *Coreopsis* likes to have some room to expand, and it looks best planted in groups of at least three.

Planting

Seeding: Direct sow in spring. Seeds may be sown indoors in winter, but soil must be kept fairly cool, at 55°–61° F, for seeds to germinate.

Planting out: Spring

Spacing: 12–18"

Growing

Grow coreopsis in **full sun**. The soil should be **average, sandy, light** and **well drained**. Plants can develop crown rot in moist, cool locations with heavy soil. Overly fertile soil causes long, floppy growth. Frequent division may be required to keep plants vigorous.

Deadhead daily to keep plants in constant summer bloom. Use scissors to snip out tall stems. Shear plants by one-half in late spring for more compact growth.

Mass plant coreopsis to fill in a dry, exposed bank where nothing else will grow, and you will enjoy the bright, sunny flowers all summer long.

C. verticillata (photos this page)

C. rosea

C. verticillata 'Moonbeam'

Tips

Coreopsis are versatile plants, useful in formal and informal borders and in meadow plantings or cottage gardens. They look best in groups.

Recommended

C. auriculata (mouse-eared tickseed) is low growing and well suited to rock gardens or fronts of borders. It grows 12–24" tall and will continue to creep outwards without becoming invasive.

C. grandiflora (large-flowered coreopsis, tickseed) forms a clump of foliage and bears bright golden yellow flowers over a long period in mid- and late summer. It grows 18–36" tall and spreads 12–18". This species and its cultivars are often grown as annuals because bearing so many flowers leaves them with little energy for surviving winter. **'Early Sunrise'** is a compact plant that grows 18–24" tall. It bears yellow, double flowers and can be started from seed.

C. lanceolata (lanceleaf coreopsis) is a mound-forming plant 12–24" tall and 12–16" wide. The yellow flowers are borne one per stem in early to mid-summer and are good cut flowers. This species self-seeds freely. Lanky, floppy foliage can be cut back hard to keep plants neat.

C. rosea (pink tickseed) is an unusual species with pink flowers. It grows 24" tall and 12" wide. This species is more shade and water tolerant than the other species, but it is not as vigorous. **'American Dream'** is even more tolerant of moisture than the species, and it bears bright pink flowers with yellow centers.

C. verticillata (thread-leaf coreopsis) is a mound-forming plant with attractive, finely divided foliage. It grows 24–32" tall and spreads 18". This long-lived species needs dividing less frequently than most others. Divide if some of the plant seem to be dying out. '**Golden Showers**' has large, golden yellow flowers and ferny foliage. '**Moonbeam**' forms a compact mound of delicate foliage. The flowers are a light creamy yellow. '**Zagreb**' grows to 12–15" tall and bears bright yellow flowers.

Problems & Pests

Occasional problems with slugs, bacterial spot, gray mold, aster yellows, powdery mildew, downy mildew, crown rot and fungal spot are possible.

C. verticillata 'Moonbeam'

C. grandiflora 'Early Sunrise'

Cornflower
Mountain Bluet
Centaurea

Height: 12–24" **Spread:** 12–24" or more **Flower color:** blue, pink, white
Blooms: late spring to mid-summer **Zones:** 3–8

CORNFLOWER IS A HARDY AND UNUSUAL PERENNIAL THAT IS worth growing from seed or ordering from a catalog. The flowers of *C. montana* are like no other; cornflower will definitely draw comments from garden visitors. In the north, under ideal growing conditions, the plant can be marginally invasive. Keep the spade handy in spring to dig up spreaders that form from underground rhizomes.

Planting

Seeding: Direct sow in late summer; protect seedlings first winter

Planting out: Spring

Spacing: 24"

Growing

Cornflower grows well in **full sun** and **light shade**. The soil should be of **poor or average fertility, moist** and **well drained**. In a rich soil, plants may develop straggly, floppy growth and may become invasive. Divide in spring or late summer every two or three years.

Deadhead to prolong blooming and prevent self-sowing. You can use a bed-edging material or bottomless flowerpot to surround the plant and limit its spread.

Tips

Cornflower makes an attractive addition to borders, informal or natural gardens and large rock gardens.

Thin the new shoots by about one-third in spring to increase air circulation through the plant.

Recommended

C. montana is a mounding or sprawling plant that bears bright cobalt blue flowers from late spring until mid-summer. Plants may self-seed. 'Alba' bears white flowers. 'Carnea' ('Rosea') bears pink flowers.

Problems & Pests

Rare problems with downy or powdery mildew, rust or mold can occur.

C. montana (photos this page)

Prompt deadheading, by cutting spent blooms back to lateral buds, extends the bloom. For a second flush of blooms in late summer, cut plants back to the basal growth as soon as blooming ceases.

Daylily

Hemerocallis

Height: 12–36" **Spread:** 12–36" **Flower color:** every color, except blue and pure white **Blooms:** summer **Zones:** 2–9

FEW PERENNIALS ARE MORE POPULAR THAN DAYLILIES, AND WHO would deny that their large, wildly colorful blooms are a glorious sight? On the other hand, don't rely too heavily on their use. A daylily takes up a lot of space, and most of its bulk, for most of the season, is composed of unexceptional, floppy green foliage, which can yellow and brown in the mid- to late-summer heat. Also, the alleged 'repeat bloomers' tend to follow up their first wave of bloom with a rather chintzy second effort. A mass planting of daylilies becomes little more than an eyesore from August through October. Choose a few varieties you love, plant them as singles and enjoy their colorful show.

Planting

Seeding: Not recommended; hybrids and cultivars don't come true to type

Planting out: Spring

Spacing: 12" for miniatures and 18–36" for taller plants

Growing

Daylilies grow in any light from **full sun** to **full shade.** The deeper the shade, the fewer flowers will be produced. The soil should be **fertile, moist** and **well drained,** but these plants adapt to most conditions and are hard to kill once established. Feed your daylilies in spring and mid-summer to produce the best display of blooms. Divide every two to three years to keep plants vigorous and to propagate them. They can be left indefinitely without dividing.

Derived from the Greek words for day, 'hemera,' and beauty, 'kallos,' the genus name, like the common name, indicates that these lovely blooms last only one day.

Tips

Plant daylilies alone or group them in borders, on banks and in ditches to control erosion. They can be naturalized in woodland or meadow gardens. Small varieties are nice in planters.

Deadhead small varieties to keep them blooming as long as possible. Be careful when deadheading purple-flowered daylilies—the sap can stain fingers and clothes.

Recommended

You can find an almost infinite number of forms, sizes and colors in a range of species, cultivars and hybrids. See your local garden center or daylily grower to find out what's available and most suitable for your garden. Several commonly available and attractive daylilies are listed here.

H. 'Barbara Mitchell' is a reblooming plant that grows 20" tall and has branched flowering stems (scapes). It bears light pink, ruffled flowers with green throats in early to mid-summer.

H. 'Fairy Tale Pink' has very narrow foliage and grows 24" tall. The ruffled flowers are light orange-pink to shell pink and are produced in early to mid-summer.

H. 'Happy Returns' bears fragrant, ruffled, yellow flowers for most of the summer. It grows about 16" tall.

H. 'Hyperion' grows 36" tall with narrow foliage and fragrant, lemon yellow flowers in early to mid-summer.

H. 'Ice Carnival' produces fluted, ruffled, white flowers with green throats in early to mid-summer. It grows 28" tall.

H. 'Little Grapette' is a wonderful, reblooming miniature plant growing 12" tall. It has grape purple flowers, with darker eyes and green throats that bloom in early summer.

H. 'Pardon Me' has branched flowering stems (scapes) and narrow foliage. This reblooming plant grows 18–24" tall and produces abundant, nocturnal, rich red flowers with green throats in early to mid-summer.

H. 'Stella d'Oro' is a repeat bloomer. The fragrant, bright golden yellow flowers are borne on modest-sized 12" plants.

H. 'Strutter's Ball' produces abundant dark purple-black flowers, with silver white markings and yellow-green throats in early to mid-summer. It grows 28" tall and has densely growing foliage.

Problems & Pests

Generally, these plants are pest free. Daylilies can have rare problems with rust, *Hemerocallis* gall midge, aphids, spider mites, thrips and slugs.

The petals of daylilies are edible. Add them to salads for a splash of color and a pleasantly peppery taste.

Delphinium
Candle Delphinium, Candle Larkspur
Delphinium

Height: 8"–6' **Spread:** 12–36" **Flower color:** blue, purple, pink, white or bicolored **Blooms:** mid-summer **Zones:** 3–7

TALL, BOLD AND ASTOUNDING IN BLOOM, DELPHINIUMS REMIND us of what growing flowers is all about. The newer Pacific hybrids have proven to be stellar performers in the north; an amazing feature of these hybrids is that they don't get some of the diseases older varieties did. Still, delphiniums are plants that require some gardening. Always deadhead spent blooms. Half the battle against fungal problems is to give delphiniums plenty of space at the time of planting, and divide them often enough that they don't become crowded. You will be rewarded with long-lived plants that deserve their status as botanical royalty.

Planting

Seeding: Direct sow in spring to produce flowers the following year. Seedlings may not be true to type.

Planting out: Spring or fall; plant with crown at soil level to avoid crown rot

Spacing: 24"

Growing

Grow in a **full sun** location that is well protected from strong winds. The soil should be **fertile, moist** and **humus rich** with **excellent drainage**. Delphiniums love well-composted manure mixed into the soil. These heavy feeders require fertilizer twice a year, in spring and summer. Each spring, delphiniums require division to keep them vigorous.

Delphis *is the Greek word for dolphin—the petals of the flowers resemble the nose and fins of a dolphin.*

D. x *belladonna* (photos this page)

D. x belladonna

To encourage a second flush of smaller blooms, remove the first flower spikes once they begin to fade and before they begin to set seed. Cut them off just above the foliage. New shoots will begin to grow, and the old foliage will fade back. The old growth may then be cut right back, allowing new growth to fill in.

Tips

Delphiniums are classic cottage-garden plants. Their height and need for staking relegate them to the back of the border, where they make a magnificent blue-toned backdrop for warmer foreground flowers such as peonies, poppies and black-eyed Susans.

The tall flower spikes of many delphiniums have hollow centers and break easily if exposed to the wind. Each flower spike needs to be individually staked. Stakes should be

installed as soon as the flower spike reaches 12" in height. You can use a wire tomato cage for a clump.

Recommended

D. x *belladonna* (belladonna hybrids, Belladonna Group) bears flowers of blue, white or mauve in loose, branched spikes. It grows 3–4' tall and spreads 12–18". **'Blue Bees'** has pale blue flowers with white centers. **'Wendy'** has dark purple-blue flowers.

D. **Pacific hybrids** (Pacific Giant Group) were originally bred in California to grow as annuals. They are tall plants, with sturdy stems, growing to 6' tall and 36" wide. They produce tall spikes of tightly packed, large, semi-double to double flowers in white and shades of pink, purple and blue in mid-summer.

D. grandiflorum (*D. chinense*) bears flowers of blue, purple or white in loose, branched clusters. It grows 8–20" tall and spreads up to 12".

Problems & Pests

Problems can be caused by slugs, powdery mildew, bacterial and fungal leaf spot, gray mold, crown and root rot, white rot, rust, white smut, leaf smut and damping off. Although this list is daunting, remember that healthy plants are less susceptible to problems.

D. Pacific hybrids (photos this page)

These plants are so gorgeous in bloom that you can build a garden or plan a party around their flowering.

Euphorbia

Cushion Spurge

Euphorbia

Height: 12–36" **Spread:** 12–24" **Flower color:** yellow, green, orange
Blooms: spring to mid-summer **Zones:** 4–9

EUPHORBIA IS NOT GROWN NEARLY ENOUGH BY GARDENERS,
except for (hint, hint) gardeners with really great-looking gardens; once you
learn that overall form and foliage are essential components to creating a
beautiful garden, you will recognize what a useful plant euphorbia is. What
one assumes are flowers are actually colorful bracts (leaves at the base of a
flower) that create more interest than the tiny flowers themselves. *E. corollata*
is a delicate, delightful variety that resembles baby's breath (p. 90). *E. dulcis*
'Chameleon' is a good one to try first; plant it as a single specimen near the
front of the bed or at the entrance to a path or patio.

Planting

Seeding: Use fresh seed for best germination rates. Start seed in cold frame in spring.

Planting out: Spring or fall

Spacing: 18"

Growing

Euphorbias grow well in **full sun** and **light shade**. The soil should be of **average fertility, moist, humus rich** and **well drained**. These plants are drought tolerant and can be invasive in too-fertile soil. Euphorbias can be propagated by stem cuttings, and they may self-seed in the garden. Division is rarely required. These plants dislike being disturbed once established.

E. polychroma

E. dulcis 'Chameleon'

E. polychroma (photos this page)

Tips

Use euphorbias in a mixed or herbaceous border, rock garden or lightly shaded woodland garden.

You may wish to wear gloves when handling these plants. Some people find the milky sap irritates their skin.

If you are cutting the stems for propagation, dip the cut ends in hot water before planting to stop the sticky white sap from running.

Don't confuse these euphorbias with the invasive, weedy leafy spurge (*E. esula*). Leafy spurge is rarely sold in garden centers, but it is common at perennial exchanges and should be strenuously avoided.

Recommended

E. corollata (flowering spurge, tramp's spurge, wild spurge) is an erect plant with slender stems that grows 24–36" tall and 12–24" wide. In summer it produces a plethora of inconspicuous flowers with showy, white bracts.

E. dulcis is a compact, upright plant that grows about 12" tall, with an equal spread. The spring flowers and bracts are yellow-green. The dark bronze-green leaves turn red and orange in fall. 'Chameleon' has purple-red foliage that turns darker purple in fall. There appear to be two plants in garden centers sharing the same cultivar name. Both have the purple foliage, but depending on where you shop, you may find yourself with an orange-flowered or a purple-tinged, yellowish, green-flowered 'Chameleon.' Ask before you buy.

E. polychroma (*E. epithimoides*) (cushion spurge) is a mounding, clump-forming plant 12–24" tall and 18–24" wide. The inconspicuous flowers are surrounded by long-lasting, yellow bracts. The foliage turns shades of purple, red or orange in fall. There are several cultivars, though the species is more commonly available.

The members of this genus hybridize easily with each other.

Problems & Pests
Aphids, spider mites and nematodes are possible problems, along with fungal root rot in poorly drained, wet soil.

E. polychroma

Feverfew
Painted Daisy
Tanacetum

Height: 9"–4' **Spread:** 9–36" **Flower color:** white, pink, purple, yellow, red
Blooms: summer to fall **Zones:** 3–8

NO DOUBT THERE ARE SOME FINE GARDENERS WHO WILL DEFEND growing *T. coccineum* as a very worthwhile horticultural experience, but this species usually transforms quickly into a floppy wreck of the high-maintenance (staking, hooping, shearing) variety. Luckily, *T. coccineum* is often short-lived. Both *T. parthenium* and *T. vulgare* (see recommended) are much finer choices for the northern garden, and they perform reasonably well in partially sunny conditions.

Planting
Seeding: Start seed in early spring; soil temperature 50°–55° F

Planting out: Spring

Spacing: 12–36"

Growing

Feverfew grows best in **full sun**. Any **well-drained** soil is suitable. Very fertile soil may encourage invasive growth. Deadheading will prolong the blooming period. Divide in spring as needed to control spread and maintain plant vigor.

Tips

Use feverfew in borders, rock gardens, wildflower gardens, cottage gardens and meadow gardens. Most of these species are quite civilized, but *T. vulgare* can become invasive. To control invasiveness, grow the non-invasive 'Crispum' or grow the species in planters and remove the flowers before the seeds ripen.

T. vulgare

Recommended

T. coccineum (painted daisy, pyrethrum) is an erect, bushy plant, growing 18–36" tall and spreading 12–18". The main flush of white, pink, purple or red, yellow-centered flowers occurs in early summer, but some flowering will continue until fall. '**Brenda**' has red or magenta flowers. 'James Kelway' bears scarlet red flowers.

T. parthenium (feverfew) is a bushy plant with fern-like, aromatic foliage. It grows 12–36" tall, spreads 12–24" and bears clusters of small, daisy-like flowers. '**Gold Ball**' forms a compact mound 9" tall and wide and bears yellow, double flowers. 'Snowball' bears white, double flowers.

T. vulgare (tansy, golden buttons) forms a large, erect, wide-spreading mound. It grows 2–4' tall, spreads 18–36" and bears clusters of bright yellow, button-like flowers from mid-summer to fall. 'Crispum' (curly tansy) is a compact plant with crinkled, lacy foliage. It is less invasive than the species.

The name 'feverfew' is a corruption of febrifuge*, which refers to a plant or medicine used to treat fevers.*

T. parthenium

Problems & Pests

These plants are generally pest free, but keep an eye open for aphids.

Flax

Linum

Height: 4–24" **Spread:** 12" **Flower color:** blue, white
Blooms: spring to fall **Zones:** 3–8

THAT FLAX IS NOT GROWN MORE OFTEN IN
northern gardens is certainly because the plant
tends to be short-lived even under ideal
conditions. It's a pity. Few perennials
can rival flax for beauty in bloom or
possess such a graceful, delicate look.
Gardeners who fall under its spell most
often grow it from seed, starting plants
under lights in mid- to late February. Combined with the fact that flax self-seeds freely,
this treatment ensures that there are always
blooming specimens in the garden.

Planting

Seeding: Direct sow in spring or fall. Early spring is best when sowing seed indoors or in cold frame.

Planting out: spring, summer

Spacing: 12"

Growing

Flax prefers **full to partial sun**. The soil should be **light, organically rich, very well drained** and of **average fertility**. Do not plant flax in a location that is consistently wet because of late melting snow. It self-seeds readily and is considered short-lived. It is very drought tolerant. Yearly propagation may be necessary to ensure longevity, and it can be done by allowing it to self-seed or by division in spring or fall.

Tips

Flax works well in wild, woodland or meadow settings. The delicate blue flowers are charming in cottage gardens, mixed beds and borders. It is commonly used in herb or medicinal gardens as well.

Shear back after flowering to encourage a new flush of growth.

Recommended

L. perenne is a clump-forming, airy perennial, with slender stems and bluish green, narrow leaves. The stems are tipped with clusters of tiny, flat, blue flowers with yellow centers. **'Diamond'** ('Diamant,' 'White Diamond') bears white to off-white flowers. **'Nanum'** ('Nanum Saphyr') grows 10–12" tall and wide and bears tiny, blue flowers. **'Sapphire'** ('Blue Sapphire,' 'Blau Saphyr') forms upright clumps, and the stems have a tendency to arch. Pale blue flowers are borne in spring through summer.

Problems & Pests

Stem rot, rust, wilt, anthracnose, damping off, slugs, snails and aphids can all cause different levels of damage.

L. perenne (photos this page)

For many years blue flax was called 'Lewis flax' in reference to Captain Meriwether Lewis (of the Lewis and Clark Expedition), who first discovered this plant in Montana.

Foamflower

Tiarella

Height: 4–12" **Spread:** 12–24" **Flower color:** white, pink **Blooms:** spring, sometimes to early summer **Zones:** 3–8

TIARELLA COMPRISES A SMALL GENUS OF VERY USEFUL SHADE plants that are grown both for their arresting flowers and pleasing foliage. Foamflower's tall, slender stems rise rapidly in spring and are soon covered with great puffs of tiny, white flowers, which from a distance resemble foam. But it's the basal mounds of lobed, maple-like leaves that remain interesting all season; some varieties turn bronze in fall. If a portion of your property contains woods, foamflowers are great to plant along the edge of the woods to ease the transition from yard to trees.

Planting
Seeding: Start seed in cold frame in spring

Planting out: Spring

Spacing: 6–24"

Growing

Foamflowers prefer **partial, light or full shade** without afternoon sun. The soil should be **humus rich, moist** and **slightly acidic**. These plants adapt to most soils. Divide in spring. Deadhead to encourage reblooming.

If the foliage fades or rusts in summer, cut it partway to the ground and new growth will emerge.

Tips

Foamflowers are excellent groundcovers for shaded and woodland gardens. They can be included in shaded borders and left to naturalize in wild gardens.

These plants spread by underground stems, which are easily pulled up to stop excessive spread.

Recommended

T. cordifolia is a low-growing, spreading plant that bears spikes of foamy, white flowers. It is attractive enough to be grown for its foliage alone, and cultivars with interesting variegation are becoming available. This species is native to eastern North America. **'Oakleaf'** forms a dense clump of dark green leaves and bears pink flowers.

T. wherryi is similar to *T. cordifolia*, but it forms a clump and bears more flowers.

Problems & Pests

Rust and slugs are possible problems.

T. cordifolia

The clusters of starry flowers make the stems look like festive sparklers.

T. wherryi

Foxglove
Digitalis

Height: 2–5' **Spread:** 12–24" **Flower color:** pink, purple, yellow, maroon, red, white **Blooms:** spring to mid-summer **Zones:** 3–8

GROWING FOXGLOVE IS ONE OF THE GREAT JOYS of gardening. Its proud, upright form provides a pleasing contrast to the mounding habits of most other garden perennials. The dramatic spikes of horn-shaped flowers, which come in a variety of colors, are breathtaking. Finally, the plants perform well in both sun and partial shade. Foxgloves are essential in the cottage garden or any informal planting. If you are creating a very small perennial garden, use one or three plants as the centerpiece.

Planting

Seeding: Direct sow or start in cold frame in early spring. Seeds need light in order to germinate. Flowering is unlikely the first year.

Planting out: Spring

Spacing: 12–24"

Growing

Foxgloves grow well in **partial or light shade.** The soil should be **fertile, humus rich** and **moist.** Purple foxglove and strawberry foxglove prefer an **acidic** soil, while yellow foxglove prefers an **alkaline** soil. These plants adapt to most soils that are neither too wet nor too dry. Division is unnecessary for purple foxglove because this plant will not live long enough to be divided. It continues to occupy your garden by virtue of its ability to self-seed. Yellow foxglove and strawberry foxglove can be divided in spring or fall.

You may wish to deadhead foxgloves once they have finished flowering, but it is a good idea to leave

some of the spikes of purple foxglove in place to self-seed.

The hybrid varieties become less vigorous with time, and self-sown seedlings may not come true to type. Sprinkle new seed in your foxglove bed each spring to ensure a steady show of the lovely flowers.

D. purpurea (photos this page)

D. purpurea 'Alba'

D. purpurea

Tips

Foxgloves are must-haves for the cottage garden or for those people interested in heritage plants. They make excellent vertical accents along the back of a border. They also make an interesting addition to a woodland garden. Some staking may be required if the plants are in a windy location. Remove the tallest spike and the side shoots will bloom on shorter stalks that may not need staking.

Recommended

D. grandiflora (yellow foxglove) is a clump-forming perennial or biennial, growing 36" tall and 18" wide. It produces pale yellow flowers with brown, netted veins on the inside of the flowers in early to mid-summer.

D. x *mertonensis* (strawberry foxglove) is also a true perennial. It forms a clump of foliage 12–16" wide with flower-bearing stems 3–4' tall. The spring and early-summer flowers are rose pink.

D. purpurea (purple foxglove) forms a basal rosette of foliage from which tall flowering spikes emerge, growing 2–5' tall and spreading 24". The flowers bloom in early summer and come in a wide range of colors. The insides of the flowers are often spotted with contrasting colors. If purple foxglove is not winter hardy in your garden, it can be grown as an annual from purchased plants. 'Alba' bears white flowers. **'Apricot'** bears apricot pink flowers. **Excelsior hybrids,** available in many colors, bear dense spikes of flowers. **Foxy hybrids,** which also come in a range of colors, are considered dwarf by foxglove standards, but they easily reach 36" in height.

D. purpurea (photos this page)

Problems & Pests

Anthracnose, fungal leaf spot, powdery mildew, root and stem rot, aphids, Japanese beetles and mealybugs are possible problems for foxgloves

Foxgloves are extremely poisonous; simply touching the plant has been known to cause rashes, headaches and nausea.

Gaillardia
Blanket Flower
Gaillardia

Height: 12–36" **Spread:** 12–24" **Flower color:** combinations of red, yellow
Blooms: early summer to early fall **Zones:** 3–10

YEARS AGO I SPOTTED GAILLARDIA IN A BOOK AND MADE AN
effort to find it at local nurseries. I couldn't find it, so I grew 'Kobold' from
seed, 12 plants or so, and now, nearly two decades later, I still enjoy gaillardia
in my garden. The availability of gaillardia has greatly increased over the
years as interest in it has grown. If you keep the plant tidy by deadheading;
don't give it too much water; and provide a winter mulch of bagged leaves or
marsh hay, you'll find this cheery native brightening the front of your border
for many years to come.

Planting

Seeding: Start seed indoors or in the garden in early spring; don't cover the seeds because they need light to germinate.

Planting out: Spring

Spacing: 18"

Growing

Gaillardia grows best in **full sun**. The soil should be **fertile, light** and **well drained**. Poor soils are tolerated, but plants will not overwinter in heavy, wet soil. Deadheading encourages the plants to bloom all summer. Cut the plants back to within 6" of the ground in late summer to encourage new growth and to promote the longevity of these often short-lived plants.

Tips

Gaillardia is a North American prairie plant that looks at home in an informal cottage garden, wildflower garden or meadow planting. It is also attractive when planted in clumps of three or four in a mixed or herbaceous border. Drought tolerant, it is ideal for neglected and rarely watered parts of the garden. Dwarf varieties make good container plantings.

Recommended

G. x grandiflora is a bushy, upright plant 24–36" tall and 12–24" wide. It bears daisy-like flowers all summer and into early fall. The petals have yellow tips and red bases. **'Burgundy'** is 24–36" tall, with dark red flowers. **'Kobold'** ('Goblin') is a compact cultivar that grows only 12" tall. The flowers are variegated red and yellow, like the ones of the species.

Problems & Pests

Powdery mildew, downy mildew, leaf spot, rust, aster yellows and leafhoppers are possible, but they rarely cause much trouble.

G. x grandiflora (photos this page)

The multi-colored petals of gaillardia *(gay-lard-ee-a) flowers add a fiery glow to cottage gardens and meadow plantings.*

Gas Plant
Burning Bush, Dittany, Fraxinella
Dictamnus

Height: 18–36" **Spread:** 12–36" **Flower color:** white, pink, pink-purple with darker veins **Blooms:** early summer **Zones:** 3–9

GAS PLANT IS AN EASY-TO-GROW, LONG-LIVED, TROUBLE-FREE perennial that requires little care. Why gas plant is not better known and more widely grown is unclear. Gardeners prize it for its foliage as well as its flowers. Depending on which variety you choose, white, pink or purplish flowers with very attractive veining start to appear in May. Gas plant's dark green, glossy leaves resemble those of an ash tree. Gas plant is very slow growing, and it can take two to three years to become established.

Gas plant is rarely troubled by pests or diseases.

Planting

Seeding: Sow seeds in garden or trays set outside in winter in colder climates. Seeds need cold treatment for germination.

Planting out: Spring

Spacing: 12–24"

Growing

Gas plant prefers **full sun** but tolerates partial shade. It prefers areas with cool nights. The soil should be **average to fertile, dry** and **well drained**.

This plant takes several years to become established and should not be divided because it resents being disturbed. It may not flower until it has become well established.

Tips

Gas plant makes a good addition to a border. You won't have to do much maintenance once it is established, so feel free to plant it in an area that is hard to reach.

Although the foliage has an appealing scent, avoid planting gas plant where you will be able to brush against it. The oils in the foliage can cause photodermatitis, which means that the oils themselves may not cause irritation, but in combination with exposure to sunlight they can cause rashes, itching and burning. The problem is often worse for people with fair skin.

Recommended

D. albus (*D. fraxinella*) is a large, clump-forming plant with lemon-scented leaves. The plant is long-lived, but it takes a few years to become established. It bears spikes of pink-veined, white or pink flowers. **Var.** *purpureus* ('Purpureus') has light pink-purple flowers with darker purple veins.

D. albus var. *purpureus*

Use care when bringing in the attractive seedpods for drying. They may explode, scattering their seeds.

D. albus

Globe Flower

Trollius

Height: 12–36" **Spread:** 16–24" **Flower color:** yellow, orange
Blooms: spring to early summer **Zones:** 3–7

GARDENERS WHO ARE INTERESTED IN GROWING COLLECTIONS
of unusual plants will want to include globe flower. This moisture-loving
plant is at home in formal and informal plantings, and it is superb as a pool-
side or streamside specimen plant. Most plants have trouble growing in clay
soil, but globe flower does not have that problem. If you can't amend your
clay soil with organic matter, globe flower will still flourish.

Planting

Seeding: Sow fresh, ripe seed in
cold frame in fall or spring. Seeds
may take up to two years to germinate.

Planting out: Spring or fall

Spacing: 18–24"

Growing

Globe flowers prefer **partial shade** but tolerate full sun if enough moisture is provided. Plants prefer **cool, moist** conditions and do not tolerate drought. The soil should be **fertile** and **heavy** and not be allowed to dry out. Globe flowers can be planted in well-drained soil as long as the soil remains moist. Prune out any yellowing leaves in summer. Division is rarely required but can be done in early spring or late fall.

Tips

Globe flower is the perfect plant for the side of a pond or stream. It will naturalize very well in a damp meadow garden or bog garden and can be used in the border as long as the soil remains moist. Globe flowers are long lasting as cut flowers.

Recommended

T. x *cultorum* (hybrid globe flower) forms perfectly globe-shaped flowers. Plants grow 24–36" tall and 16–18" wide. **'Earliest of All'** grows 18–20" tall and produces pale yellow-orange flowers earlier than the other globe flowers. **'Orange Princess'** has large, deep orange flowers on plants 12–24" in height.

T. europaeus (common globe flower) has dark green foliage and grows 24" tall and wide, bearing lemon yellow flowers that resemble those of buttercups. **'Superbus'** produces a plethora of 1–2" wide blooms.

Problems & Pests

Powdery mildew may cause occasional problems.

T. europaeus

T. x *cultorum* 'Orange Princess'

Globe Thistle
Small Globe Thistle
Echinops

Height: 2–4' **Spread:** 24" **Flower color:** blue, purple **Blooms:** late summer
Zones: 3–8

I ADMIT TO BEING SMITTEN BY *ECHINOPS* FROM THE MOMENT OF
my first encounter with it, but I readily understand the reasoning of those
who say 'No thanks.' It is a big, steely, tough-looking plant,
and gardeners will either love it or leave it. I love it
because in bloom it gives you large, blue, perfect
spheres, and about the only other option for that
similar look is spring-blooming *Alliums* (nodding onions). The flowers are wonderful in
dried arrangements. The leaves are big, long,
lobed and leathery, and the tiny thorns on them
will prick the ungloved hand. *Echinops* is best
grown as a single; I first grew it as a wave of three
plants, and that was too much, even for me.

Planting
Seeding: Direct sow in spring

Planting out: Spring or fall

Spacing: 18–24"

Growing
Globe thistle prefers **full sun** but tolerates partial shade.
The soil should be of **poor to average fertility** and **well
drained.** Divide in spring when the clump appears
dense or overgrown, is less vigorous and begins to
show dead areas. Wear gloves and long sleeves to protect yourself from the prickles.

Deadheading prevents self-seeding. Cutting back to the basal foliage after flowering may result in a second round of blooms.

Tips

Globe thistle is a striking plant for the back or center of the border and for neglected areas of the garden that often miss watering.

Recommended

E. ritro forms a compact clump of spiny foliage. It bears round clusters of purple or blue flowers in late summer. 'Vietch's Blue' has smaller but more abundant flowers.

Problems & Pests

Globe thistle rarely has any problems, but aphids can show up from time to time.

This plant is a good choice for gardeners who need a large, low-maintenance specimen to fill an unused corner.

E. ritro (photos this page)

Goat's Beard

Aruncus

Height: 6"–6' **Spread:** 1–6' **Flower color:** cream, white **Blooms:** early summer, mid-summer **Zones:** 3–7

ARUNCUS IS AN OUTSTANDING NORTH AMERICAN NATIVE PLANT that gains in popularity with each new season. The list of tall, lush, shade-loving perennials that exhibit eye-catching blooms is relatively short, and this plant belongs at the top of that list. *A. dioicus* exhibits handsome, 12" spires of creamy white flowers that shimmy in the slightest breeze and glow with a yellowish tinge in the June moonlight. *A. aethusifolius*, the dwarf, provides exceptional lace-like foliage that turns a rusty red in fall.

Planting

Seeding: Use fresh seed and keep soil moist and conditions humid. Soil temperature should be 70°–75° F.

Planting out: Spring or fall

Spacing: 1$^1/_2$–6'

Growing

These plants prefer **partial to full shade.** If they are planted in deep shade, they bear fewer blooms. They also tolerate full sun as long as the soil is kept evenly moist. The soil should be **rich** and **moist,** with plenty of **humus** mixed in. Divide in spring or fall, though goat's beard plants may be difficult to divide because they develop a thick root mass. Use a sharp knife to cut the root mass into pieces.

A. dioicus (photos this page)

A. dioicus

Male goat's beard plants have full, fuzzy flowers; female plants have more pendulous flowers.

A. aethusifolius

Goat's beards will self-seed if flowers are left in place, but deadheading maintains an attractive appearance and encourages a longer blooming period. If you want to start some new plants from seed, allow the seedheads to ripen before removing them. You will need to have both male and female plants in order to produce seeds that will sprout. Don't save male flowerheads—they will not produce seeds.

Tips

These plants look very natural growing at the sunny entrance or edge of a woodland garden, in a native plant garden or in a large island planting. They may also be used in a border or alongside a stream or pond.

Recommended

A. aethusifolius (dwarf Korean goat's beard) forms a low-growing, compact mound. It grows 6–16" tall and spreads up to 12". Branched spikes of loosely held, cream flowers are produced in early summer. This plant looks similar to astilbe (p. 86) and is sometimes sold by that name.

A. dioicus (common goat's beard, giant goat's beard) forms a large, bushy, shrub-like perennial 3–6' tall, with an equal spread. Large plumes of cream white flowers are borne from early to mid-summer.

There are several cultivars, though some can be hard to find. **'Kneiffii'** is a dainty cultivar with finely divided leaves and arching stems with nodding plumes. It grows about 36" tall and spreads 18". **'Zweiweltkind'** ('Child of Two Worlds') is a compact plant with drooping, white flowers.

Problems & Pests

Occasional problems with fly larvae and tarnished plant bugs are possible.

A. dioicus

Goldenrod

Solidago

Height: 2–4' **Spread:** 18" **Flower color:** yellow **Blooms:** mid-summer to fall **Zones:** 2–8

HERE'S AN ATTRACTIVE, TERRIFICALLY USEFUL PERENNIAL THAT gets no respect, which is not the fault of the plant. Goldenrod is in the same plant family that harbors ragweed (*Ambrosia*). The showier goldenrod has the misfortune of blooming at the peak of allergy season along with ragweed, and it is therefore seen as one of the causes of allergies—which it isn't. It is a great plant, bestowing arching spires of golden yellow blooms to the fall landscape. Plant three in a curving line in front of *Aster novae-angliae* 'Purple Dome' or *Aster* x *frikartii* (pp. 82–85) to learn all there is to know about appealing color and foliage combinations.

Planting

Seeding: Not recommended; desirable cultivars do not come true to type from seed

Planting out: Spring or fall

Spacing: 12"

Growing

Goldenrods prefer **full sun** but tolerate partial shade. The soil should be of **poor to average fertility, light** and **well drained**. Too fertile a soil will result in lush, invasive growth but few flowers. Divide in spring or fall when needed to control growth and keep plants vigorous.

Tips

Goldenrods are good plants for late-season color. They look at home in a large border, cottage garden or wildflower garden. Don't plant them near less vigorous plants because goldenrods can quickly overwhelm them.

Recommended

S. **hybrids** have been developed for their improved habit and flowering over the common wild goldenrods. Plants form a clump of strong stems with narrow leaves. They generally grow about 24–36" tall and spread about 18". The plume-like clusters of yellow flowers are produced from mid-summer to fall. **'Crown of Rays'** holds its flower clusters in horizontal spikes. **'Golden Shower'** bears flowers in horizontal or drooping plumes. This taller cultivar reaches 3–4' in height.

Problems & Pests

Goldenrods seldom have major problems, though stem galls, leaf spot, rust and powdery mildew may occur from time to time.

'Crown of Rays' (right)

Goutweed
Snow on the Mountain, Bishop's Goutweed
Aegopodium

Height: 8–24" **Spread:** indefinite **Flower color:** white, but inconspicuous, grown for foliage **Blooms:** summer **Zones:** 3–8

FOR GARDENERS IN SEARCH OF A LEAFY GROUNDCOVER TO GROW in sun or shade, few perennials are as reliable and easy to grow as goutweed. It's important, however, that the warning bell be sounded early: a little goutweed goes a long way. Goutweed is as often cursed as it is praised because it can spread at a full gallop through the landscape. Few garden club discussions about the plant will end without at least one veteran member recounting an insidious infestation of the plant launched from the neighbor's side of a communal picket fence. Despite these complaints, 'Variegatum,' the variety most often found in the trade, provides a quick and easy answer to the age-old question 'What can I grow underneath my (fill in the blank) trees?'

Planting

Seeding: Not recommended

Planting out: Spring, summer, fall

Spacing: 12–24"

Growing

Goutweed grows well in any light conditions from **full sun** to **full shade**. Soil of **poor fertility** is recommended to curb invasiveness, but any **well-drained** soil is fine. This plant is drought tolerant and thrives on neglect. If the foliage starts to look bedraggled during summer, cut goutweed plants back completely. They will sprout fresh new growth. Division is rarely required, but you will have to dig up any parts of the plants that are venturing into undesired areas.

A. podagraria 'Variegatum'

Tips

It is best to plant goutweed where it has lots of room to spread or is severely restricted from spreading. Good places include on steep banks that are difficult to mow, in dry shade under a tree where nothing else will grow, in planters or where a natural barrier is created such as the area between a house, walkway and driveway.

Goutweed is an excellent choice for growing at a cottage or other infrequently used property, where there isn't much time to maintain a lawn. Avoid planting this perennial near a lawn because it will quickly creep in.

Goutweed was reputedly cultivated in medieval times for medicinal purposes, particularly to treat gout.

A. podagraria 'Variegatum'

Recommended

A. podagraria is rarely grown because it is unstoppably invasive. The cultivar **'Variegatum'** has attractive, white-margined foliage. It is reputed to be less invasive than the species, but it is still very prone to spreading if left unchecked.

Problems & Pests

Goutweed may be afflicted by leaf blight; cut back the damaged foliage to renew the plants.

Hardy Geranium

Cranesbill Geranium
Geranium

Height: 2–36" **Spread:** 12–36" **Flower color:** white, red, pink, purple, blue
Blooms: spring, summer, fall **Zones:** 3–8

ONCE YOU START GROWING HARDY GERANIUMS, YOUR LOVE FOR these plants will never wane. Veteran gardeners are probably familiar with *G.* 'Johnson's Blue.' I still grow it and always ensure I whack it back by two-thirds after it blooms so I will enjoy a tighter mound of fresh foliage. I have started to explore the many newer cultivars. Wonderful, intricate patterns on the various sizes of lobed or toothed foliage keep this easy-to-grow perennial handsome before and after bloom.

Planting

Seeding: Species are easy to start from seed in early fall or spring. Cultivars and hybrids may not come true to type.

Planting out: Spring or fall

Spacing: 12–24"

Growing

Hardy geraniums grow well in **full sun, partial shade** and **light shade.** Some tolerate heavier shade. These plants dislike hot weather. Soil of **average fertility** and **good drainage** is preferred, but most conditions are tolerated except waterlogged soil.

Divide in spring. Shear back spent blooms for a second set of flowers. If the foliage looks tatty in late summer, prune it back by two-thirds to rejuvenate.

Tips

These long-flowering plants are great in the border, filling in the spaces between shrubs and other larger plants and keeping the weeds down. They can be included in rock gardens and woodland gardens and mass planted as groundcovers.

G. sanguineum

G. x *oxonianum*

G. pratense

G. sanguineum var. striatum

Recommended

G. 'Brookside' is a clump-forming, drought-tolerant geranium with finely cut leaves. It grows 12–18" tall and spreads about 24". The deep blue to violet blue flowers appear in summer. (Zones 3–8)

G. x *cantabrigiense* (Cambridge geranium) is a vigorous grower that spreads slowly by runners to form a groundcover. Individual plants grow about 24" wide. The 8–12" tall stems bear rose pink to white flowers in spring and summer. It retains its foliage, creating a nice winter effect. 'Biokovo' has red foliage in fall and grows only 4–5" tall with white to pale pink flowers. Plants spread 24–36". (Zones 3–8)

G. cinereum (grayleaf geranium) forms a basal rosette of gray-green foliage. It grows 4–6" tall and spreads about 12". It produces small clusters

of white- or pink-veined flowers in early summer. It is often grown in rock gardens and other well-drained spots. 'Ballerina' has silvery foliage and pink flowers that are darkly veined in purple. (Zones 5–8)

G. endressii is a clump-forming, evergreen perennial that spreads by rhizomes. It grows 18–20" tall and 24" wide bearing clusters of erect, funnel-shaped, bright pink flowers for a long period in summer. The flowers darken with age. 'Wargrave Pink' is a very vigorous cultivar that grows 24" tall, spreads about 36" and bears salmon pink flowers. (Zones 3–8)

G. himalayense is a mat-forming perennial that spreads by rhizomes. It grows 12–18" tall and 24" wide with mid-green leaves that turn a

G. pratense

G. sanguineum cultivar

nice reddish fall color. It produces violet blue to dark blue flowers, with darker veins in mid-summer, that occasionally bloom into fall. **'Plenum'** ('Birch Double') has double, dark purple-blue flowers with darker veins. (Zones 4–7)

G. **'Johnson's Blue'** is a slowly spreading perennial 12–18" tall and 24–36" wide with narrowly divided foliage. It produces lavender blue flowers with darker veins in early summer. The 2" wide flowers are tinged pinkish in the centers. This plant is a sterile hybrid first introduced in the 1950s. There may be plants offered under this name that are not the true 'Johnson's Blue.' (Zones 4–8)

G. macrorrhizum (bigroot geranium, scented cranesbill) forms a spreading mound of fragrant foliage. It grows 12–20" tall and

spreads 16–24". This plant is quite drought tolerant. Flowers in variable shades of pink are borne in spring and early summer. **'Bevan's Variety'** bears magenta flowers. **'Ingwersen's Variety'** has shiny, light green foliage and light pink flowers. (Zones 4–8)

G. x *oxonianum* is a vigorous, mound-forming plant with attractive evergreen foliage; it bears pink flowers from spring to fall. It grows up to 30" tall and spreads about 24". **'A.T. Johnson'** bears many silvery pink flowers. **'Claridge Druce'** is a vigorous, clump-forming plant with gray-green foliage. The funnel-shaped flowers are rose pink with darker veins. This cultivar self-seeds freely and plants come mostly true from seed. (Zones 5–8)

G. phaeum (dusky cranesbill, mourning widow) forms clumps 24–30" tall and 18" wide. The foliage

G. sanguineum

often has brown or purple-brown markings. Clusters of pendant, white-centered, dusky purple to deep maroon to almost black flowers bloom from late spring to early summer. This plant prefers a moist, shady location. (Zones 4–8)

G. pratense (meadow cranesbill) forms an upright clump, growing 24–36" tall and spreading about 24". Many white, blue or light purple flowers are borne for a short period in early summer. It self-seeds freely. '**Mrs. Kendall Clarke**' bears rose pink flowers with blue-gray veining. (Zones 3–8)

G. sanguineum (bloody cranesbill, bloodred cranesbill) forms a dense, mounding clump. It grows 6–12" tall and spreads 12–24". Bright magenta flowers are borne mostly in early summer and sporadically until fall. '**Album**' has white flowers and a more open habit than other cultivars. '**Alpenglow**' has bright rosy red flowers and dense foliage. '**John Elsley**' is 2–4" tall with dark green leaves and carmine red to rose pink flowers. '**Max Frei**' bears bright carmine pink to magenta pink flowers. '**New Hampshire Purple**' bears flowers that are large and dark rose-purple. **Var.** *striatum* is heat and drought tolerant. It has pale pink blooms with blood red veins. (Zones 3–8)

Problems & Pests
Rare problems with leaf spot and rust can occur.

These plants are often called cranesbills because the distinctive seed capsule resembles a crane's long bill.

G. sanguineum cultivar

Hens and Chicks
Roof Houseleek
Sempervivum

Height: 3–6" **Spread:** 12" to indefinite **Flower color:** red, yellow, white, purple; grown mainly for foliage **Blooms:** summer **Zones:** 3–8

AS A CHILD, I FIRST ENCOUNTERED HENS AND CHICKS GROWING wild on the rocky cliffs and shorelines of northwest Ontario, Canada. I thought it was a delight then, and I still think that today. The only problem is finding a place to grow the plant. This succulent will flat-out die in good gardening soil. So tuck it into sunny rock gardens and anywhere you have created rock outcroppings or built a retaining wall made of boulders. Oh, and don't forget the roof. I spotted clusters of hens and chicks growing amidst the mossy shingles of a rustic potting shed, and my childhood enchantment was renewed.

Planting

Seeding: Not recommended. Remove and replant young rosettes to propagate.

Planting out: Spring

Spacing: 10–12"

Growing

Grow these plants in **full sun** or **partial shade**. The soil should be of **poor to average fertility** and very **well drained**. Add fine gravel or grit to the soil to provide adequate drainage. Once a plant blooms, it dies. When you deadhead the faded flower, pull up the soft parent plant as well to provide space for the new daughter rosettes that sprout up, seemingly by magic. Divide by removing these new rosettes and rooting them.

S. tectorum (photos this page)

Tips

These plants make excellent additions to rock gardens and rock walls, where they will even grow right on the rocks.

Recommended

S. arachnoideum (cobweb houseleek) is identical to *S. tectorum,* except that the tips of the leaves are entwined with hairy fibers, giving the appearance of cobwebs. This plant may need protection during wet weather. (Zones 5–8)

S. tectorum forms a low-growing mat of fleshy-leaved rosettes, each about 6–10" across. Small new rosettes are quickly produced and grow and multiply to fill almost any space. Flowers may be produced in summer but are not as common in colder climates. **'Atropurpureum'** has dark reddish purple leaves. **'Limelight'** has yellow-green, pink-tipped foliage. **'Pacific Hawk'** has dark red leaves that are edged with silvery hairs. (Zones 3–8)

Problems & Pests

Hens and chicks are generally pest free, although some problems with rust and root rot can occur.

Heuchera
Coral Bells, Alum Root
Heuchera

Height: 6"–4' **Spread:** 12–18" **Flower color:** red, pink, white
Blooms: spring, summer **Zones:** 3–9

FEW PERENNIALS THAT ARE AVAILABLE TO
northern gardeners offer the tremendous variety
of foliage sizes, shapes and colors as heuchera. I
place the plant on my very short list of perennials that are essential to the creation of a
beautiful garden. After all, the main problem with any perennial is that the bloom
comes and goes, while the rest of the
plant sits there all season long. So why not
grow plants that remain positively stunning
when not in bloom? 'Ruby Veil,' 'Coral
Cloud,' 'Chocolate Ruffles,' 'Pewter Moon'
and a dozen more varieties will put
you well down the path to discovering the importance of growing
plants for their leaves, not just for
their blooms.

Planting
Seeding: Species, but not cultivars, may be started from
seed in spring in cold frame

Planting out: Spring

Spacing: 12–18"

Growing

Heucheras grow best in **light or partial shade**. The foliage colors can bleach out in full sun, and plants become leggy in full shade. The soil should be of **average to rich fertility, humus rich, neutral to alkaline, moist** and **well drained**. Good air circulation is essential.

The spent flowers should be removed to prolong the blooming period. Every two or three years, heucheras should be dug up to remove the oldest, woodiest roots and stems. Plants may be divided at this time, if desired, then replanted with the crown at or just above soil level. Cultivars may be propagated by division in spring or fall.

H. sanguinea

These delicate woodland plants will enhance your garden with their bright colors, attractive foliage and airy sprays of flowers.

H. micrantha 'Palace Purple'

H. micrantha 'Palace Purple' (photos this page)

Tips

Use heuchera as edging plants, in clusters in woodland gardens or as groundcovers in low traffic areas. Combine different foliage types for an interesting display.

Heucheras have a strange habit of pushing themselves up out of the soil. Mulch in fall if the plants begin heaving from the ground.

Recommended

Most of the cultivars listed are hybrids developed from crosses between the various species. They are grouped with one of their acknowledged parents in the following list.

H. americana is a mound-forming plant about 18" tall and 12" in spread. Its heart-shaped foliage is marbled and bronze-veined when it is young and matures to deep green. Cultivars have been developed for their attractive and variable foliage. **'Ruby Veil'** has low mounds 6–10" tall and 15" wide of large, ruby red leaves with silver highlights and slate gray venation. The tiny, greenish white flowers are held aloft on 26" tall stems.

H. **Bressingham hybrids** are compact hybrids, 12–18" tall and wide, that can be started from seed. The flowers are pink or red, blooming in late spring to mid-summer.

H. x *brizioides* is a group of mound-forming hybrids developed for their attractive flowers. They grow 12–30" tall and 12–18" wide. **'Coral Cloud'** has pinkish red flowers and glossy, crinkled leaves. **'June Bride'** has large, white flowers. **'Mount St. Helens'** has large, cardinal red flowers. 'Raspberry Regal' is a larger plant, growing up to 4' tall. The foliage is strongly marbled, and the flowers are bright red.

H. micrantha is a mounding, clump-forming plant up to 36" tall. The foliage is gray-green, and the flowers are white. The species is not common in gardens, but many cultivars are very common. 'Chocolate Ruffles' has ruffled, glossy, brown foliage with purple undersides that give the leaves a bronzed appearance. **Var.** *diversifolia* 'Palace Purple' is one of the best-known cultivars of all the coral bells. This compact cultivar has deep purple foliage and white blooms. It grows 18–20" tall. It can be started from seed, but only some of the seedlings will be true to type. 'Pewter Moon' has light pink flowers and silvery leaves with bronzy purple veins.

H. 'Plum Pudding'

H. 'Pewter Veil' has 12–16" tall and wide clumps of silvery purple leaves with dark gray veins that are copper pink when young. Its flowers are white flushed with pink on stems 16–24" tall.

Cut flowers of heuchera (hew-ker-uh) species can be used in arrangements.

H. 'Plum Pudding' forms mounds of shiny, silvery, ruffled, plum purple foliage with darker veins, 8–12" tall and 12–16" wide. Open clusters of small, pink to white flowers bloom in late spring to mid-summer on 26" wiry stems.

H. sanguinea is the hardiest species. It forms a low-growing mat of foliage. It grows 12–18" tall, with an equal spread. The dark green foliage is marbled with silver. The red, pink or white flowers are borne in summer. 'Frosty' has red flowers and silver-variegated foliage.

Problems & Pests

Healthy heucheras have very few problems. In stressful situations, they can be afflicted with foliar nematodes, powdery mildew, rust or leaf spot.

H. x *brizioides* cultivar

Hollyhock

Alcea

Height: 3–9' **Spread:** 12" **Flower color:** yellow, white, apricot, pink, red, purple, reddish black **Blooms:** mid-summer to fall **Zones:** 3–7

BIG, BOLD AND BRASSY, HOLLYHOCK SEEMS TO REVEL IN being the life of the party, and there's nothing wrong with that. There's little to nothing wrong with the plant. I've seen it, tall, stout and glorious in bloom, erupting from a wide crack in a city sidewalk, so there's no great trick to growing it. Holly-hock does tend to be short-lived. The trick to keeping blooming specimens in the garden is to give them ample space and allow them to go to seed in addition to remov-ing and replanting daughter plants as described under Growing.

Planting

Seeding: Direct sow in fall or start indoors in mid-winter. Flowers should be produced the first sum-mer. Plants started in spring or sum-mer should flower the following summer.

Planting out: Spring or fall

Spacing: 12"

Growing

Hollyhock prefers **full sun** but tolerates some shade. The soil should be of **average fertility** and **well drained**. Plant in an area that is sheltered from strong winds. Division is unnecessary for this short-lived perennial. Rotate the planting site each year or two to help keep rust problems at bay.

Many hollyhock cultivars will self-seed, or you can collect the seeds yourself for planting. To propagate cultivars that don't come true to type from self-sown seed (or to propagate any hollyhock you enjoy), carefully detach the small daughter plants that develop around the base of the plant and replant them where you want them. With one or both of these techniques, you should be able to keep strong, healthy hollyhock plants coming back year after year in your garden.

A. rosea

Hollyhock was originally grown as a food plant. The leaves were added to salads.

'Nigra'

Promptly remove leaves peppered with tiny, orange dots of rust to help keep the disease under control. In fall, leave healthy basal growth intact but remove and burn any tatty leaves.

Tips

Use hollyhock as a background plant or in the center of an island bed. A fence or wall will provide shelter and support. Stake plants in a windy location.

Hollyhock plants become shorter and bushier if the main stem is pinched out early in the season, when it is about 6–12" tall. The flowers are smaller, but the plant is less likely to be broken by the wind and can therefore be left unstaked.

Old-fashioned hollyhock varieties commonly have single flowers and grow very tall. The main advantage of using older varieties is a higher resistance to disease.

A. rosea (photos this page)

Recommended

A. rosea is a short-lived perennial
that bears flowers on tall spikes. It
reappears in the garden by virtue of
being a prolific self-seeder. It grows
3–9' tall and about 12" wide. From
mid- or late summer to fall, it bears
flowers in shades of yellow, white,
pink or purple. **Chater's Double
hybrids** bear ruffled, double flowers
in many bright and pastel shades.
This cultivar grows 6–8' tall and is
more consistently perennial than the
species. **'Nigra'** bears single flowers
in a unique shade of dark reddish
black, with yellow throats. **'Summer
Carnival'** is an early-blooming,
double-flowered cultivar with flowers in a wide range of colors.

Problems & Pests

Hollyhock rust is the worst problem
for hollyhocks, but they can also
have trouble with leaf spot, mallow
flea beetles, aphids, slugs, Japanese
beetles and, when plants are young,
cutworms.

*The powdered roots of plants in
the mallow family, to which
hollyhock belongs, were once
used to make a soft lozenge for
sore throats. Though popular
around the campfire, marsh-
mallows no longer contain the
throat-soothing properties they
originally did.*

A. rosea Chater's Double hybrids (right)

Hosta
Plantain Lily
Hosta

Height: 4"–6' **Spread:** 16"–6' **Flower color:** white or purple; plants grown mainly for foliage **Blooms:** late spring, summer **Zones:** 3–8

ENTERING THE WORLD OF HOSTAS CAN BE INTIMIDATING. HOW can one possibly choose from one of the largest and most diverse group of perennials on the planet? My advice is to cover the basics. Hosta foliage is either green, blue, yellow-gold or variegated, so start out by purchasing a blue, a gold, a green and a variegated. Yes, variegated does involve about 86 billion combinations; just pick what you like. When planting, remember that hostas look great planted by themselves and in groupings. When planting in groups, vary the leaf size and color so that no two hostas of the same color or leaf size are next to each other.

Once established, these hardy plants need little attention other than occasional watering and mulching with a rich organic layer.

Planting

Seeding: Direct sow or start in cold frame in spring. Young plants can take three or more years to reach flowering size.

Planting out: Spring

Spacing: 1–4'

Growing

Hostas prefer **light or partial shade** but will grow in full shade. Some newer varieties tolerate full sun. Morning sun is preferable to afternoon sun. The soil should be **fertile, moist** and **well drained,** but most soils are tolerated. Hostas are fairly drought tolerant, especially if given a mulch to help retain moisture.

Division is not required but can be done every few years in spring or summer to propagate new plants.

Tips

Hostas make wonderful woodland plants, especially when combined with ferns and other fine-textured plants. Hostas are also good plants for a mixed border, particularly when used to hide the ugly, leggy lower stems and branches of some shrubs. The dense growth and thick, shade-providing leaves of hostas make them useful for suppressing weeds.

Although hostas are commonly grown as foliage plants, they are becoming more appreciated for the spikes of lily-like flowers, some of which are fragrant and make lovely cut flowers. Some gardeners, however, find that the flower color clashes with the leaves, which are the main decorative feature of the plant. If you don't like the look of the flowers, feel free to remove them before they open—this will not harm the plant.

Recommended

Hostas have been subjected to a great deal of crossbreeding and hybridizing, resulting in hundreds of cultivars, many whose exact parentage is uncertain.

H. **'August Moon'** is a vigorous, sun-tolerant plant with pale golden yellow foliage. The foliage grows 20" tall and $2^1/_2$–$3^1/_2$' wide. White flowers bloom in summer on 28" tall scapes.

H. **'Blue Angel'** grows 18–30" tall and 3–4' wide producing heart-shaped, wavy, blue-green to gray-blue foliage. White flowers appear in mid-summer on 36" scapes.

H. fortunei (fortune's hosta) is the parent of many hybrids and cultivars. It has broad, dark green foliage and bears lavender purple flowers in mid-summer. It quickly forms a dense clump of foliage 12–24" tall and 24–36" in spread. '**Aureomarginata**' has yellow-margined leaves and is more tolerant of sun than many cultivars.

H. '**Francee**' has puckered, dark green leaves with a narrow, white margin. It grows 15–21" tall and 30–36" wide. In early summer, it bears lavender flowers on 30" scapes.

H. '**Golden Tiara**' forms clumps 12" tall and 16–20" wide of heart-shaped, mid-green foliage with a thin gold edge. Purple flowers bloom in summer on 24–30" tall scapes.

H. '**Gold Standard**' has chartreuse to bright yellow leaves with narrow, irregular, green margins. Plants grow 24–30" tall and 24–36" wide and bear lavender flowers on 3¹/₂' scapes in mid-summer.

H. '**Guacamole**' has gold to chartreuse leaves with green margins. It is a sun-tolerant plant 18–22" tall and 3–4' wide. Large, very fragrant, lavender flowers bloom in late summer on 30" scapes. The variegations are most pronounced with some sun.

H. '**Halcyon**' is a slug-resistant selection with heart-shaped, blue foliage. Plants grow 14–16" tall and 28" wide with lavender gray flowers in dense clusters on 18" scapes. It blooms in mid- to late summer.

Hosta leaves develop best if the plants are left undivided for many years.

Hostas are considered by some gardeners to be the ultimate in shade plants. They are available in a wide variety of leaf shapes, colors and textures.

H. 'Honeybells' has sweetly fragrant, light purple flowers that bloom in late summer on 36" scapes. It is a vigorous selection growing 30" tall and 4' wide. The foliage is heart-shaped, pale green and shiny.

H. 'June' grows 8–12" tall and 24–30" wide. Foliage is greenish gold with blue margins. Pale lavender flowers are produced in summer on 20" scapes.

H. 'Krossa Regal' is a vase-shaped plant with tall, arching stems and frosted, deeply ribbed, blue-gray foliage. Plants grow 30–36" tall and wide. Wavy clusters of pale lavender flowers bloom in summer on 4–5' scapes.

H. 'Love Pat' has frosted blue, roundish, puckered, cupped foliage. It grows 18–20" tall and 24–36" wide bearing whitish flowers in early to mid-summer on 22" scapes.

H. montana forma *aureomarginata* has deeply veined, thick, shiny, dark green foliage with a wide, irregular, yellow margin. It grows 30" tall and 36" wide with white to pale lavender flowers on 36" scapes, appearing in late spring to early summer.

H. 'Patriot' grows 15–20" tall and 24" wide. It has dark green foliage with wide, crisp, white margins. Lavender flowers bloom in mid-summer on 30" scapes.

H. 'Paul's Glory' has gold leaves with a wide blue margin. The gold fades to white over the growing season. Plants grow 17–20" tall and 26–36" wide. White to light lavender flowers bloom on 24" scapes in late spring to early summer.

H. plantaginea (fragrant hosta) has glossy, bright green leaves with distinctive veins; it grows 18–30" tall, spreads to about 36" and bears large, white, fragrant flowers in late summer. 'Aphrodite' has white, double flowers.

H. 'Regal Splendor' is a vase-shaped plant 36" tall and wide. The foliage is frosted blue with creamy yellow margins. Lavender flowers appear in mid-summer on 5–6' scapes.

H. 'Royal Standard' is durable and low-growing. It grows 4–8" tall and spreads up to 36". The dark green leaves are deeply veined, and the flowers are light purple.

H. sieboldiana (Siebold's hosta) forms a large, impressive clump of blue-green foliage. It grows about 36" tall and spreads up to 4'. The early-summer flowers are a light grayish purple that fades to white.

H. 'Sum & Substance' is a sun-tolerant, pest-resistant plant 24–36" tall and 5–6' wide with thick,

smooth, pale yellow to chartreuse foliage. Pale lavender flowers bloom in mid-summer on 30–36" scapes.

Problems & Pests

Slugs, snails, leaf spot, crown rot and chewing insects such as black vine weevils are all possible problems for hostas. Varieties with thick leaves tend to be more slug resistant.

Iris

Iris

Height: 6"–4' **Spread:** 6"–4' **Flower color:** many shades of pink, red, purple, blue, white, brown, yellow **Blooms:** spring, summer, sometimes fall **Zones:** 3–10

YEARS AGO, WHEN I WAS JUST A YOUNG AND IMPRESSIONABLE gardener, I heard a much-respected veteran horticulturist dismiss irises as 'frivolous plants, not worthy of space in the garden, what with their brief little "pffft" of bloom.' Like an idiot, I took him at his word. So for nearly 10 years I missed out on growing what I now consider one of the great marvels of the garden. The sharp, vertical slash of iris foliage is an essential component of plant design, and the bloom, even if somewhat brief, is something I do not ever wish to live without.

Planting

Seeding: Not recommended; germination is erratic and hybrids and cultivars may not come true to type

Planting out: Late summer or early fall

Spacing: 2"–4'

Growing

Irises prefer **full sun** but tolerate very light or dappled shade. The soil should be **average to fertile** and **well drained**. Blue flag, Japanese iris and Siberian iris prefer a moist but still well-drained soil.

Divide in late summer or early fall. Bearded iris are best divided yearly to maintain good condition. When dividing bearded iris rhizomes, replant with the flat side of the foliage fan facing the garden. Dust the

I. germanica cultivar

The wall of a 3500-year-old Egyptian temple features an iris, making this plant one of the oldest cultivated ornamentals.

I. sibirica

toe-shaped rhizome with a powder cleanser before planting to help prevent soft rot. Plant rhizomes of bearded iris so that $1/3$ to $1/2$ of the rhizome is visible above the soil.

Deadhead irises to keep them tidy. Cut the foliage of Siberian iris back in spring.

Tips

Irises are popular border plants, but Japanese iris, blue flag and Siberian iris are also useful alongside a stream or pond, and dwarf cultivars make attractive additions to rock gardens.

It is a good idea to wash your hands after handling irises because they can cause severe internal irritation if ingested. Make sure they are not planted close to places where children play.

Iris is Greek for 'rainbow,' along which a goddess was thought to travel when she carried messages from the gods to humans.

I. germanica cultivars (photos this page)

Recommended

I. ensata (*I. kaempferi*) (Japanese iris) is a water-loving species. It grows up to 36" tall and spreads about 18". White, blue, purple or pink flowers are borne from early to mid-summer. It rarely needs dividing. This species is resistant to iris borers.

I. germanica (Germanica Group) (bearded iris) produces flowers in all colors. This iris has been used as the parent plant for many desirable cultivars. Cultivars may vary in height and width from 6" to 4'. Flowering periods range from mid-spring to mid-summer, and some cultivars flower again in fall.

I. sibirica (Siberian iris) is more resistant to iris borers than other species. It grows 2–4' tall and 36" wide. It flowers in early summer; cultivars are available in many shades, mostly purple, blue and white. Plants take a year or two to recover after dividing.

I. versicolor (blue flag, poison flag, wild iris) is also a water-loving iris growing 24–36" tall and 12–18" wide. Branched flowering stems are 36" tall, each producing 2–5 lavender, violet, violet blue or red violet flowers with yellow and white markings at the base of the sepals in mid-spring to early summer.

Problems & Pests

Irises have several problems that can be prevented or mitigated through close observation. Iris borers are a potentially lethal pest. They burrow their way down the leaf until they reach the root, where they continue eating until there is no root left at all. The tunnels they make in the leaves are easy to spot, and if infected leaves are removed and destroyed or the borers squished within the leaf, the borers will never reach the roots.

Leaf spot is another problem that can be controlled by removing and destroying infected leaves. Be sure to give irises the correct growing conditions. Too much moisture for some species will allow rot diseases to settle in and kill the plants. Plant rhizomes high in the soil to deter root rot. Slugs, snails and aphids may also cause some trouble.

I. germanica cultivar

Powdered iris root, called orris, smells like violets when crushed and can be added to perfumes and potpourris as a fixative.

I. sibirica

Jacob's Ladder
Polemonium

Height: 8–36" **Spread:** 8–16" **Flower color:** purple, white, blue
Blooms: late spring, summer **Zones:** 3–7

THERE IS NO SHADY SPOT THAT will not benefit from the addition of this wonderful North American native, with its charming spring display of small, cupped flowers and intricate leaves that rise, ladder-like, from attractive basal clumps. Take care to provide the proper soil for Jacob's ladder, as described in this account. Once the plant takes a liking to its location, its foliage remains an asset to any woodland scene from spring to frost.

Planting

Seeding: Start seed in spring or fall. Keep soil temperature at about 70° F. Seed can take up to a month to germinate.

Planting out: Spring

Spacing: About 12"

Growing

Jacob's ladder species grow best in **partial shade** or very **light shade**. The soil should be **fertile, humus rich, moist** and **well drained**. Dead-head regularly to prolong blooming. These plants self-seed readily. Division is rarely required but should be done in late summer if desired.

Tips

Include Jacob's ladder plants in borders and woodland gardens. Use *P. caeruleum* as a tall focal point in planters. *P. reptans* can be used in rock gardens and as an edging along paths.

Recommended

P. caeruleum is the commonly grown Jacob's ladder. This plant grows 18–36" tall and spreads about 12". It forms a dense clump of basal foliage, with leafy, upright stems that are topped with clusters of purple flowers. **'Album'** has white flowers. **'Apricot Delight'** produces many mauve flowers with apricot pink centers. **'Brise d'Anjou'** has cream white leaflet margins. It does not bear as many flowers as the species.

P. reptans (creeping Jacob's ladder) is a very hardy, mounding perennial 8–16" tall, with an equal spread. It bears small, blue or lilac flowers in late spring and early summer.

Problems & Pests

Powdery mildew, leaf spot and rust are occasional problems.

P. caeruleum 'Album'

The leaflets of the foliage are organized in a neat, dense, ladder-like formation, giving these plants their common name.

P. caeruleum

Joe-Pye Weed

Boneset, Snakeroot

Eupatorium

Height: 2–9' **Spread:** 2–4' **Flower color:** white, purple, pink
Blooms: mid-summer to early fall **Zones:** 3–9

MANY VARIETIES OF *EUPATORIUM* ARE SUCH BIG, FOREBODING lunkers that I think many gardeners didn't appreciate their great value to the modern American garden. You saw Joe-Pye in large, naturalized settings (it is native to the eastern and central U.S.), and nowhere else. That's changing, and if you want to start growing a bold, beautiful perennial, here's your chance. Joe-Pye looks great around lakes and ponds, at the back of the border and mixed in with tall grasses and prairie plants like *Rudbeckia* (p. 100), *Echinacea* (p. 140) and *Liatris* (p. 230). The more refined *E. rugosum* 'Chocolate' thrives in partial shade, and it is one of my favorite perennials.

Planting

Seeding: Start seed indoors in late winter or early spring; soil temperature should be 59°–68° F

Planting out: Spring

Spacing: 18–36"

Growing

Joe-Pye weed plants prefer **full sun** but tolerate partial shade. The soil should be **fertile** and **moist**. Wet soils are tolerated. Divide plants in spring when clumps become overgrown. Don't put off dividing if space is a problem, because dividing over-sized clumps is a tough job.

Pruning growth back in May encourages branching and lower, denser growth, but it can delay flowering.

Tips

These plants can be used in a moist border or near a pond or other water feature. The tall types are ideal in the back of a border or center of a bed where they will create a backdrop for lower-growing plants.

It may take a couple of seasons for these plants to mature, so don't crowd them.

Recommended

E. maculatum is a huge plant. It grows 5–7' tall and spreads 3–4'. In late summer it bears clusters of purple flowers. 'Gateway' is slightly shorter, growing up to 6' tall. The large flower clusters are rose pink, and the plant's stems are reddish.

E. perfoliatum (common boneset, thoroughwort) is a clump-forming

E. rugosum 'Chocolate'

E. maculatum

E. rugosum (photos this page)

plant 5' tall and 24–36" wide with large, mid-green foliage with softly hairy undersides. In late summer to fall it produces large clusters of purple-tinged, white flowers.

E. purpureum (sweet Joe-Pye weed) is clump-forming. It grows 7–9' tall and 36" wide. It has purple-tinged stems and large, purple-tinged, mid-green foliage that has a slight vanilla aroma when bruised. Domed clusters of pink to purple-pink flowers bloom from mid-summer to early fall.

E. rugosum (*Ageratina altissima*) (boneset, white snakeroot) forms a bushy, mounding clump of foliage. It grows 3–4' tall, or taller, and spreads 24–36". Clusters of white flowers appear in late summer and early fall. 'Chocolate' grows 24–36" tall and has dark bronzy purple leaves that mature to dark green. This cultivar performs best in partial shade.

Problems & Pests

These plants may have occasional problems with powdery mildew, fungal leaf spot, rust, aphids, whiteflies and leaf miners.

'Joe-Pye' may refer to a 19th-century Native American healer who is said to have cured settlers of typhus with these plants.

E. maculatum (facing page)

Jupiter's Beard
Red Valerian
Centranthus

Height: 24–36" **Spread:** 12–24" **Flower color:** red, pink, white
Blooms: summer **Zones:** 4–8

THOUGH NOT COMMON AT NURSERIES, *CENTRANTHUS* IS A
perfectly charming, light and airy plant, which was once very common in the
cottage and cutting gardens of Europe after its introduction from its native
Mediterranean region. It is a violent reseeder, to the point where care should
be taken to cut back blooms as they fade. Doing so results in a rebloom that
can carry into fall. The best use of the plant I've ever seen was growing it
along the base of a stone wall, where the delicate, star-shaped, red flowers
and stems of slender, light green foliage contrasted strikingly with the dark,
brutish stone.

Planting

Seeding: Start seed in spring indoors or in cold frame

Planting out: Spring or fall

Spacing: 12–18"

Growing

Jupiter's beard grows best in **full sun**. The soil should be of **average fertility, neutral to alkaline** and **well drained**. Too rich a soil or too much fertilizer will encourage floppy, disease-prone growth. Division is rarely required but can be done in spring or fall to propagate desirable plants. Deadheading will extend the blooming season and prevent excessive self-seeding.

If flowering slows during the summer months, cut the plant back by up to half to encourage new growth and more flowering. Cut the plant back in fall, leaving the basal foliage in place, to give it time to harden off before winter.

'Albus'

C. ruber

Tips

Jupiter's beard can be included in borders. It looks particularly impressive when left to self-seed into an unused corner of the garden, where it will form a sea of bright flowers. The flowers are popular for fresh arrangements.

Recommended

C. ruber forms a bushy, upright plant. It bears large clusters of red, pink or white flowers on and off over the whole summer. Deadheading will encourage sporadic blooming through fall, but extending the bloom too long will shorten the life of the plant. **'Albus'** bears white flowers.

Jupiter's beard is rarely plagued by any pests or diseases.

Lady's Mantle

Alchemilla

Height: 6–18" **Spread:** 8–24" **Flower color:** yellow, yellowish green
Blooms: summer, early fall **Zones:** 3–7

AS A REGIONAL GARDEN SCOUT FOR NATIONAL GARDENING
magazines, I don't believe I've ever found a garden that was assigned for
photo publication that didn't include lady's mantle. It is what I call a 'complete' plant, meaning that the flower color and form and the foliage color
and form contrast so beautifully that the plant is an utter spectacle in and of
itself. I especially like the tiny baubles of chartreuse flowers that bob above
soft, lobed, light green foliage in June. Do remember to cut back the flowers
as they fade, then the foliage by mid-August, to reveal fresh mounds of
attractive basal foliage.

Planting

Seeding: Direct sow fresh seed or start in containers; transplant while seedlings are small

Planting out: Spring

Spacing: 8–24"

Growing

Lady's mantle plants prefer **light shade** or **partial shade,** with protection from the afternoon sun. They dislike hot locations, and excessive sun will cause scorching of the leaves. The soil should be **fertile, humus rich, moist and well drained.** These plants are drought resistant once established. Division is rarely required but can be done in spring before flowering starts or in fall once flowering is complete. If more plants are desired, move some

Poets and alchemists were inspired by the crystal-like dew that collects on the leaves; the dew was reputed to have magical and medicinal qualities.

A. mollis (photos this page)

of the self-seeded plants that are bound to show up to where you want them. Deadhead to keep the plants tidy and to prevent excessive reseeding.

Tips

Lady's mantles are ideal for grouping under trees in woodland gardens and along border edges where they soften the bright colors of other plants. A wonderful location is alongside a pathway that winds through a lightly wooded area.

If your lady's mantle begins to look tired and heat stressed during summer, rejuvenate it in one of two ways. Trim the whole plant back, encouraging new foliage to fill in, or remove the dead leaves and then trim the plant back once the new foliage has started to fill in. Leave plants intact over the winter, then clean them up in spring.

A. mollis (photos this page)

Recommended

A. erythropoda is a clump-forming plant with dense, blue-green to gray foliage. It grows 6–8" tall and 8–12" wide, and the plant stems turn red in the sun. Tiny clusters of chartreuse flowers bloom in summer and are held above the foliage. The flowers and stems turn orange-red in fall.

A. mollis (common lady's mantle) is the most frequently grown species. It grows 8–18" tall and spreads up to about 24". Plants form a mound of soft, rounded foliage, above which are held sprays of frothy, yellowish green flowers in early summer. Deadheading may encourage a second flush of flowers in late summer or fall.

Problems & Pests

Lady's mantles rarely suffer from any problems, though fungi may be troublesome during warm, wet summers. These plants are deer resistant.

The airy flowers make a fabulous filler for fresh and dried flower arrangements, and the leaves can be boiled to make a green dye for wool.

Lamb's Ears
Woolly Betony
Stachys

Height: 6–18" **Spread:** 18–24" **Flower color:** pink, purple
Blooms: summer **Zones:** 3–8

HERE'S ANOTHER PLANT THAT SHOULD BE GROWN FOR THE simple fact that the leaves aren't green. When choosing plants for a garden, the priority should be sharply contrasting colors in the foliage. Here in our two great states we are limited in the number of choices we have for these kinds of plants. With that in mind, what's going to be cooler than a plant with silvery white leaves?

Planting
Seeding: Direct sow or start in containers in cold frame in spring

Planting out: Spring

Spacing: 18–24"

Growing

Lamb's ears grows best in **full sun**. The soil should be of **poor or average fertility** and **well drained**. Leaves can rot in humid weather if the soil is poorly drained. Divide in spring.

Remove spent flower spikes to keep plants looking neat. Select a flowerless cultivar if you don't want to deadhead. Cut back diseased or damaged foliage; new foliage will sprout when the weather cools down.

Tips

Lamb's ears makes a great groundcover in a new garden where the soil has not yet been amended. It can be used to edge borders and pathways, providing a soft, silvery backdrop for more vibrant colors in the border.

Leaves can look tatty by mid-summer. The more of this plant you use, the more you will have to clean up. Plant only as much as you can tend, or plant in an out-of-the-way spot where the stressed foliage will not be as noticeable.

Recommended

S. byzantina (*S. lanata*) forms a mat of thick, woolly rosettes of leaves. Pinkish purple flowers are borne all summer. **'Big Ears'** ('Helen von Stein') has greenish silver leaves that are twice as big as those of the species. **'Silver Carpet'** has silvery white, fuzzy foliage; it rarely, if ever, produces flowers.

Problems & Pests

Fungal leaf problems are rare, but they can occur in hot, humid weather.

Cut flowerheads when they are in bud or after they bloom, and hang them to dry for use in dried flower arrangements.

Lamium
Dead Nettle, Yellow Archangel
Lamium

Height: 8–24" **Spread:** indefinite **Flower color:** white, pink, yellow, mauve
Blooms: spring, summer **Zones:** 3–8

A SPLENDID SHADE GROUNDCOVER WITH ONE UNFORTUNATE common name (dead nettle), lamium is an essential perennial for northern gardeners. Once you start growing it, you'll want lamium everywhere, and it will even handle a half-day of direct sun if not allowed to dry out. In flower it is wonderful, but the key to lamium's value is its weaving mounds of fabulously attractive, variegated foliage. Planted around shrubs, under trees and amongst ferns, hosta, astilbe, pulmonaria and any shade-loving plant you can think of, it's always perfect. Lamium spreads quickly without being invasive; after a few years you will have plenty to divide and replant.

Planting

Seeding: Not recommended; cultivars don't come true to type

Planting out: Spring

Spacing: 12–18"

Growing

Lamiums prefer **partial to light shade.** They tolerate full shade but may become leggy. The soil should be of **average fertility, humus rich, moist** and **well drained.** The more fertile the soil, the more vigorously the plants will grow. These plants are drought tolerant when grown in the shade but can develop bare patches if the soil is allowed to dry out for extended periods.

Divide and replant in fall if bare spots become unsightly.

Lamiums remain more compact if sheared back after flowering.

With their strikingly variegated leaves, these plants are useful for lighting up dark spaces in the garden. They look especially lovely at dusk and in the moonlight.

L. galeobdolon 'Florentinum' (photos this page)

L. maculatum cultivar with phlox

L. maculatum 'Anne Greenaway'

Tips

These plants can be useful ground-covers for woodland or shade gardens or under shrubs in a border, where lamiums can keep weeds down.

Keep in mind that lamiums can be quite invasive and are likely to overwhelm less vigorous plants. If they become invasive, pull some of them up, making sure to remove the fleshy roots.

Recommended

L. galeobdolon (*Lamiastrum galeobdolon*) (yellow archangel) can be quite invasive, though the cultivars are less so. It grows 12–24" tall and spreads indefinitely. The flowers are yellow. '**Florentinum**' ('Variegatum') has silver foliage with green margins. '**Herman's Pride**' forms dense mats of coarsely toothed, green foliage, heavily streaked with silver.

L. maculatum (dead nettle) grows 8" tall and spreads at least 36". The green leaves often have white or silvery markings. White, pink or mauve flowers are borne in summer. **'Anne Greenaway'** has green leaves with gold margins and silver centers. It bears light purple flowers in spring. **'Beacon Silver'** has green-edged, silver foliage and pink flowers. **'Beedham's White'** has chartreuse to gold foliage and white flowers. **'Chequers'** has green leaves with silver stripes down the centers. The flowers are mauve. **'White Nancy'** has white flowers and silver leaves with green margins.

L. galeobdolon 'Florentinum'

Problems & Pests

Rare problems with slugs, powdery mildew, downy mildew and leaf spot are possible.

Dead nettle (the alternate common name for lamium) is so named because its leaves resemble those of stinging nettle but have no sting.

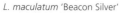

L. maculatum 'Beacon Silver'

Liatris

Blazing Star, Spike Gayfeather, Gayfeather
Liatris

Height: 1½–6' **Spread:** 18–24" **Flower color:** purple, white **Blooms:** mid-summer to fall **Zones:** 3–9

TOO OFTEN NEW GARDENERS CONSIDER FLOWER color, but not plant form. Forget color for a moment: what shapes are needed to mix up the plantings so there is contrast in form? Well, vertical spikes, for one, are needed, and therein lies the supreme value of liatris. Its stems rocket up from the ground producing dense, bushy spikes of flowers that bloom from the top down. Liatris is a bee and butterfly magnet, and clumps of liatris are always dazzling additions to sunny and hot spots in the garden.

Planting

Seeding: Direct sow in fall. Plants may take two to four years to bloom from seed.

Planting out: Spring

Spacing: 18–24"

Growing

Liatris prefers **full sun**. The soil should be of **average fertility, sandy, well drained** and **humus rich**. Water well during the growing season, but don't allow the plants to stand in water during cool weather. Mulch during summer to prevent moisture loss. Divide every three or four years in fall. The clump will appear crowded when it is time to divide.

L. spicata 'Kobold'

Trim off the spent flower spikes to promote a longer blooming period and to keep liatris looking tidy.

Tips

Use this plant in borders and meadow plantings. Plant in a location that has good drainage to avoid root rot in winter. Liatris does well when grown in planters.

The spikes make excellent, long-lasting cut flowers.

Recommended

L. aspera (rough gayfeather, royal blazing star) is an erect, clump-forming plant 6' tall and 18" wide, with narrow, grass-like foliage. It bears purple flowers in open spikes in late summer to early fall.

L. punctata (snakeroot) is a clump-forming plant 24–32" tall and 24" wide. Dense, 12" long spikes of purple flowers are produced in late summer to fall.

L. pycnostachya (button snakeroot, Kansas gayfeather, prairie blazing star) grows 4–5' tall and 18" wide. Dense, 12–18" long spikes of mauve to lilac purple flowers are produced from mid-summer to early fall. The

bracts are purple tinged. **'Alba'** has creamy white flowers.

L. spicata is an erect, clump-forming plant 18–36" tall and 18–24" wide. The flowers are pinkish purple or white. **'Floristan Violet'** has purple flowers. **'Floristan White'** has white flowers. **'Kobold'** has deep purple flowers.

Problems & Pests

Slugs, stem rot, root rot, rust and leaf spot are possible problems.

L. spicata 'Floristan White'

Ligularia

Ligularia

Height: 3–6' **Spread:** 2–5' **Flower color:** yellow, orange; ornamental foliage
Blooms: summer, early fall **Zones:** 4–8

SIMILAR TO *ALCHEMILLA*, THE PERENNIAL LIGULARIA MAKES MY list as a 'complete' plant; its flowering habit contrasts splendidly with the foliage of the same plant. Both *L. przewalskii* and *L. stenocephala* produce impressive, tall spikes of yellow flowers that rocket up from large, very handsome leaves. Lately I've become a huge fan of *L. dentata* 'Desdemona,' primarily for its immense, rounded, purplish foliage. Don't be afraid to plant ligularias in the middle or front of a border, where they can be viewed all season long.

Planting

Seeding: Species can be started out-doors in spring in containers; culti-vars rarely come true to type

Planting out: Spring

Spacing: 2–5'

Growing

Ligularias should be grown in **light shade** or **partial shade** with protec-tion from the afternoon sun. The soil should be of **average fertility, humus rich** and consistently **moist.** Division is rarely, if ever, required but can be done in spring or fall to propagate a desirable cultivar

Tips

Use ligularias alongside a pond or stream. They can also be used in a well-watered border or naturalized in a moist meadow or woodland garden.

L. dentata

L. stenocephala

The foliage can wilt in hot sun, even in moist soil. The leaves will revive at night, but they will still look horrible during the day. If your ligularia looks wilted, it is best to move the plant to a cooler, more shaded position in the garden.

Recommended

L. dentata (bigleaf ligularia, golden groundsel) forms a clump of rounded, heart-shaped leaves. It grows 3–5' tall and spreads 3–4'. In summer and early fall it bears clusters of orange-yellow flowers, held above the foliage. '**Desdemona**' and '**Othello**' are two similar cultivars, with orange-yellow flowers and purple-green foliage. They come fairly true to type when grown from seed.

L. przewalskii (Shevalski's ligularia) also forms a clump but has deeply incised leaves. It grows 4–6' tall and spreads 2–4'. In mid- and late summer it produces yellow flowers on long, purple spikes.

L. stenocephala 'The Rocket'

L. dentata

L. stenocephala (narrow-spiked ligularia) has toothed rather than incised foliage and bears bright yellow flowers on dark purple-green spikes. It grows 3–5' in height and width. This species is closely related to the previous one, and 'The Rocket' may be a hybrid of the two. This cultivar has heart-shaped leaves with ragged-toothed margins. The leaf veins are dark, becoming purple at the leaf base.

Problems & Pests

Ligularias have no serious problems, though slugs can damage young foliage.

L. dentata 'Desdemona'

L. dentata

Loosestrife

Lysimachia

Height: 2"–4' **Spread:** 24" to indefinite **Flower color:** yellow, white
Blooms: summer **Zones:** 3–9

THOUGH *LYSIMACHIA* HAS BEEN KNOWN
to be somewhat annoying because of the
aggressive nature of some of its cultivars,
Lysimachia is a fine perennial for northern
gardens. The low-growing *L. nummularia* is
a superior groundcover for ornate areas of
light shade. *L. punctata* has the somewhat
unusual habit of producing its star-shaped
flowers tight to the stem of the plant, just
above each set of leaves. If you are growing
a variety that spreads quicker than you'd
like, consider growing a clump in a large
plastic nursery container, which is set into
the ground.

Planting

Seeding: Sow seed indoors or directly outside in early spring

Planting out: spring, summer

Spacing: 24"

Growing

Loosestrife grows well in **full sun to partial shade**. The soil should be **humus rich, fertile, moist** and **well drained**. It is best not to allow the soil to dry out during the long, hot summer, especially when planted in full sun. *L. punctata* is tolerant of very short dry periods. Divide in spring or fall.

L. punctata

Tips

Loosestrife works well in a herbaceous border, bog garden or pond margin. The low-growing species is best suited for use as a groundcover.

Tall, upright varieties are frequently used in fresh floral arranging.

L. clethroides

L. punctata 'Alexander'

L. clethroides

Recommended

L. ciliata (fringed loosestrife) is an erect, rhizomatous, vigorously growing perennial 24–36" tall, occasionally to 4' tall, and 24" wide. It bears slightly nodding, star-shaped, yellow flowers with reddish brown centers in mid-summer. **'Firecracker'** ('Purpurea') grows 24–30" tall and has dark purple foliage that contrasts superbly with the yellow flowers.

L. clethroides (gooseneck loosestrife, Japanese loosestrife) is an erect perennial with mid- to gray-green foliage, growing 24–36" tall and wide and spreading by rhizomes. Tall, dense, spike-like clusters of white flowers are borne on thick, purple stems in mid- to late summer. The flower clusters are slightly bent, resembling a goose's neck. The foliage may turn bronzy red in fall. This species is best suited to bog or waterside plantings.

L. nummularia (creeping Jenny, moneywort) is a prostrate, evergreen perennial growing 2–4" tall and spreading indefinitely. It has small, round leaves and stems that root where the stem nodes touch the soil. Fragrant, yellow flowers are borne throughout the summer. It can become invasive, but it is easily kept in check by gently cultivating the runners out. **'Aurea'** has golden foliage. This cultivar needs morning or afternoon sun to keep its golden yellow color.

L. punctata (yellow loosestrife, garden loosestrife) is a bushy, upright perennial that spreads by rhizomes, and it grows 24–36" tall and wide. Bright yellow, cupped flowers are borne in the leaf axils in mid- to late summer. **'Alexander'** has variegated foliage with creamy white edges and green centers. It grows slightly smaller than the species.

Problems & Pests

Mites, rust and leaf spot are possible problems.

Smoke from a burning plant was believed to drive snakes away.

It is unclear what the connection is, but the common and botanical names both translate to 'ending strife.'

L. ciliata cultivar

L. punctata

Lungwort

Pulmonaria

Height: 8–24" **Spread:** 8–36" **Flower color:** blue, red, pink, white, purple
Blooms: spring **Zones:** 3–8

HERE'S A HIGHLY USEFUL SHADE PLANT THAT SHOULD BE
included anywhere one grows tired of seeing hostas. While lovely in
flower, lungwort brings fabulous foliage to the party. New cultivars
seem to arrive each season, offering tremendous choice in leaf size
and coloration. Lungwort combines wonderfully with ferns,
Heuchera (p. 194), *Polygonatum* (p. 316), *Polemonium* (p. 212),
Hosta (p. 202) and most other denizens of shady spaces.

Planting

Seeding: Start seed in containers
outdoors in spring; plants don't consistently come true to type

Planting out: Spring or fall

Spacing: 12–18"

Growing

Lungworts prefer **partial to full shade**. The soil should be **fertile, humus rich, moist** and **well drained**. Rot can occur in very wet soil.

Divide in early summer after flowering or in fall. Provide the newly planted divisions with lots of water to help them reestablish. Shear plants back lightly after flowering to deadhead and show off the fabulous foliage and to keep the plants tidy.

Tips

Lungworts make useful and attractive groundcovers for shady borders, woodland gardens and edges of ponds and streams.

P. saccharata

Pulmonaria *species (usually* P. officinalis) *are traditional culinary and medicinal herbs. The young leaves may be added to soups and stews to flavor and thicken the broth. When dried, the spotted leaves also make an attractive addition to potpourri.*

P. longifolia 'E.B. Anderson'

P. longifolia (above)

Recommended

P. angustifolia (blue lungwort) forms a mounded clump of foliage. The leaves have no spots. This plant grows 8–12" tall and spreads 18–24". Clusters of bright blue flowers, held above the foliage, are borne from early to late spring.

P. 'Ice Ballet' is a vigorous plant with silver-spotted, mid-green foliage and large, white flowers held above the foliage. It grows 12" tall and 18–20" wide and prefers partial shade.

P. longifolia (long-leaved lungwort) forms a dense clump of long, narrow, white-spotted, green leaves. It grows 8–12" tall and spreads 8–24". It bears clusters of blue flowers in spring or even earlier, as the foliage emerges. **'Diana Clare'** has apple green foliage with a silver sheen and large, violet blue flowers. This cultivar does not like to be cut back. **'E. B. Anderson'** ('Bertram Anderson') has silver-spotted foliage and vivid cobalt to violet blue flowers.

P. 'Majeste' has solid, glossy, silver leaves with a narrow, green margin. It grows 10–14" tall and wide. Blue buds open to reveal pink flowers that fade back to blue with age. Keep this plant in partial to full shade.

P. montana (*P. rubra*) (red lungwort) forms a loose clump of unspotted, softly hairy leaves. It grows 12–24" tall and spreads 24–36". Bright red flowers appear in early spring. **'Redstart'** has pinkish red flowers.

P. officinalis (common lungwort, spotted dog) forms a loose clump of evergreen foliage, spotted with white. It grows 10–12" tall and spreads about 18". The spring flowers open pink and mature to blue. This species was once grown for its reputed medicinal properties, but it is now valued for its ornamental qualities. '**Cambridge Blue**' bears many blue flowers.

P. '**Raspberry Splash**' has upright growth to 15" tall and 24" wide. It prefers full sun to partial shade. It has raspberry pink flowers and strongly silver-marked, narrow, pointed foliage.

P. '**Roy Davidson**' grows 12" tall and 18" wide, bearing pale blue flowers and silver-marked, blue-green foliage.

P. saccharata (Bethlehem sage) forms a compact clump of large, white-spotted, evergreen leaves. It grows 12–18" tall, with a spread of about 24". The spring flowers may be purple, red or white. This species has given rise to many cultivars and hybrids. '**Janet Fisk**' is very heavily spotted and appears almost silvery in the garden. Its pink flowers change to blue as they age. '**Mrs. Moon**' has pink buds that open to a light purple-blue. The leaves are dappled with silvery white spots. '**Pierre's Pure Pink**' has white-spotted foliage and pale salmon pink to shell pink flowers.

Problems & Pests

Lungworts may become susceptible to powdery mildew if the soil dries out for extended periods. Remove and destroy damaged leaves. These plants are generally problem free.

P. saccharata (photos this page)

This plant has more than 20 common names. Many are Biblical references, such as Abraham, Isaac and Jacob, Adam and Eve, Children of Israel and Virgin Mary.

Lupine

Lupinus

Height: 18–36" **Spread:** 12–18" **Flower color:** white, yellow, pink, red, blue, some bicolored **Blooms:** early to mid-summer **Zones:** 3–6

GARDENERS WILLING TO GIVE THE EXTRA EFFORT REQUIRED TO keep lupines healthy are typically happy to do so—these stately perennials are at ease in the formal garden, cottage garden or naturalized setting. While lupines are magnificent in flower, their bloom period is brief. However, the extremely attractive foliage more than makes up for this shortfall. Unfortunately, in less than ideal conditions, plants are usually short-lived and prone to a goodly spectrum of pests and diseases. Growing lupines in acidic (pH 6–6.5) soil, providing summer mulch to keep roots cool and providing some shade from intense midday sun will greatly increase the plants' vigor.

Planting

Seeding: Soak seeds in warm water for 24 hours then direct sow in mid-fall or mid-spring. If you start seeds indoors, you may need to place planted seeds in the refrigerator for four to six weeks after soaking and planting.

Planting out: Spring or fall

Spacing: 12–18"

Growing

Lupines grow best in **full sun** but tolerate light to partial shade. The soil should be of **average to high fertility, moist, light, well drained** and **slightly acidic**. Protect plants from drying winds.

Division is not required. Lupines dislike having their roots disturbed. Deadhead as the season progresses to encourage more flowering.

Tips

Lupines are wonderful when massed together in borders or in cottage and natural gardens.

These perennials can be rather short-lived. One solution is to leave just a couple of spikes in place once flowering is finished to allow some seedlings to fill in as the older plants die out. The self-seeded plants will not likely resemble the parents. You can also propagate by carefully removing the small offsets that develop at the base of the plants and replant them.

Recommended

There are many species of lupines, but they are rarely grown in favor of the many popular hybrids. Most lupines form a dense basal mound of foliage from which tall spikes emerge, bearing many colorful pea-like flowers.

Gallery hybrids are dwarf hybrids. They grow about 18–24" tall and spread about 12–18". They are available with flowers in blue, red, pink, yellow or white.

Russell hybrids were among the first groups of hybrids developed. They grow about 24–36" tall and 12–18" wide and produce flowers in a wide range of solids and bicolors.

Problems & Pests

Lupines are susceptible to aphids and powdery mildew. Provide good air circulation to the plants to avoid mildew problems. Problems with slugs, snails, leaf spot, stem rot and damping off (in seedlings) can also occur, though infrequently.

Lupines are in the same plant family as beans and peas. Do not eat lupine pods or seeds, however, because they will cause stomach upset.

Lychnis
Maltese Cross, Rose Campion
Lychnis

Height: 2–4' **Spread:** 12–18" **Flower color:** magenta, white, red
Blooms: summer **Zones:** 3–8

FEW PERENNIALS ARE AS BREATHTAKING IN BLOOM AS LYCHNIS, and if not for the fact that this northern native is often short-lived, it would most certainly be one of gardening's most popular plants. The contrast between the eye-popping, magenta blooms that hover over the plant and the plant's light, silvery gray foliage is sheer delight. I much prefer *L. coronaria* to *L. chalcedonica*. The excessive height of the latter usually requires cumbersome staking, while its foliage tends to brown out and drop during midsummer heat waves.

Planting
Seeding: Start seeds in late spring; soil temperature should be 68°–70° F

Planting out: Spring

Spacing: 12–18"

Growing

Lychnis plants grow well in **full sun** but enjoy some afternoon shade to protect them from excessive heat. The soil should be of **average fertility** and **well drained**. These plants do not tolerate heavy soils; if you garden in clay, use raised beds or amend the planting space with lots of organic material such as peat moss, compost, composted manure or all three. Division can be done in spring, though lychnis plants may not live long enough to need it.

Although these plants are short-lived and should almost be treated as annuals or biennials, in light or gravelly soils they reseed prolifically. Basal cuttings can also be taken to propagate the plants.

Tips

Lychnis plants make beautiful, carefree additions to a border, cottage garden or naturalized garden.

These tall plants may need some support, particularly in a windy location. Peony supports or twiggy branches pushed into the soil are best and are less noticeable than having the plants tied to stakes.

Recommended

L. chalcedonica (Maltese cross) is a stiff, upright plant growing 3–4' tall and 12–18" wide. The scarlet flowers are borne in clusters in early to mid-summer. Some support may be required to keep this plant standing upright. '**Alba**' has white flowers.

L. coronaria (rose campion) is a biennial or short-lived perennial that forms an upright mass of silvery gray leaves and branching stems. It grows 24–36" tall and about 18" wide. In late summer the plant is dotted with magenta pink flowers, which are very striking against the silvery foliage. '**Alba**' has white flowers. '**Angel's Blush**' has white flowers with reddish pink centers. '**Atrosanguinea**' has red flowers.

L. coronaria

L. chalcedonica

Mallow

Malva

Height: 8"–4' **Spread:** 12–24" **Flower color:** purple, pink, white, purple-blue
Blooms: summer, fall **Zones:** 4–9

THIS SUPERB PERENNIAL IS NOT WIDELY GROWN BY
northern gardeners because it is rather short-lived. It should
be given serious consideration, however, because in bloom,
at the back of the flowerbed, *Malva* is stunning. Plants
bloom profusely for an extended period in summer. For several years I grew a swath of pink-
blooming *M. alcea* in front of a stand of dark
green arborvitae, and it was the most com-
mented upon feature of my garden. Allow
plants to go to seed, and you'll find that
keeping blooming specimens at your dis-
posal is not much of a chore.

Planting

Seeding: Direct sow indoors or out in spring or early summer

Planting out: Spring, summer

Spacing: 12–24"

Growing

Mallows grow well in **full sun** or **partial shade**. The soil should be of **low to average fertility, moist** and **well drained**. Mallows are drought tolerant. In rich soils the plants may require staking. Mallows do not need dividing. Propagate by basal cuttings taken in spring.

Mallows readily self-seed. Cutting plants back by about half in late May will encourage more compact, bushy growth but will delay flowering by a couple of weeks. Transplant or thin out seedlings if they are too crowded.

M. sylvestris 'Bibor Felho'

Some types of mallow are reputed to have a calming effect when ingested and were used in the Middle Ages as antidotes for aphrodisiacs and love potions.

M. sylvestris 'Primley Blue'

Tips

Use mallows in a mixed border or in a wildflower or cottage garden. Deadhead to keep the plants blooming until October. Mallows also make good cut flowers.

Recommended

M. alcea (hollyhock mallow) is a loose, upright branching plant. It grows 2–4' tall and spreads 18–24". This plant bears pink flowers with notched petals all summer. '**Fastigiata**' has a neat, upright form. If deadheaded, it continues to produce flowers well into fall.

M. moschata (musk mallow) is a bushy, upright plant with musk-scented leaves. It grows about 36" tall, spreads about 24" and bears pale pink or white flowers all summer.

M. moschata
M. alcea 'Fastigiata'

M. sylvestris (cheeses) is a biennial or short-lived perennial that is upright or spreading in habit. Plants of this species grow 8"–4' tall and spread about 12–24". The pink flowers have darker veins and are produced all summer. Many cultivars are available. '**Bibor Felho**' has an upright form and rose purple flowers with darker purple veins. '**Braveheart**,' also an upright cultivar, has light purple-pink flowers with dark purple veins. '**Primley Blue**' has light purple-blue flowers. It is a prostrate cultivar, growing only about 8" tall. '**Zebrina**' has pale pink or white flowers with purple veins and is an upright grower.

Problems & Pests

Problems with rust, leaf spot, Japanese beetles and spider mites can occur occasionally.

M. sylvestris 'Zebrina' (photos this page)

Marguerite
Golden Marguerite, Marguerite Daisy
Anthemis

Height: 8–36" **Spread:** 24–36" **Flower color:** yellow, orange, cream
Blooms: summer **Zones:** 3–7

THOUGH SOMEWHAT OBSCURE IN THE GARDENING TRADE, *Anthemis* is a worthy, long-blooming perennial. Golden yellow flowers are borne atop fern-like foliage that emits a pleasant aroma when brushed against. This plant will take it hot and dry, and the fact that it is one of the best reseeders of all time makes it a great choice for wide, open spaces, hillsides and meadows.

Planting
Seeding: Direct sow in spring

Planting out: Spring

Spacing: 18–24"

Growing

Marguerites prefer **full sun**. The soil should be of **average fertility** and **well drained**. These plants are drought tolerant. The clumps tend to die out in the middle and should be divided every two or three years in spring or fall.

Flowering tends to occur in waves. Cut off the dead flowers to encourage continual flowering all summer. If the plants begins to look thin and spread out, cut them back hard to promote new growth and flowers. These plants are avid self-seeders, so deadhead if you don't want new plants popping up all over.

A. tinctoria (photos this page)

To avoid the need for staking, cut plants back in May or group several plants together so they can support each other. Otherwise, when the plants are young, insert small, twiggy branches as supports.

Tips

Marguerites form attractive clumps that blend wonderfully into a cottage-style garden. Their drought tolerance makes them ideal for rock gardens and exposed slopes.

Recommended

A. tinctoria forms a mounded clump of foliage that is completely covered in bright or pale yellow, daisy-like flowers in summer. '**Beauty of Grallach**' has deep orange-yellow flowers. '**E.C. Buxton**' has flowers with creamy yellow petals and yellow centers. '**Grallach Gold**' has bright golden yellow flowers. '**Moonlight**' has large, pale yellow flowers.

Problems & Pests

Marguerites may occasionally have problems with aphids and fungal problems such as powdery or downy mildew.

Meadow Rue

Thalictrum

Height: 4"–5' **Spread:** 12–36" **Flower color:** pink, purple, yellow, white
Blooms: summer, fall **Zones:** 3–8

MORE AND MORE NORTHERN GARDENERS ARE DISCOVERING THIS
diverse and useful plant family, which consists of over 100 species native to
many parts of the world. Meadow rue has a light, finely textured appearance
in both foliage and flower, providing strong contrast to the bolder foliage
and form of most other perennials. I've gone nuts over *T. kiusianum*, one of
the tiniest, most delicate little groundcovers you'll ever see. Combine it with
dwarf hostas and small ferns. Taller varieties are wonderful for use in
arrangements.

Planting

Seeding: Direct sow in fall or start indoors in early spring; soil temperature should be 70° F

Planting out: Spring

Spacing: 12–24"

Growing

Meadow rues prefer **light or partial shade** but tolerate full sun if the soil remains moist. The soil should be **humus rich, moist** and **well drained.** These plants rarely need to be divided. If necessary for propagation, divide in spring as the foliage begins to develop. Plants may take a while to reestablish once they have been divided or have had their roots disturbed.

T. aquilegifolium with goutweed

T. aquilegifolium

T. *rochebruneanum* 'Lavender Mist'

T. *delvayi* 'Hewitt's Double'

Tips

In the middle or at the back of a border, meadow rues make a soft backdrop for bolder plants and flowers and are beautiful when naturalized in an open woodland or meadow garden.

These plants often do not emerge until quite late in spring. Mark the location where they are planted so that you do not inadvertently disturb the roots if you are cultivating their bed before they begin to grow.

Do not place individual plants too close together because their stems can become tangled.

Recommended

T. aquilegifolium (columbine meadow rue) forms an upright mound 24–36" tall, with an equal spread. Pink or white plumes of flowers are borne in early summer. The leaves are similar in appearance to those of columbines. '**Thundercloud**' ('Purple Cloud') has dark purple flowers. (Zones 3–8)

T. delvayi (Yunnan meadow rue) forms a clump of narrow stems that usually need staking. It grows 4–5' tall and spreads about 24". It bears fluffy, purple or white flowers from mid-summer to fall. '**Hewitt's Double**' is a popular cultivar that produces many tiny, purple, pom-pom-like flowers. (Zones 3–8)

T. flavum subsp. *glucum* (dusty meadow rue) is a clump-forming plant with creeping rhizomes. It grows 36" tall and 24" wide. The leaves and stems are a white-dusted blue-green. Clusters of fragrant, glowing, sulfur yellow flowers bloom in summer. (Zones 3–8)

T. kiusianum (Kyushu meadow rue) is native to Japan and grows only 4–6" tall and 12" wide. The tiny leaves are tinged with purple. Small clusters of airy, pinkish purple flowers cover the plant for an extended period in summer. (Zones 4–8)

T. rochebruneanum '**Lavender Mist**' (lavender mist meadow rue) forms a narrow, upright clump. It grows 3–5' tall and spreads 12–24". The late-summer blooms are lavender purple and have numerous distinctive yellow stamens. (Zones 3–8)

Problems & Pests

Infrequent problems with powdery mildew, rust, smut and leaf spot can occur.

Meadow rue flowers are generally petal-less. The unique flowers consist of showy sepals and stamens.

T. delvayi 'Hewitt's Double'

Meadowsweet

Filipendula

Height: 2–8' **Spread:** 1½–4' **Flower color:** white, cream, pink, red
Blooms: late spring, summer, fall **Zones:** 3–8

HERE IS A GREATLY UNDERUSED GEM THAT HAS PROVED ITSELF
reliable in even the northernmost stretches of Wisconsin and Minnesota.
The charms of meadowsweet extend from the formal garden to meadow
plantings, cottage gardens and pondside placements. The frothy flower clusters float above highly attractive, deep green foliage. Cut stems to the ground
after flowering to trigger lush new foliage growth that looks great through to
season's end.

Planting

Seeding: Germination can be erratic; start seed in cold frame in fall and keep soil evenly moist

Planting out: Spring

Spacing: 18–36"

Growing

Meadowsweet plants prefer **partial or light shade**. Full sun is tolerated if the soil remains sufficiently moist. The soil should be **fertile, deep, humus rich** and **moist**. Divide in spring or fall. You may need a sharp knife to divide these plants, because they grow thick, tough roots. Meadowsweets tend to self-seed, and if dividing these perennials seems daunting, transplanting the seedlings could be an easier way to get new plants. These plants can be deadheaded if desired, but the faded seedheads are quite attractive when left in place.

F. ulmaria cultivar

The flowers of F. ulmaria *were often used to flavor ales and mead in medieval times, giving rise to the name meadowsweet, from the Anglo-Saxon* medesweete.

F. ulmaria

F. ulmaria

In the 16th century it was customary to strew rushes and herbs to insulate the floor underfoot, freshen the air and combat infections. Meadowsweet was the herb Queen Elizabeth I preferred for these purposes.

F. ulmaria 'Plena'; F. rubra (facing page)

Tips

Most meadowsweets are excellent plants for bog gardens or wet sites. Grow them alongside streams or in moist meadows. Meadowsweets may also be grown in the back of a border, as long as they are kept well watered.

F. vulgaris prefers dry soil. It is a good choice if you can't provide the moisture the other species need.

The flowers of *F. ulmaria*, once used to flavor mead and ale, are now becoming popular as a flavoring for vinegars and jams. They may also be made into a pleasant wine, which is concocted in much the same way as dandelion wine.

Recommended

F. rubra (queen-of-the-prairie) forms a large, spreading clump 6–8' tall and 4' in spread. It bears clusters of fragrant, pink flowers from early to mid-summer. **'Venusta'** bears very showy, pink flowers that fade to light pink in fall.

F. ulmaria (meadowsweet, queen-of-the-meadow) bears cream white flowers in large clusters. It grows to be 24–36" tall and 24" wide. **'Aurea'** has yellow foliage that matures to light green as summer progresses. **'Plena'** ('Flore Pleno') has double flowers.

F. vulgaris (dropwort, meadowsweet) is a low-growing species up to 24" tall and 18" wide. **'Plena'** ('Flore Pleno') has white, double flowers.

Problems & Pests

Powdery mildew, rust and leaf spot can be troublesome.

Monarda
Bee Balm, Bergamot
Monarda

Height: 2–4' **Spread:** 15–36" **Flower color:** red, pink, light purple
Blooms: late spring, summer, fall **Zones:** 3–9

THE RIOTOUS WAVES OF COLOR PUT FORTH BY THE CURIOUSLY shaped flowers of monarda have long made the plant a favorite of gardeners, despite the fact that this member of the mint family has several drawbacks. For years, to love bee balm was to hate it, because it seemed impossible to grow a variety that wouldn't succumb to powdery mildew by mid-summer. Newer introductions have lessened this disease aspect somewhat, but the plant remains a quick spreader, and it must be divided and dug up with frequency. Give monarda plants plenty of space—they will just take it anyway, if you don't—and you'll be rewarded by heavy mid-season blooms and frequent visits to your garden by bees, butterflies and hummingbirds.

The genus name honors Spanish botanist and physician Nicholas Monardes (1493–1588).

Planting

Seeding: Start seeds outdoors in cold frame or indoors in early spring

Planting out: Spring or fall

Spacing: 18–24"

Growing

Monarda grows well in **full sun, partial shade** or **light shade**. The soil should be of **average fertility, humus rich, moist** and **well drained**. Dry conditions encourage mildew and loss of leaves, so regular watering is a must. Divide every two or three years in spring just as new growth emerges.

M. didyma hybrids (photos this page)

M. didyma hybrids (photos this page)

Cut back some of the stems by half in May to extend the flowering period and encourage compact growth. Thinning the stems in spring also helps prevent powdery mildew. If mildew strikes after flowering, cut the plants back to 6" to increase air circulation.

Tips

Use monarda beside a stream or pond or in a lightly shaded, well-watered border.

The fresh or dried leaves may be used to make a refreshing, minty, citrus-scented tea. Put a handful of fresh leaves in a teapot, pour boiling water over them and let steep for at least five minutes. Sweeten the tea with honey to taste.

Monarda attract bees, butterflies and hummingbirds to your garden. Avoid using pesticides, which can seriously harm or kill these creatures and which will prevent you from using the plant for culinary or medicinal purposes.

Recommended

M. didyma is a bushy, mounding plant that forms a thick clump of stems with red or pink flowers. The following selections are hybrids that have *M. didyma* as one of the parents. Many of these hybrids have *M. fistulosa* as the other parent. **'Beauty of Cobham'** grows 36" tall and 18" wide. It has purple-tinged, green foliage and lilac pink to pale pink flowers with purple bracts. It blooms from mid-summer to early fall. **'Blaustrumph'** ('Blue Stocking') is a heat- and drought-tolerant plant bearing vibrant, deep violet flowers with purple bracts. It grows 2–4' tall and 24–36" wide. 'Gardenview Scarlet' bears large, scarlet flowers and is resistant to powdery mildew. 'Jacob Cline' ('Jacob Kline') produces deep red flowers in late spring to early summer. It grows 3–4' tall and 18–24" wide and is mildew resistant. 'Marshall's Delight' doesn't come true to type from seed and must be propagated by cuttings or divisions. It is very resistant to powdery mildew and bears pink flowers. The following two selections grow 24–36" tall and 18–24" wide and grow true from seed. They have lightly aromatic, mildew-resistant foliage and produce flowers in summer. 'Panorama Mixed' flowers in scarlet, bright red, pink, crimson or salmon. 'Panorama Red Shades' has bright red flowers. 'Raspberry Wine' has wine red flowers and dark green foliage. It grows 2½–4' tall and 15–24" wide.

M. fistulosa (wild bee balm) is a clump-forming, bushy plant with well-branched stems. It grows to 4' tall and 18–24" wide and bears lavender, lilac purple or pale pink flowers with pink- or purple-tinged bracts from mid-summer to fall.

Problems & Pests

Powdery mildew is the worst problem for monarda, but rust, leaf spot and leafhoppers can cause trouble. Don't allow the plant to dry out for extended periods.

M. didyma 'Marshall's Delight'

*The common name 'bergamot' comes from the similarity of this plant's scent to that of Italian bergamot orange (*Citrus bergamia*), often used in aromatherapy.*

M. didyma hybrid

Monkshood

Aconitum

Height: 2–6' **Spread:** 12–18" **Flower color:** purple, blue, white
Blooms: mid- to late summer **Zones:** 3–8

ACONITUM IS ON THE SHORT LIST OF PERENNIALS THAT
bloom in August in our region. The fact that the common bloom
color is a purplish blue makes it a highly valuable addition to the
garden. *A. charmichaelii* is a knockout, with bold, deep green
foliage that is attractive all season. I grow it in combination
with *Astilbe* (p. 86), *Ligularia* (p. 232) and *Rodgersia* to create
a bed of moisture-loving plants that welcome twice-weekly
watering. Be aware that all parts of all varieties are poisonous if eaten.

Planting

Seeding: Germination may be irregular. Seeds direct sown in spring may
bloom the following summer; seeds
sown later will not likely bloom
until the third year.

Planting out: Spring; bare-
rooted tubers may be
planted in fall

Spacing: 18"

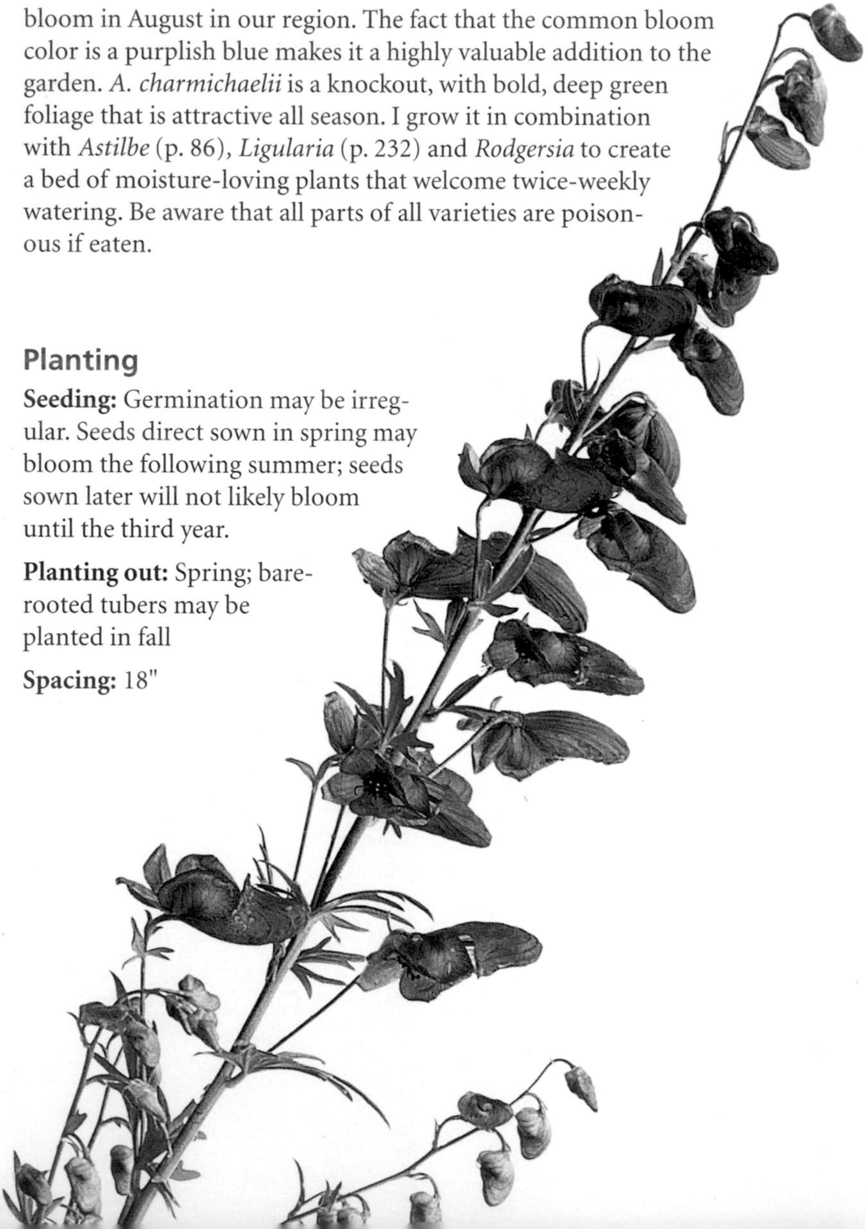

Growing

Monkshoods prefer to grow in **light or partial shade** but tolerate sun if the climate is cool. These plants will grow in any **moist** soil but prefer to be in a **rich** soil with lots of **organic matter** worked in.

Monkshoods prefer not to be divided, because they may be a bit slow to reestablish. If division is desired to increase the number of plants, it should be done in late fall or early spring. When dividing or transplanting monkshoods, the crown of the plant should never be planted at a depth lower than where it was previously growing. Burying the crown any deeper will cause it to rot and the plant to die.

Tall monkshoods may need to be staked. Peony hoops or tomato cages inserted around young plants will be hidden as the plants fill in.

A. napellus

A. x cammarum 'Bicolor'

A. x *cammarum* 'Bicolor'

A. *napellus*

Tips

Monkshood plants are perfect for cool, boggy locations along streams or next to ponds. They make tall, elegant additions to a woodland garden in combination with lower-growing plants. Do not plant monkshoods near tree roots because these plants cannot compete with trees.

Monkshoods prefer conditions to be on the cool side. They will do poorly when the weather gets hot, particularly if conditions do not cool down at night. Mulch the roots to keep them cool.

Recommended

A. x *cammarum* (Cammarum hybrids) is a group of hybrids that contains several of the more popular cultivars. **'Bicolor'** (bicolor monkshood) bears blue and white flowers. The flower spikes are often branched. **'Bressingham Spire'** bears

dark purple-blue flowers on strong spikes. It grows up to 36" tall but needs no staking.

A. charmichaelii (azure monkshood) forms a low mound of basal leaves from which the flower spikes emerge. The foliage generally grows to about 24" in height, but the plant can grow 6' tall when in flower. Purple or blue flowers are borne a week or so later than those of other species. 'Arendsii' bears dark blue flowers on strong spikes that need no staking.

A. napellus (common monkshood) is an erect plant that forms a basal mound of finely divided foliage. It grows 3–5' tall, spreads 12–18" and bears dark purple-blue flowers.

Problems & Pests

Problems with aphids, root rot, stem rot, powdery mildew, downy mildew, wilt and rust can occur.

Aconitum may come from the Greek akoniton, *meaning 'dart.' The ancient Chinese and the Arabs used the juice of monkshood to poison arrow tips.*

A. napellus (photos this page)

Obedient Plant
False Dragonhead
Physostegia

Height: 1–4' **Spread:** 12–24" or more **Flower color:** pink, purple, white
Blooms: mid-summer to fall **Zones:** 2–9

EXTREMELY EASY TO GROW AND HARDY TO
the most northern extremes, *Physostegia* looks
great massed in waves in a large garden. If you
plant just one or two, this borderline invasive
perennial will soon create a goodly mass.
Keep it in check each spring to be rewarded
with showy spikes of tubular flowers that
are wonderful for cutting. If the plant
gets floppy on you, prune or pinch by
one-half in spring, and you'll grow
sturdier, only slightly shorter
plants come bloom time.

Planting

Seeding: Direct sow in early fall or in spring with soil temperature 70°–75° F. Protect fall-started seedlings from winter cold the first year.

Planting out: Spring or fall

Spacing: 12–24"

Growing

Obedient plants prefer **full sun** but tolerate partial or light shade. The soil should be **moist** and of **average to high fertility**. In a fertile soil these plants are more vigorous and may need staking. Choose a compact cultivar to avoid the need for staking. Plants can become invasive. Divide in early to mid-spring, once the ground can be worked, every two years or so to curtail invasiveness.

Tips

Use these plants in borders, cottage gardens, informal borders and naturalistic gardens. The flowers of obedient plants can be cut for use in fresh arrangements.

The individual flowers can be bent around on the stems and will stay put where you leave them. It is this unusual habit that gives the plant its common name.

Recommended

P. virginiana has a spreading root system from which upright stems sprout. It grows 2–4' tall and spreads 24" or more. 'Bouquet Rose' bears lilac pink flowers. 'Summer Snow' is a more compact, less invasive plant with white flowers. 'Variegata' is a desirable variegated

P. virginiana

specimen with cream-margined leaves and bright pink flowers.

P. 'Vivid' bears bright purple-pink flowers. This compact hybrid grows 12–24" tall and spreads 12".

Problems & Pests

Rare problems with rust and slugs are possible.

P. virginiana 'Variegata'

Oriental Poppy

Papaver

Height: 1½–4' **Spread:** 18–36" **Flower color:** red, pink, white
Blooms: late spring to early summer **Zones:** 3–7

CHILDREN LOVE THE COLORFUL, CRINKLY FLOWERS OF ORIENTAL poppies. In fact, their paper-like blooms seem to bring out the child in us all. These old-fashioned favorites continue to impress new gardeners because there is no other perennial with blooms like them. You learn to place poppies where their mid-season disappearing act is hidden by other leafy perennials or annuals grown in front.

Planting

Seeding: Direct sow in spring or fall

Planting out: Spring

Spacing: 24"

Growing

Grow Oriental poppy in **full sun**. The soil should be **average to fertile** and must be **well drained**. Division is rarely required but may be done in late summer to early fall once new rosettes begin to form. Plants die back after flowering and send up fresh new growth in late summer, which should be left in place for winter insulation.

P. orientale cultivars (photos this page)

Tips

Small groups of Oriental poppy look attractive in an early-summer border, although they may leave a bare spot during the dormant period in summer. Baby's breath and catmint plants make good companions and will fill in any blank spaces.

Use of poppy seeds in cooking and baking can be traced as far back as the ancient Egyptians.

Recommended

P. orientale forms an upright, oval clump $1^1/_2$–4' tall and 24–36" wide. Red, scarlet, pink or white flowers, with prominent black stamens, are borne in late spring and early summer. '**Allegro**' has bright scarlet red flowers. '**Black and White**' bears white flowers with black markings at the base of the petals. '**Pizzicato**' is a dwarf cultivar, with flowers in a wide range of colors. It forms a mound 18–24" tall, with an equal spread.

Problems & Pests

Problems with powdery mildew, leaf smut, gray mold, root rot and damping off are possible but rare in well-drained soil.

Ox-Eye

False Sunflower, Orange Sunflower
Heliopsis

Height: 36" **Spread:** 18–36" **Flower color:** yellow, orange
Blooms: mid-summer to mid-fall **Zones:** 2–9

IF ONLY NORTHERN GARDENERS COULD GROW A BUSHY, FREE-flowing perennial featuring big, bountiful, bright yellow blooms that lasted for a good part of summer, was virtually pest- and disease-free, didn't care much about soil and would thrive in sun to light shade. Hey, wait a minute, we can, and the plant is *Heliopsis*. Individual flowers can be up to 4" across, and they are prized for cutting. Combine *Heliopsis* with purple coneflower, mid-season blooming aster, *Liatris* and butterfly weed in a large setting, and you will be sure to have the butterflies bopping and the bees a-buzzing.

Planting

Seeding: Start seed in spring, with soil temperature at about 68° F

Planting out: Spring

Spacing: 24"

Growing

Ox-eye prefers **full sun,** but it tolerates partial shade. The soil should be **average to fertile, humus rich, moist** and **well drained.** Most soil conditions are tolerated, including poor, dry soils. Divide every two or so years.

Deadhead to prolong the blooming period. Cut plants back once flowering is complete.

Tips

Use ox-eye at the back or in the middle of mixed or herbaceous borders. This plant is easy to grow and popular with novice gardeners.

Recommended

H. helianthoides forms an upright clump of stems and foliage and bears yellow or orange, daisy-like flowers. '**Ballerina**' grows 36" tall and has single, golden yellow flowers. '**Incomparabilis**' has double, bright golden yellow flowers. '**Summer Sun**' ('Sommersonne') bears single or semi-double, bright golden yellow flowers. It grows about 36" tall.

Problems & Pests

Occasional trouble with aphids and powdery mildew can occur.

H. helianthoides (photos this page)

The stems of ox-eye are stiff, making the blooms useful in fresh arrangements.

Pachysandra

Japanese Spurge, Allegheny Spurge

Pachysandra

Height: 8–12" **Spread:** indefinite **Flower color:** white, fairly inconspicuous; plant grown for foliage **Blooms:** early spring **Zones:** 4–9

PACHYSANDRA IS A VERSATILE, FORGIVING GROUNDCOVER THAT looks great anywhere a low, dense mat of green is desired. It is one of the classic groundcovers for areas under trees, benches and decks, but I find it pleasing as an edging to shady pathways and in the woodland garden border. To cover large areas around trees, buy it in flats, then plant on a 12" grid. In just a few years you'll have a lush carpet, with ample plants to dig in spring and move to other spots in the garden.

Planting

Seeding: Not recommended

Planting out: Spring or fall

Spacing: 12–18"

Growing

Pachysandras prefer **light to full shade** and tolerate partial shade. The soil should be **moist, humus
rich** and **well drained**. Division is not required
but can be done in spring for propagation.

Tips

Pachysandras are durable groundcovers to use
under trees, along north-facing walls, in shady borders and in woodland gardens. Try Allegheny
spurge as an accent plant or in a naturalized, wood
land setting.

These plants are evergreen and generally need little attention. Shearing back any winter damage in
spring will quickly result in a flush of new growth.

Recommended

P. procumbens (Allegheny spurge, Allegheny
pachysandra) is a clump-forming, spreading
species native to the southeastern United States.
It grows 12" tall and spreads indefinitely. The
semi-evergreen leaves emerge a light green,
mature to bronze-green and turn reddish in fall.
(Zones 5–9)

P. terminalis (Japanese spurge) forms a low mass
of foliage rosettes. It grows about 8" tall and can
spread almost indefinitely. **'Variegata'** has white
margins or silver-mottled foliage. It is not as vigorous as the species. (Zones 4–9)

Problems & Pests

Problems with leaf blight, root rot and scale
insects can occur. The fungal root rots can devas-
tate a bed. Regularly thinning plants and trimming back overgrown plants will encourage air
circulation and help prevent the onset of disease.

P. terminalis (photos this page)

*The unusual name
pachysandra comes
from the Greek
pachys, 'thick,' and
andros, 'male,'
referring to the thick
stamens in the
flowers.*

Pasqueflower

Pulsatilla

Height: 4–12" **Spread:** 8–12" **Flower color:** purple, blue, red, white
Blooms: early to mid-spring **Zones:** 3–7

PRETTY LITTLE *PULSATILLA* IS ONE OF THE SUBTLE WONDERS OF
spring—its cupped, purplish red flowers appear soon after the last of the
snow has disappeared. With silky hairs rising from clean, lobed foliage, this
exotic-looking European native could pass as a desert wildflower. I grow *Pulsatilla* here and there at the front of a shade bed that receives afternoon sun.
It has been telling me spring has arrived for as long as I can remember.

Planting

Seeding: Sow seed as soon as it is ripe (mid-summer to fall)

Planting out: Spring

Spacing: 8–12"

Growing

Pasqueflower grows well in **full sun** or **partial shade**. The soil should be **fertile** and very **well drained**. Poorly drained, wet soil can quickly kill this plant. Pasqueflower resents being disturbed. Plant it while it is very small, and don't divide it.

Propagate pasqueflower by carefully taking root cuttings in early spring. You may have to soak the soil around the plant to loosen it and get at the roots. Dig carefully to expose a root, then remove it and replant it. See the 'Propagating Perennials' section in the introduction for more information about starting root cuttings. Be sure to protect the remaining plant from spring frosts with mulch if you have taken cuttings from it.

Tips

Pasqueflower can be grown in rock gardens, woodland gardens, borders and on gravelly banks. It also works well in pots and planters but should be moved to a sheltered location for the winter. An unheated garage or porch will offer some protection from the freeze-thaw cycles and excessive moisture of winter. Make sure the pots get some light once the plants begin to show signs of growth.

Pasqueflower is harmful if eaten, and repeated handling may cause skin irritation.

Recommended

P. vulgaris (*Anemone pulsatilla*) forms a mounded clump of lacy foliage. Flowers in shades of blue, purple or occasionally white are borne in early spring, before the foliage emerges. The seed-heads are very fluffy and provide interest when the flowers are gone. '**Alba**' (var. *alba*) has white flowers. '**Rubra**' has bright purple-red flowers.

Pasqueflower is one of the first perennials to bloom in spring.

'Rubra'

The early blooming time of many Pulsatilla *species gave rise to the common name.* 'Pasque' *refers to the* Paschal, *or Easter, season.*

P. vulgaris

Penstemon
Beard-Tongue
Penstemon

Height: 1–5' **Spread:** 6–24" **Flower color:** white, pink, purple, red
Blooms: late spring, summer, early fall **Zones:** 3–9

A TRUE NORTH AMERICAN NATIVE, PENSTEMON TYPICALLY NEEDS
ideal growing conditions. A few varieties developed by plant breeders are relatively easy to establish. 'Husker Red' was named Perennial Plant Association
perennial of the year in 1996, and deservedly so. Spikes of white, tubular
flowers contrast spectacularly with the plant's reddish
stems and leaves. All varieties do well in hot, sunny
locations, and they are quite drought tolerant
once established. They are easily
propagated from seed and
divisions.

Planting

Seeding: Start indoors in late summer or early spring; soil temperature should be 55°–64° F

Planting out: Spring or fall

Spacing: 12–24"

Growing

Penstemons prefer **full sun** but tolerate some shade. The soil should be of **average to rich fertility, sandy** and **well drained**. These plants are drought tolerant and will rot in wet soil. Mulch in winter with chicken grit or pea gravel to protect the crowns from excessive moisture and cold.

Divide every two to three years in spring. Pinch plants when they are 12" tall to encourage bushy growth.

P. digitalis 'Husker Red'

Tips

Use penstemons in a mixed or herbaceous border, a cottage garden or a rock garden.

Twiggy branches pushed into the ground around young penstemon plants will support them as they grow.

Recommended

P. barbatus is an upright, rounded perennial. It grows 18–36" tall and spreads 12–18". The red or pink flowers are borne from early summer to early fall. '**Elfin Pink**' is very reliable and has compact spikes of pink flowers. It grows up to 18" tall. '**Prairie Dusk**' has tall spikes of tubular, rose purple flowers; it blooms over a long season. (Zones 3–8)

P. digitalis is a very hardy, upright, semi-evergreen perennial. It grows 2–5' tall and spreads 18–24". It bears white flowers, often veined with

purple, all summer. **'Husker Red'** combines white flowers with vibrant burgundy foliage that adds interest for more than one season and makes an attractive mass planting. (Zones 4–8)

P. gracilis (slender beard-tongue) grows 12–24" tall and spreads 6–12" wide. It produces pale violet flowers with a dense, yellow beard from late spring to mid-summer. (Zones 3–8)

P. grandiflorus (large beard-tongue) has thick, fleshy foliage. It grows 3–3^1/$_2$' tall and 10" wide and bears pink to blue lavender flowers in summer. (Zones 3–9)

Problems & Pests

Powdery mildew, rust and leaf spot can occur but are rarely serious.

Over 200 species of Penstemon *are native to varied habitats from mountains to open plains throughout North and South America.*

The mashed wet leaves of some Penstemon *species have been used to treat rattlesnake bites.*

Peony

Paeonia

Height: 24–36" **Spread:** 24–36" **Flower color:** white, pink, red
Blooms: spring, early summer **Zones:** 2–7

DO YOU HAVE MANY FOND CHILDHOOD MEMORIES OF YOUR grandmother's peonies? Chances are good that decades later, those plants are still alive and blooming. Easy to grow and tough as nails, peonies are among the longest-lived perennials. Peonies add backbone to the garden that few other perennials can match. Let's thank our lucky stars we live in the north, where the plant thrives; peonies turn to goo in the Deep South and southwest, and gardeners there look northward with envy.

Planting

Seeding: Not recommended; seeds may take two to three years to germinate and many more years to grow to flowering size

Planting out: Fall or spring

Spacing: 24–36"

Growing

Peonies prefer **full sun** but tolerate some shade. The planting site should be well prepared before the plants are introduced. Peonies like **fertile, humus-rich, moist, well-drained** soil, to which lots of compost has been added. Too much fertilizer, particularly nitrogen, causes floppy growth and retards blooming. Division is not required, but it is usually the best way to propagate new plants and should be done in fall.

Cut back the flowers after blooming and remove any blackened leaves to prevent the spread of gray mold. Red peonies are more susceptible to disease.

Whether you choose to clean your perennial garden in fall or spring, it is essential to deal with peonies in fall. To reduce the possibility of disease, clean up and discard or destroy all leaf litter before the snow falls.

P. lactiflora cultivars (photos this page)

P. lactiflora cultivar (photos both pages)

Peonies are slow growers and often take a couple of years to bloom, but once established they may well outlive their owners.

Tips

These are wonderful plants that look great in a border when combined with other early-flowering plants. They may be underplanted with bulbs and other plants that will die down by mid-summer, when the emerging foliage of peonies will hide the dying foliage of spring plants. Avoid planting peonies under trees where they will have to compete for moisture and nutrients.

Planting depth is a very important factor in determining whether or not a peony will flower. Tubers planted too shallowly or, more commonly, too deeply will not flower. The buds or eyes on the tuber should be 1–2" below the soil surface.

Place wire tomato or peony cages around the plants in early spring to support heavy flowers. The cage will be hidden by the foliage as it grows up into the wires.

Recommended

Peonies may be listed as cultivars of a certain species or as interspecies hybrids. Hundreds are available.

P. lactiflora (common garden peony, Chinese peony) forms a clump of red-tinged stems and dark green foliage. It grows 24–36" tall, with an equal spread, and bears single, fragrant, white or pink flowers with yellow stamens. The following selections are some popular hybrid cultivars: **'Bowl of Cream'** has 8" wide, bowl-shaped, double, white flowers with hidden gold stamens; **'Duchess de Nemours'** has fragrant, white, double flowers tinged yellow at the bases of the inner petals; and

'Kansas' bears large, double, bright red flowers that don't fade in the intense sun. 'Krinkled White' has crinkled, single, cup-shaped, white flowers with gold stamens. 'Miss America' produces large, semi-double, white flowers with ruffled petals. 'Raspberry Sundae' has large, double, fragrant, pale pink flowers. 'Red Charm' bears very ruffled, double, dark red flowers. 'Sara Bernhardt' has large, fragrant, pink, double flowers. 'Scarlet O'Hara' has large, single, scarlet flowers with gold stamens. The flowers fade to bright pink with age. 'Seashell' bears single, shell pink flowers with yellow stamens. These cultivars may also be sold as hybrids and not as cultivars of this species.

P. officinalis (common peony) forms a clump of slightly hairy stems and deeply lobed foliage 24–30" tall and wide. It bears single, red or pink flowers with yellow stamens.

Problems & Pests

Peonies may have trouble with *Verticillium* wilt, ringspot virus, tip blight, stem rot, gray mold, leaf blotch, nematodes and Japanese beetles.

Despite their exotic appearance, peonies are tough perennials that can survive winter temperatures as low as –40° F.

To use peonies as cut flowers, cut when the flower is in full color and the bloom is fully open. The foliage is long lasting and can be used as a base for arrangements all summer. Cutting more than one-third of the flowers produced in a year can reduce flower production the following year.

Perennial Salvia
Sage
Salvia

Height: 12–36" **Spread:** 12–36" **Flower color:** purple, blue, pink, cream
Blooms: late spring, summer, early fall **Zones:** 3–9

SPIKY SALVIAS COMBINE BEAUTIFULLY WITH VIRTUALLY ALL perennials that have a mounding habit. They work particular wonders when grown in front of or beside geraniums, yarrows, euphorbias, coreopsis and taller sedums. Don't confuse perennial salvia with annual salvia (wonderful plant that it is), which is sold as a bedding plant. Same genus, different species. Perennial salvia is darn hardy, returning in a larger clump each year as long as it is grown in ample sun and soil that drains well.

Planting

Seeding: Cultivars do not come true to type; species can be started in early spring

Planting out: Spring

Spacing: 18–24"

Growing

Salvias prefer **full sun** but tolerate light shade. The soil should be of **average fertility** and **well drained**. These plants benefit from a light mulch of compost each year. They are drought tolerant once established. Division can be done in spring, but the plants are slow to reestablish and resent having their roots disturbed. They are easily propagated by tip cuttings.

Deadhead to prolong blooming. Trim plants back in spring to encourage new growth and keep plants tidy. New shoots will sprout from old, woody growth.

S. officinalis 'Icterina'

S. officinalis *has aromatic foliage that is used as a flavoring in many dishes.*

S. officinalis 'Tricolor'

S. x *sylvestris* 'May Night'

S. x *sylvestris* cultivar

Tips

All *Salvia* species are attractive plants for the border. Taller species and cultivars add volume to the middle or back of the border, and the smaller specimens make an attractive edging or feature near the front. Perennial salvias can also be grown in mixed planters.

Recommended

S. nemorosa (*S.* x *superba*) is a clump-forming, branching plant with gray-green leaves. It grows 18–36" tall and spreads 18–24". The spikes of blue or purple flowers are produced in summer. **'Lubeca'** bears long-lasting, purple flowers. (Zones 3–7)

S. officinalis (common sage) is a woody, mounding plant with soft gray-green leaves. It grows 12–24" tall and spreads 18–36". The spikes of light purple flowers appear in early and mid-summer. **'Berggarten'** ('Bergarden') has silvery leaves

about the size and shape of a quarter. '**Icterina**' ('Aurea') has yellow-margined foliage. '**Purpurea**' has purple stems. The new foliage emerges purple, and it matures to purple-green. '**Tricolor**' has green or purple-green foliage outlined in cream. New growth emerges pinkish purple. It is the least hardy of the variegated sages. (Zones 4–7)

S. sclarea (clary sage) is a short-lived perennial or biennial up to 36" tall and about 12" in spread. It forms a mound of large, fuzzy leaves, and it bears large, loose spikes of purple-bracted cream, purple, pink or blue flowers in late spring and early summer. (Zones 4–9)

S. x *sylvestris* 'May Night'

S. x *sylvestris* (perennial salvia) grows 30–36" tall and about 12" in spread. It is often confused with the very similar *S. nemorosa*. Cultivars have been listed under both species at different times. '**May Night**' bears deep purple-blue flowers. '**Rose Queen**' bears unique rosy purple flowers, but the growth is somewhat floppier than that of the other cultivars. (Zones 3–7)

The genus name Salvia *comes from the Latin* salvus, *'save,' referring to the medicinal properties of several species.*

S. nemorosa 'Lubeca'

S. verticillata '**Purple Rain**' is a low, mounding plant that grows 18" tall, with an equal spread. It bears purple blooms in late summer and early fall. The colorful bracts remain long after the flowers fade. (Zones 5–8)

Problems & Pests

Scale insects, whiteflies and root rot (in wet soils) are the most likely problems.

Phlox

Phlox

Height: 2"–4' **Spread:** 12–36" **Flower color:** white, red, purple, pink
Blooms: spring, summer, fall **Zones:** 3–8

GARDEN FOR ANY LENGTH OF TIME, AND IT'S SAFE TO SAY THAT
you will eventually grow phlox because the genus comprises a widely diverse
group of beautiful plants that grow in sun to partial shade. The sun-loving
P. paniculata is a mainstay of cottage gardens and formal and informal
flowerbeds. While gorgeous in bloom, the foliage adds nothing to the overall
result—plant *P. paniculata* where it's hidden pre- and post-bloom. I edge all
my beds with stone, and always grow *P. stolonifera* at points along the front
edge, where it twists, tumbles and looks terrific, in bloom or not.

Planting

Seeding: Not recommended

Planting out: Spring

Spacing: 12–36"

Growing

Garden phlox and early phlox prefer **full sun** and moss phlox prefers **partial shade.** Creeping phlox prefers **light to partial shade** but tolerates heavy shade. All like **fertile, humus-rich, moist, well-drained** soil. Divide in fall or spring. Creeping phlox spreads out horizontally as it grows. The stems grow roots where they touch the ground. These plants are easily propagated by detaching the rooted stems in spring or early fall. Do not prune creeping phlox in fall—it is an early-season bloomer and will have next spring's flowers already forming.

P. subulata

Tips

Low-growing species are useful in a rock garden or at the front of a border. Taller species may be used in the middle of a border, where they are particularly effective if planted in groups.

Garden phlox requires good air circulation to help prevent mildew. Thin out large stands to help keep the air flowing. Early phlox is more resistant to powdery mildew than garden phlox.

P. paniculata

P. paniculata 'Eva Cullum'

The name Phlox *is from the Greek word for 'flame,' referring to the colorful flowers of many species.*

P. paniculata

Recommended

P. maculata (Maculata Group) (early phlox, wild sweet William) forms an upright clump of hairy stems and narrow leaves that are sometimes spotted with red. It grows 24–36" tall and spreads 18–24". Pink, purple or white flowers are borne in conical clusters in the first half of summer. This species has good resistance to powdery mildew. '**Delta**' bears fragrant, pinkish white flowers with a dark pink eye. '**Omega**' bears white flowers with light pink centers. '**Rosalinde**' bears dark pink flowers. These cultivars are taller than the species, usually 30" or more.

P. paniculata (Paniculata Group) (garden phlox) blooms in summer and fall. It has many cultivars, which vary greatly in size, growing 20"–4' tall and spreading 12–36". Many colors are available, often with contrasting centers. '**Crème de Menthe**' grows 24–36" tall and 12" wide. It has mildew-resistant, green and white variegated foliage and white flowers with a pink eye. '**David**' grows to $3^1/_2$' tall and bears white flowers and is resistant to powdery mildew. '**Eva Cullum**' grows to 36" tall and bears pink flowers with red centers. '**Franz Shubert**' also grows to 36" tall. It bears dense clusters of lilac pink flowers with star-shaped, dark pink eyes. '**Katherine**' is a long-blooming, mildew-resistant plant growing 3–4' tall. It bears pale lavender flowers with white, star-shaped eyes. '**Laura**' grows 24–30" tall and has lavender purple flowers with white, star-shaped eyes. '**Starfire**' bears crimson red flowers on 36" tall plants.

P. stolonifera (creeping phlox) is a low, spreading plant. It grows 4–6" tall, spreads about 12" and bears flowers in shades of purple in spring. This species is a former Perennial Plant of the Year.

P. subulata (moss phlox, creeping phlox, moss pinks) is very low growing, only 2–6" tall, with a spread of 20". Its cultivars bloom in various colors from late spring to early summer. 'Candy Stripe' bears bicolored pink and white flowers.

Problems & Pests

Occasional problems with powdery mildew, stem canker, rust, leaf spot, leaf miners and caterpillars are possible.

P. paniculata 'Crème de Menthe'

Phloxes come in many forms, from low-growing creepers to tall, clump-forming uprights. The many species can be found in diverse climates, including dry, exposed mountainsides and moist, sheltered woodlands.

P. subulata

Pincushion Flower

Scabiosa

Height: 12–24" **Spread:** 12–24" **Flower color:** purple, blue, white, pink
Blooms: summer, fall **Zones:** 3–7

IF CREATING AN OLD-FASHIONED, SIMPLE STYLE OF GARDEN, BE
sure to include *Scabiosa*. The plant's very distinctive flowers feature broad,
tufted centers of florets ringed by small, floppy petals that are reminiscent of
an embroidered pincushion. *Scabiosa* will indeed flower in partial shade, but
I've found it becomes more stragglier than is its regular habit; full sun makes
the plant much happier.

Planting

Seeding: Direct sow in spring or summer

Planting out: Spring

Spacing: 12–24"

Growing

Pincushion flowers prefer **full sun** but tolerate partial shade. The soil should be **light, moderately fertile, neutral** or **alkaline** and **well drained.** Divide in early spring, whenever the clumps become overgrown.

Deadhead as the flowers fade to promote a longer flowering period. Cutting flowers at their peak every few days for indoor use will make this maintenance chore more enjoyable. Leave the evergreen foliage intact over the winter and remove dead and tattered leaves in spring.

Tips

Pincushion flowers look best planted in groups of three or more in a bed or border. They are also used as cut flowers.

Recommended

S. caucasica forms a basal rosette of narrow leaves. Blue or lavender flowers are borne in summer on long stems that grow up to 24" tall; the plant spreads 24" as well. **'Fama'** bears sky blue flowers with silvery white centers. **Isaac House hybrids** is a group of slightly smaller plants with large, shaggy, blue flowers. **'Perfecta Alba'** bears large, frilly, pure white flowers.

S. columbaria (small scabious) forms a low mound of gray-green foliage 12–18" wide. Lavender blue flowers bloom from summer to frost atop 12–18" stems. Several hybrids have been developed from crosses between *S. caucasica* and *S. columbaria*. These hybrids may be listed as cultivars of either species.

S. columbaria 'Butterfly Blue'

'Butterfly Blue' bears lavender blue flowers from early summer until frost. **'Pink Mist'** grows about 12" tall and bears many pink blooms from summer to frost.

Problems & Pests

Pincushion flowers rarely have problems, though aphids may be troublesome.

S. caucasica

Pinks

Dianthus

Height: 4–18" **Spread:** 12–24" **Flower color:** pink, red, white, lilac purple
Blooms: spring, summer **Zones:** 3–9

DIANTHUS IS NOT ONLY A GREAT AND POPULAR CHOICE FOR
gardens in the U.S., it is one of the most widely loved garden perennials on
the planet. Few upright perennials grace the garden with cool blue-green
foliage, and these stout trooper holds their rich color all season. The species
D. gratianopolitanus is an outstanding low-maintenance variety that all new
gardeners should grow. Combine it with other varieties of pinks and with
silvery leaved lamb's ears (p. 224), artemisias (p. 78) and catmints (p. 124).

Planting

Seeding: Not recommended; cultivars do not come true to type from seed

Planting out: Spring

Spacing: 10–20"

Growing

Pinks prefer **full sun** but tolerate some light shade. A **well-drained, neutral** or **alkaline** soil is required. The most important factor in the successful cultivation of pinks is drainage––they hate to stand in water. Mix sharp sand or gravel into their area of the flowerbed to encourage good drainage.

Pinks may be difficult to propagate by division. It is often easier to take

D. deltoides

cuttings in summer, once flowering has finished. Cuttings should be 1–3" long. Strip the lower leaves from the cutting. The cuttings should be kept humid, but be sure to give them some ventilation so that fungal problems do not set in.

D. plumarius

D. gratianopolitanus

Cheddar pink is a rare and protected species in Britain. It was discovered in the 18th century by British botanist Samuel Brewer, and it became as locally famous as cheddar cheese.

Tips

Pinks make excellent plants for rock gardens and rock walls and for edging flower borders and walkways. They can also be used in cutting gardens and even as groundcovers.

Deadhead as the flowers fade to prolong blooming, but leave a few flowers in place to go to seed. Pinks self-seed quite easily. Seedlings may differ from the parent plants, often with new and interesting results.

Recommended

D. x *allwoodii* (allwood pinks) forms a compact mound and bears flowers in a wide range of colors. 'Frosty Fire' grows 4–8" tall and 12" wide bearing double, dark crimson red flowers with occasional white flecks in late spring to early summer. 'Helen' grows 12" tall and 18" wide and bears salmon pink, double flowers in mid- to late spring.

D. deltoides (maiden pink) grows 6–12" tall and about 12" wide. The plant forms a mat of foliage and flowers in spring. It is a popular species to use in rock gardens. 'Brilliant' ('Brilliancy,' 'Brilliance') bears dark red flowers.

D. gratianopolitanus (cheddar pink) usually grows about 6" tall and 12" wide, but it can grow up to 12" tall and 18" wide. This plant is long-lived and forms a very dense mat of evergreen, silver gray foliage with sweet-scented flowers borne in summer. 'Bath's Pink' bears plentiful, light pink flowers and tolerates warm, humid conditions. 'Feuerhexe' ('Firewitch') has clove-scented, bright magenta flowers. '**Mountain Mist**' grows to 10" tall and has smoky pink flowers. '**Tiny Rubies**' is a popular selection bearing double, deep pink flowers. It grows 4–6" tall.

D. plumarius (cottage pink) is noteworthy for its role in the development of many popular cultivars known as garden pinks. They are generally 12–18" tall and 24" wide, although smaller cultivars are available. They all flower in spring and into summer if deadheaded regularly. The flowers can be single, semi-double or fully double and are available in many colors. '**Doris**' has semi-double, salmon pink flowers with darker pink centers. It is popular as a cut flower. '**Spring Beauty**' bears double flowers in many colors with more strongly frilled edges than the species. '**Sonata**' bears fragrant, double flowers in many colors all summer.

D. plumarius with spirea

D. plumarius

Problems & Pests

Providing good drainage and air circulation will keep most fungal problems away. Occasional problems with slugs, blister beetles, sow bugs and grasshoppers are possible.

The tiny, delicate petals of pinks can be used to decorate cakes. Be sure to remove the white part at the base of the petal before using the petals or they will be bitter.

Rose Mallow
Hardy Hibiscus
Hibiscus

Height: 1¹/₂–8' **Spread:** 18–36" **Flower color:** white, red, pink
Blooms: mid-summer to frost **Zones:** 4–9

FEW PERENNIALS CAN MATCH ROSE MALLOW FOR IN-YOUR-FACE displays of huge (up to 12" across), colorful blooms. Gardeners moving to Wisconsin and Minnesota from warmer climates are always delighted (after recovering from shock) to discover that, yes, we can grow rose mallow up here in the tundra. But make it easy on the plant—the more contained and protected the location, the better, not only to keep the plants from toppling over in the wind, but to ensure winter survival.

Planting

Seeding: Direct sow indoors or out in spring. Ensure soil temperature is 55°–64° F.

Planting out: Spring

Spacing: 36"

Growing

Grow rose mallow in **full sun.** The soil should be **humus rich, moist** and **well drained.** Rose mallow is a heavy feeder and benefits from a side dressing of fertilizer when it begins to leaf out. Divide in spring.

Prune by one-half in June for bushier, more compact growth. Deadhead to keep the plant tidy. If you cut your rose mallow back in fall, be sure to mark its location as this plant is slow to emerge in spring.

Tips

Rose mallow is an interesting plant for the back of an informal border or mixed into a pondside planting. The large flowers create a bold focal point in late-summer gardens.

Recommended

H. moscheutos is a large, vigorous plant with strong stems. It grows 3–8' tall and spreads about 36". The huge flowers can be up to 12" across. **'Blue River II'** grows about 4' tall. It bears pure white flowers. **'Disco Belle'** is a small plant 18–24" tall and wide. It is often grown as an annual, and its flowers can be red, pink or white. **'Lord Baltimore'** bears red flowers. **'Southern Belle'** bears red, pink or white flowers on large plants 4–6' tall.

'Southern Belle'

Problems & Pests

Rose mallow may develop problems with rust, fungal leaf spot, bacterial blight, *Verticillium* wilt, viruses and stem or root rot. A few possible insect pests are whiteflies, aphids, scale insects, mites and caterpillars.

'Blue River II'

Russian Sage

Perovskia

Height: 3–4' **Spread:** 3–4' **Flower color:** blue, purple **Blooms:** mid- or late summer to fall **Zones:** 4–9

ONE OF MY GREAT REGRETS AS A GARDENER IS THAT I can no longer grow proper, robust specimens of this most desirable perennial in my increasingly shady yard. I may have to sell my house and build on a new, sunny lot, which isn't a crazy notion if it means I can reclaim the supreme splendor of Russian sage. Attractive all season, glorious in bloom, Russian sage is an easy-to-grow, long-lived perennial that possesses a lengthy bloom period throughout late summer. Always plant Russian sage as a single, at the front of large flowerbeds and in key spots wherever a focal point is desired. I am envious.

Planting

Seeding: Not recommended; germination can be very erratic

Planting out: Spring

Spacing: 36"

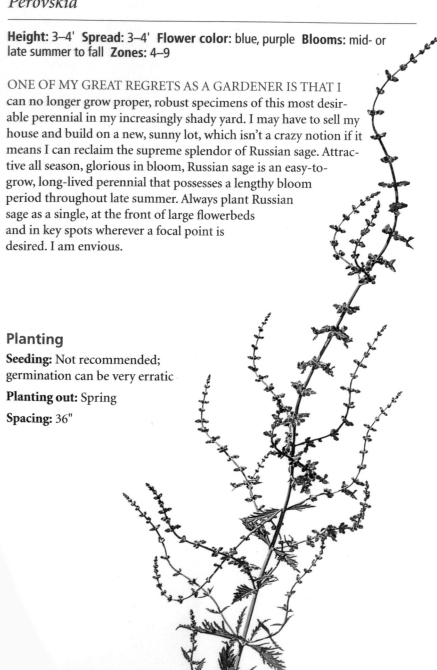

Growing

Russian sage prefers a location with **full sun**. The soil should be **poor to moderately fertile** and **well drained**. Too much water and nitrogen will cause the growth to flop, so take care when growing this plant next to heavy feeders. Russian sage does not need dividing.

In spring, when new growth appears low on the branches, or in fall, cut the plant back hard to about 6–12" to encourage vigorous, bushy growth.

Tips

The silvery foliage and blue flowers combine well with other plants in the back of a mixed border and soften the appearance of daylilies. Russian sage may also be used to create a soft screen in a natural garden or on a dry bank.

Recommended

P. atriplicifolia is a loose, upright plant with silvery white, finely divided foliage. The small, lavender blue flowers are loosely held on silvery, branched stems. **'Filigran'** has delicate foliage and an upright habit. **'Longin'** is narrow and erect and has more smoothly edged leaves than other cultivars.

The airy habit of this plant creates a mist of silver purple in the garden.

'Longin'

The flowers make a nice addition to fresh and dried flower arrangements.

P. atriplicifolia

Sea Holly
Eryngium

Height: 2–5' **Spread:** 12–24" **Flower color:** blue, white, creamy green
Blooms: mid-summer to fall **Zones:** 2–8

IF YOU ARE A PROGRESSIVE, CUTTING EDGE SORT OF GARDENER, grow sea holly. The great rage these days is to grow something the neighbors don't have, and sea holly will fill this need quite well. The best of the bunch, *E. alpinum* is hardy to zone 2, for Pete's sake. The distinctive, bug-eyed flowerheads fuzz into long-lasting, globe-shaped flowers that are highly valuable in fresh and dried flower arrangements. Sea hollies are outstanding in rock gardens, because their overall appearance is that of some exotic desert plant, yet the very striking *E. yuccifolium* is native to our region.

Planting

Seeding: Not recommended, though direct sowing in fall may produce spring seedlings

Planting out: Spring

Spacing: 12–24"

Growing

Grow sea hollies in **full sun**. The soil should be **average to fertile** and **well drained**. These plants have a long taproot and are fairly drought tolerant, but they will suffer if left more than two weeks without water. Sea hollies are very slow to reestablish after dividing. Root cuttings can be taken in late winter.

The leaves of these plants are edged with small spines, making dead-heading a pain—literally. It is not necessary unless you are very fussy about keeping plants neat.

Tips

Try to mix sea hollies with other late-season bloomers in a border. They make an interesting addition to naturalized gardens.

Recommended

E. alpinum (alpine sea holly, blue-top eryngo) grows 2–4' tall. This species has soft and feathery-looking but spiny bracts and steel blue or white flowers. There are several cultivars available in different shades of blue. (Zones 2–8)

E. amethystinum (amethyst sea holly) grows 4–5' tall. The flowers are steel blue with silvery gray bracts. (Zones 3–8)

E. alpinum

E. yuccifolium (rattlesnake master) grows 3–4' tall. This North American native forms a rosette of long, narrow, spiny, blue-gray leaves. From mid-summer to fall it bears creamy green or pale blue flowers with gray-green bracts. (Zones 4–8)

Problems & Pests

Roots may rot if the plants are left in standing water for long periods of time. Slugs, snails and powdery mildew may be problems.

E. yuccifolium

Sedum

Stonecrop

Sedum, Hylotelephium

Height: 2–30" **Spread:** 12" to indefinite **Flower color:** yellow-green, white, red, pink; plant also grown for foliage **Blooms:** summer, fall **Zones:** 2–9

THE ONLY NEGATIVE ASPECT TO THE GREAT PUBLICITY AND widespread acceptance enjoyed by wonderful sedum varieties such as 'Bertram Anderson' and 'Autumn Joy' is that some gardeners aren't aware of just how huge and useful this diverse family of plants is. Sedum has wonderful, low-growing varieties that are well suited to rock gardens, stone walls, steps and crevices, in addition to the uses for more commonly grown upright varieties. All varieties feature outstanding foliage that complement surrounding plants throughout the season.

Planting

Seeding: Sow indoors in early spring. Seed sold is often a mix of different species; you may not get what you expected, but you may be pleasantly surprised.

Planting out: Spring

Spacing: 18"

Growing

Sedums prefer **full sun** but tolerate partial shade. The soil should be of **average fertility**, very **well drained** and **neutral to alkaline**. Divide in spring when needed. Prune back 'Autumn Joy' in May by one-half and insert pruned-off parts into soft soil; cuttings root quickly. Early-summer pruning of upright species and hybrids gives compact, bushy plants but can delay flowering.

Tips

Low-growing sedums make both wonderful groundcovers and rock-garden or rock-wall plants. They also edge beds and borders beautifully. The taller types give a lovely late-season display in a bed or border.

A recent change in taxonomy has seen many of the taller sedums split away from the genus *Sedum* to form their own genus, *Hylotelephium*. We include the taller sedums (*Hylotelephium*) here under the genus *Sedum* because many gardeners are unaware of the taxonomic change.

'Autumn Joy' (photos this page)

S. spectabile 'Brilliant'

'Autumn Joy' brings color to the late-season garden, when few flowers are in bloom.

S. spurium

Recommended

S. acre (gold moss stonecrop) grows 2" high and spreads indefinitely. The small, yellow-green flowers are borne in summer. It is often sold as 'Golden Carpet.' (Zones 3–8)

S. 'Autumn Joy' (*Hylotelephium* 'Autumn Joy') (autumn joy sedum) is a popular upright hybrid. The flowers open pink or red and later fade to deep bronze over a long period in late summer and fall. The plant forms a clump 24" tall, with an equal spread. (Zones 3–8)

S. 'Bertram Anderson' is a mound-forming plant 8–12" tall and 12–15" wide. It has shiny, purple stems with dusty, dark lilac blue foliage and bears rose pink flowers in late summer. (Zones 2–9)

S. 'Matrona' is an erect plant 24–30" tall and 12–24" wide with purple-tinged, gray-green foliage and dark purple stems. The large clusters of rose pink flowers bloom in late summer and fade to a bronze hue in fall. (Zones 3–9)

S. 'Mohrchen' forms an upright clump of stems. It grows about 24" tall, with an equal spread. Bronze-red summer foliage brightens to ruby red in fall. The clusters of pink flowers are borne in late summer and fall. (Zones 3–8)

S. spectabile (*Hylotelephium spectabile*) (showy stonecrop) is an upright species with pink flowers borne in late summer. It forms a clump 16–24" tall and wide. 'Brilliant' bears bright pink flowers and typically flowers two weeks earlier than 'Autumn Joy'. 'Meteor' bears slightly domed clusters of rose pink flowers. (Zones 3–8)

S. spurium (two-row stonecrop) forms a mat about 4" tall and 24" wide. The mid-summer flowers are deep pink or white. **'Red Carpet'** bears deep red flowers above reddish foliage, which deepens in fall and winter. (Zones 3–8)

S. **'Vera Jameson'** (*Hylotelephium* 'Vera Jameson') is a low, mounding plant with purple-tinged stems and pinkish purple foliage. It grows up to 12" tall and spreads 18". The clusters of dark pink flowers are borne in late summer and fall. (Zones 3–8)

Problems & Pests

Slugs, snails and scale insects may cause trouble for these plants.

S. 'Vera Jameson'

Low-growing sedums make an excellent groundcover under trees. Their shallow roots survive well in the competition for space and moisture.

S. spurium 'Red Carpet'

Shasta Daisy
Leucanthemum

Height: 12–40" **Spread:** 12–24" **Flower color:** white with yellow centers
Blooms: early summer to fall **Zones:** 4–9

THOUGH THE COMMON NAME CAN LEAD TO SOME CONFUSION—
many people call lots of different, white, daisy-like flowers 'shasta daisies'—you
should find this plant correctly labeled *Leucanthemum* and readily available at
nurseries. Flowers that bloom in white are essential to the creation of an attractive garden, and these robust bloomers certainly keep the flowers coming.

Planting

Seeding: Start seeds
indoors or direct sow in
spring with soil tempera-
ture at about 70°–75° F

Planting out: Spring

Spacing: 24"

Growing

Shasta daisy grows well in **full sun** and **partial shade**. The soil should be **fertile, moist** and **well drained**. Divide every year or two, in spring, to maintain plant vigor. Shasta daisy planted in fall may not become established in time to survive winter. Plants can be short-lived in Zones 4 and 5.

Pinch or trim plants back in spring to encourage compact, bushy growth. Regular deadheading extends the bloom by several weeks, but it may also lead to death by exhaustion.

Tips

Use this perennial in the border, where it can be grown as a single plant or massed in groups. The flowers can be cut for fresh arrangements.

Recommended

L. x *superbum* forms a large clump of dark green leaves and stems. It bears white, daisy-like flowers with yellow centers all summer, often until the first frost. 'Becky' is a vigorous, tough-as-nails plant growing 36–40" tall, and it begins blooming later than the other selections. It bears single, white flowers with a bright gold centers for a extended period. 'Marconi' grows 36" tall and has large, semi-double or double flowers. It should be protected from the hot afternoon sun. 'Snowcap' is a smaller plant growing 12–16" tall and 12" wide with large, pure white flowers. 'Thomas Killen' is a thick-stemmed selection 30" tall and 18"

L. x *superbum* (photos this page)

wide, bearing flowers with a double row of white petals and raised golden centers. It is a great cut flower.

Problems & Pests

Occasional problems with aphids, leaf spot and leaf miners are possible.

Solomon's Seal

Polygonatum

Height: 1–5' **Spread:** 12–24" **Flower color:** white, greenish white, creamy
Blooms: spring, summer **Zones:** 3–9

FEW PERENNIALS CONTRIBUTE THE ARCHING, SCULPTURAL
composition of *Polygonatum*, and there is no woodland setting where the
plant should not be found. It is a plant grown for its form and foliage, which
combine effortlessly with ferns, hostas, geraniums, heucheras and any and all
wildflowers found in light to full shade.

Planting

Seeding: Sow seed in cold frame in early spring

Planting out: Spring

Spacing: 12–24"

Growing

Solomon's seal prefers **partial to full shade**. The soil should be **fertile, humus rich, moist** and **well drained**. Propagate by division in spring once the rhizomes have begun to grow. Do not damage the young shoots. Division can also be done in fall. When division of the rhizomes is necessary, be sure that each division has at least one bud eye.

Tips

Solomon's seal seems to brighten up the dullest shade garden. It works well in mixed beds and borders but looks most at home in woodland settings or naturalized areas. It is suitable as a groundcover when mass planted.

Dark blue-black to black, round berries follow the waxy flowers. The berries are highly poisonous. Do not plant in areas that are easily accessible to children or pets.

Recommended

P. biflorum (*P. canaliculatum*) (smooth Solomon's seal) is a rhizomatous plant with slender, arching stems growing 12–36" tall and 12–24" wide, but it may reach 5' in height. It has pendant, greenish white flowers blooming in late spring to mid-summer. (Zones 3–9)

P. hirtum is a erect, rhizomatous plant growing 16"–4' tall and 24" wide. It has pendant, green-tipped, creamy white, tubular flowers appearing in late spring to mid-summer. (Zones 5–8)

P. odoratum (fragrant Solomon's seal) grows 24–36" tall and 12–24"

wide. It has arching stems and spreads slowly by rhizomes. Pendent, green-tipped, white flowers are borne along the stem in spring to early summer. '**Variegatum**' has white-edged variegated foliage. New stems are red. (Zones 4–8)

Problems & Pests

Slugs and sawfly larvae are possible problems.

Speedwell
Veronica
Veronica

Height: 3–30" **Spread:** 3–18" **Flower color:** pink, purple, blue
Blooms: spring, summer **Zones:** 3–8

VERONICA HOLDS A SPECIAL PLACE IN MY HEART, FOR IT WAS THE
first perennial I purchased when I first became a gardener. A highly regarded
specialty nursery had been recommended by a friend, and when I asked the
proprietor what perennial I should start with, he sold me three pots of
'Sunny Border Blue.' Divisions from those three plants thrive in my garden
to this day. The newer variety I'm excited about is 'Blue Charm,' which has a
softer, more mounding habit, even though—just between you and me—
I haven't seen one yet that comes close to approaching the 30–36" heights
listed in some reference material.

Planting

Seeding: Not recommended; seedlings do not always come true to type. Seeds germinate quickly when started indoors in early spring.

Planting out: Spring

Spacing: 18"

Growing

Speedwells prefer **full sun** but tolerate partial shade. The soil should be of **average fertility, moist** and **well drained**. Lack of sun and excessive moisture and nitrogen may be partly to blame for the sloppy habits of some plants. Frequent dividing ensures strong, vigorous growth and decreases the chances of flopping. Divide in fall or spring every two to three years.

The genus name honors St. Veronica, who is said to have wiped the tears from the face of Jesus as he marched to Calvary.

V. spicata cultivars (photos this page)

When the spikes begin to fade, remove the entire spike to the point where it sprouted from the plant to encourage rapid reblooming. For tidier plants, shear back to 6" in June.

Tips

Speedwell is a beautiful plant for edging borders. Low-growing speed-wells are useful in a rock garden or at the front of a perennial border. Upright speedwells work well in masses in a bed or border. 'Goodness Grows' is useful in a rock garden or at the front of a perennial border.

Recommended

V. 'Giles van Hees' is a dwarf selection growing 3–6" tall and wide. It produces dense spikes of reddish pink to bright pink flowers in late spring to early summer. (Zones 4–8)

V. spicata (photos both pages)

V. **'Goodness Grows'** (spike speedwell) is a popular, easy, long-blooming plant that grows to about 12" tall and wide and produces long, tapering spikes of small, blue violet flowers throughout summer. (Zones 3–8)

V. prostrata (prostrate speedwell) is a low-growing, spreading plant. It grows 6" tall and spreads 16". Its flowers may be blue or occasionally pink. Many cultivars are available.

V. spicata (spike speedwell) is a low, mounding plant with stems that flop over when they get too tall. It grows 12–24" tall, spreads 18" and bears spikes of blue flowers in summer. Many cultivars of different colors are available. **'Blue Charm'** grows 24–30" tall and has lavender blue flowers. Subsp. *incana* (*V. incana*) has soft, hairy, silvery green leaves and deep purple-blue flowers. **'Sunny Border Blue'** was the 1993 Perennial Plant of the Year. It grows 15–20" tall and has bright blue flowers.

V. **'Waterperry Blue'** is a prostrate, groundcover type perennial growing 4–6" tall and 12" wide. It has deep to light purple-blue flowers that bloom in spring to early summer. The new foliage is reddish and bronze-tinged.

Problems & Pests

Problems with scale insects are possible, as are fungal problems such as downy and powdery mildew, rust, leaf smut and root rot.

Speedwells often attract hummingbirds, butterflies and bees to the garden.

Spiderwort

Tradescantia

Height: 12–24" **Spread:** 18–24" **Flower color:** purple, blue, pink, red, white
Blooms: early summer to fall **Zones:** 3–9

HERE'S AN OUT-OF-THE-ORDINARY, EAGER-TO-PLEASE WOODLAND
sprite that possesses graceful form and a wide range of colors in bloom.
Flowers last only one day, but they are borne with great abundance across
the season and drop neatly without deadheading. Spiderwort tolerates a
wide range of soil types, and it doesn't seem to distinguish between sunny
spots and those in partial shade, which makes it a low-maintenance favorite.

Planting

Seeding: Not recommended

Planting out: Spring or fall

Spacing: 18–24"

Growing

Spiderwort grows equally well in **full sun** or **partial shade**. Spiderwort grows easily in **average, well-drained, moist** soils. Spiderwort tolerates poor soil, drainage and light and still flowers for the better part of the summer. In fertile soil the plant becomes borderline invasive. Divide in spring or fall every four or so years.

After flowering has ceased and the leaves fade, cutting the plants back will produce a fresh flush of foliage and possibly a second round of blooms late in the season. Dead-heading is not required during the flowering flush.

Tips

Spiderwort does well in a well-watered border, and it looks very attractive next to a pond or other water feature, where the grassy foliage softens the sometimes unnatural edges of the pond. This plant is also attractive in a lightly shaded woodland or natural garden. Once established, spiderwort will grow almost anywhere.

Recommended

T. x *andersoniana* (*T. virginiana*, Andersoniana hybrids) forms a large clump of grassy foliage. Clusters of three-petaled flowers are produced on long stems. **'Charlotte'** has pink flowers. **'Isis'** has bright blue flowers. **'Purple Dome'** has dark purple flowers. **'Red Cloud'** has red flowers. **'Snowcap'** has white flowers.

Recent studies by botanists have found that Tradescantia *species do not naturally hybridize with each other; therefore* T. x andersoniana *is not considered by them to be a valid name. The botanists now think* T. virginiana, *a native to most of the eastern United States, is just a very variable species.*

Problems & Pests

Problems are rarely severe enough to warrant control. Aphids, spider mites, caterpillars, rot and leaf spot may afflict plants from time to time.

T. x *andersoniana* hybrid

Thyme

Thymus

Height: 2–18" **Spread:** 8–24" **Flower color:** purple, red, pink, white; plant grown mainly for foliage **Blooms:** late spring, summer **Zones:** 4–8

THYME WILL TELL EVERYONE ENTERING YOUR GARDEN THAT you're at the forefront of fashionable gardening trends, for this lovely petite perennial has left the herb jar and moved front and center as a highly valuable ornamental plant. If you need marvelous foliage for a small space, *T.* x *citriodorus* is your plant; *T. serpyllum* is a great choice for the gaps between flagstones in pathways and patios. Most varieties are gorgeous in bloom, proving that even in the plant word, less can be more.

Planting

Seeding: Many popular hybrids, particularly those with variegated leaves, cannot be grown from seed. Common thyme and mother of thyme can be started from seed. Start indoors in early spring.

Planting out: Spring

Spacing: 16–20"

Growing

Thyme prefers **full sun.** The soil should be **average or poor** and very **well drained;** it helps to work leaf mold into it. Divide plants in spring.

It is easy to propagate thyme cultivars that cannot be started from seed. As the plant grows outwards, the branches touch the ground and send out new roots. These rooted stems may be removed and grown in pots to be planted out the following spring. Unrooted stem cuttings may be taken in early spring, before flowering.

T. pseudolanguinosus

This large genus has species throughout the world that were used in various ways in several cultures. Ancient Egyptians used it in embalming, the Greeks added it to baths and the Romans purified their rooms with it.

T. x citriodorus cultivar

Tips

Thymes are useful plants for sunny, dry locations at the front of borders, between or beside paving stones and on rock gardens and rock walls.

Once the plants have finished flowering, it is a good idea to shear them back by about half to encourage new growth and prevent the plants from becoming too woody.

Recommended

T. x *citriodorus* (lemon-scented thyme) forms a mound 12" tall and 10" wide. The foliage smells of lemon, and the flowers are pale pink. The cultivars are more ornamental. 'Aureus' has golden yellow variegated leaves. 'Silver Queen' has cream to dull silver variegated foliage.

T. x *citriodorus* cultivar

T. serpyllum

T. Coccineus Group include creeping thymes that have red-purple to crimson flowers with darker centers and small, oval to rounded, dark green foliage. Plants grow 3–5" tall and 12" wide or more. Included in this group are 'Atropurpureus,' 'Purpurteppich,' 'Purple Beauty' and 'Red Elf.'

T. praecox is a creeping, mat-forming plant with dark green foliage, growing 2–4" tall and 18–24" wide or more. Mauve to dark purple flowers bloom in summer.

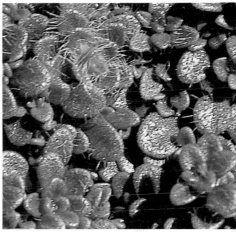

T. pseudolanguinosus

T. pseudolanguinosus (woolly thyme) is a mat-forming plant up to 3" high and 8–10" in spread, with fuzzy, gray-green leaves. It bears pink or purplish flowers in summer.

In the Middle Ages, it was believed that drinking a thyme infusion would enable one to see fairies.

T. serpyllum (mother of thyme, creeping thyme, wild thyme) is a popular low-growing species. It usually grows about 5" tall and spreads 12" or more. The flowers are purple. There are many cultivars available. 'Snowdrift' has white flowers.

T. vulgaris

T. vulgaris (common thyme) forms a bushy mound of dark green leaves. The flowers may be purple, pink or white. It usually grows about 12–18" tall and spreads about 16". '**Compactus**' grows 4–6" tall producing gray-tinged, pale green foliage and pale lilac flowers. '**Silver Posie**' is a good cultivar with pale pink flowers and silver-edged leaves.

Problems & Pests

Thyme plants rarely have problems. Seedlings may suffer from damping off, and plants may get gray mold or root rot. Good circulation and adequate drainage are good ways to avoid these problems.

Turtlehead

Chelone

Height: 16–36" **Spread:** 18–24" **Flower color:** pink, purple, white
Blooms: mid-summer to fall **Zones:** 3–7

TO THE LIST OF UNDERUSED, EXTREMELY WORTHY PERENNIALS,
let's add *Chelone*, an exceedingly easy-to-grow North American native plant.
Chelone's primary assets are its glossy, dark green foliage, lovely clusters of
softly colored, rounded flowers and the fact that flowering begins in August
and can extend well into September, when fresh new bloom is needed most.
Because it is a moisture-lover, you may spot 'Alba' growing in wild, boggy
areas of Minnesota and Wisconsin.

Planting

Seeding: Indoors in January, outdoors in late spring; soil temperature
should be 59°–68° F

Planting out: Spring

Spacing: 18"

Growing

Turtlehead grows best in **partial shade** or **full sun**. The soil should be **fertile, humus rich, moist** and **well drained**, but this plant tolerates clay soil and boggy conditions. Plants may become weak and floppy in too shaded a spot, so pinch tips in spring to encourage bushy growth.

Divide plants in spring or fall. They can be propagated from stem cuttings taken in early summer.

Tips

Turtlehead can be used in a pondside or streamside planting. It also does well in a bog garden or in a moist part of the garden where plants requiring better drainage won't grow.

Recommended

C. lyonii (pink turtlehead) is an erect plant with square stems. This popular species is almost identical to *C. obliqua*, except that the flowers are a slightly darker pink, blooming from late summer to fall. *C. lyonii* is more commonly grown and possibly the more adaptable species.

C. obliqua (rose turtlehead) is an upright plant that grows 16–36" tall and 18–24" wide, forming a dense mound of foliage. From late summer to fall, the plants bear pink or purple flowers. 'Alba' (*C. glabra*) bears white flowers slightly earlier than the species.

Problems & Pests

Rare problems with powdery mildew, rust and fungal leaf spot can occur.

C. lyonii

The common name of this plant is derived from the fact that the flowers resemble turtle's heads with their mouths open.

C. obliqua

Vinca
Myrtle, Periwinkle
Vinca

Height: 4–8" **Spread:** indefinite **Flower color:** blue, purple, white
Blooms: summer, fall **Zones:** 4–9

VINCA IS A PLANT THAT MAKES YOU LOOK LIKE
a savvy garden designer—I've never planted it where
it didn't combine perfectly with surrounding
plants. It is an extremely low-growing groundcover, with dark green, glossy leaves that
quickly form a dense mat. Because vinca is
extremely shallow-rooted, there's no
harm in letting it roam freely throughout the shade garden.

Planting
Seeding: Not recommended
Planting out: Spring or fall
Spacing: 24–36"

Growing

Grow vinca in **partial to full shade**.
It will grow in **any type of soil** as
long as it is not too dry. The plants
turn yellow if the soil is too dry or
the sun too hot. Divide vinca in
early spring or mid- to late fall,
whenever it becomes overgrown.
One plant can cover almost any area.

After planting, mulch the soil surface with shredded leaves and compost to prevent weeds from
sprouting among the groundcover.
The mulch will also help keep the
soil moist to hasten vinca's estab-
lishment and encourage it to fill in
quickly.

Tips

Vinca is a useful and attractive
groundcover in a shrub border,
under trees or on a shady bank, and
it prevents soil erosion. Vinca is
shallow-rooted and able to outcompete weeds but won't interfere with
deeper-rooted shrubs.

If vinca begins to outgrow its space,
shear it back hard in early spring. If
the sheared-off ends have rooted
along the stems, these cuttings may
be potted and given away as gifts or
may be introduced to new areas of
the garden.

Recommended

V. minor (lesser periwinkle) forms a
low, loose mat of trailing stems.
Purple or blue flowers are borne in
a flush in spring and sporadically all
summer and into fall. '**Alba**' bears
white flowers. '**Atropurpurea**' bears
reddish purple flowers.

*The glossy green foliage of vinca
remains attractive and cooling in
the heat of summer, long after the
early flush of flowers has
finished.*

V. minor (photos this page)

Wild Ginger

Asarum

Height: 3–6" **Spread:** 12" or more **Flower color:** burgundy or green, incon-spicuous; plant grown for foliage **Blooms:** early summer **Zones:** 4–8

IT'S ODD THAT MORE NORTHERN GARDENERS DON'T GROW THIS trouble-free, native groundcover. Everyone who visits my garden asks me what it is, so it certainly does the job of adding interest to shady areas. We grow wild ginger for its big, heart-shaped leaves that are produced in such numbers that weeds never stand a chance. The flowers of this plant are noth-ing short of ugly, but by a neat bit of nature's design, they remain unseen under the foliage.

Planting
Seeding: Not recommended

Planting out: Spring or fall

Spacing: 12"

Growing

Wild gingers need **full shade** or **partial shade.** The soil should be **moist** and **humus rich.** All *Asarum* species prefer **acidic** soils, but *A. canadense* will tolerate alkaline conditions. Wild gingers tolerate dry conditions for a while in good shade, but prolonged drought will eventually cause the plants to wilt and die back. Division is unlikely to be necessary, except to propagate more plants.

Tips

Use wild gingers in a shady rock garden, border or woodland garden.

The thick, fleshy rhizomes grow along the soil or just under it, and pairs of leaves grow up from the rhizomes. Cuttings can be made by removing sections of rhizome with leaves growing from them and planting each section separately. When taking cuttings, you must be careful not to damage the tiny, thread-like roots that grow from the stem below the point where the leaves attach.

Recommended

A. canadense (Canada wild ginger) is native to eastern North America. The heart-shaped leaves are slightly hairy.

A. europaeum (European wild ginger) is a European native with very glossy leaves, quite often distinctively silver-veined. It is the quickest species to spread over an area. This species is not as heat tolerant as *A. canadense.*

A. canadense (photos this page)

The heart-shaped leaves can be tucked into simple flower arrangements.

Yarrow

Achillea

Height: 1–5' **Spread:** 12–36" **Flower color:** white, yellow, red, orange, pink, purple **Blooms:** early summer to fall **Zones:** 3–9

YARROWS ARE EXCEPTIONAL PERENNIALS, AND THERE IS NO sunny garden where they should not be found. Their fern-like foliage gives the eye a much-needed break from the usual oblong, rounded leaves hanging off most plants, while their rounded, horizontal clusters of flowers give a look mimicked by few other plants. Combine yellow- and gold-flowering varieties with *Veronica*, *Nepeta*, *Perovskia* and other blue bloomers. Plant a few where they lean over into pathways; yarrows release a pleasant fragrance when brushed by a pantleg.

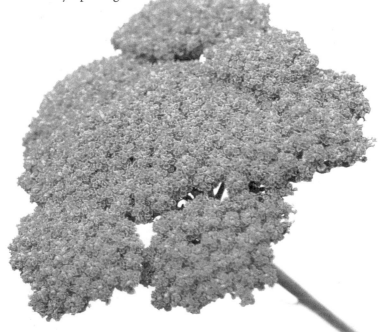

Planting

Seeding: Direct sow in spring. Don't cover seeds; they need light to germinate.

Planting out: Spring

Spacing: 12–24"

Growing

Yarrows grow best in **full sun**. They do well in an **average to sandy** soil that is **well drained**. These plants tolerate drought and poor soil but do not do well in a heavy, wet soil or in very humid conditions. Excessively rich soil or too much nitrogen results in weak, floppy growth. Good drainage is the key to the survival of these plants. *A. millefolium* and *A. filipendula* often needs staking. Divide every two or three years in spring.

Once the flowerheads begin to fade, cut them back to the lateral buds; yarrows will flower more profusely and longer. Basal foliage should be left in place over the winter and tidied up in spring.

A. 'Moonshine'

Yarrows have blood-coagulating properties that were recognized by the ancient Greeks. Achillea *is named after the legendary Achilles, because during the battle of Troy he is said to have treated his warriors' wounds with this herb.*

A. millefolium

A. *millefolium* cultivar
A. 'Moonshine'

Tips

Yarrows are informal plants. Cottage gardens, wildflower gardens and mixed borders are perfect places to grow yarrows. These plants thrive in hot, dry locations where nothing else will grow.

Yarrow plants make excellent groundcovers, despite being quite tall. The plants send up shoots and flowers from a low basal point, and they may be mowed periodically without excessive damage to the plant. Mower blades should be kept at least 4" high. Keep in mind that you are mowing off the flowerheads. Do not mow more often than once a month, or you will have short yarrow with no flowers!

Yarrows are used in fresh or dried arrangements. Pick flowerheads only after pollen is visible, or they will die very quickly once cut.

Recommended

A. **'Coronation Gold'** has bright golden yellow flowers and fern-like foliage. It grows about 36" tall, with a 12" spread. This plant is quite heat tolerant.

A. filipendulina has yellow flowers and grows up to 4' tall. It has been used to develop several hybrids and cultivars. Cultivars come in various heights, with flowers in shades of yellow. '**Cloth of Gold**' grows to 5' tall and has flat clusters of deep, golden yellow flowers. '**Gold Plate**' has slightly domed flowerheads up to 6" across.

A. **Galaxy hybrids** are crosses between *A. millefolium* and *A.* 'Taygetea,' a clump-forming garden hybrid that grows 24" tall and bears lemon yellow flowers in large clusters. Galaxy hybrids have sturdy stems, growing 12–36" tall, and large flower clusters, 4–6" across, in a wide range of colors including cream, yellow, salmon, orange, mauve, pink, red and white.

A. millefolium (common yarrow) grows 12–36" tall, with an equal spread, and has white flowers. The foliage is soft and very finely divided. Because it is quite aggressive, the species is almost never grown in favor of the many cultivars that have been developed. '**Cerise Queen**' has pinkish red flowers. '**Summer Pastels**' has flowers of many colors, including white, yellow, pink and purple. It is a very heat- and drought-tolerant cultivar and has fade-resistant flowers.

A. '**Moonshine**' bears bright yellow flowers all summer. The foliage is silvery gray. It grows 18–24" tall and spreads 12–24".

Problems & Pests

Rare problems with powdery mildew and stem rot are possible.

A. filipendulina 'Gold Plate'

The ancient Druids used yarrow to divine seasonal weather, and the ancient Chinese used the stems to foretell the future.

A. millefolium 'Summer Pastels'

Height Legend: Low: < 12" • Medium: 12–24" • Tall: > 24"

SPECIES by Common Name	COLOR								BLOOMING			HEIGHT		
	White	Pink	Red	Orange	Yellow	Blue	Purple	Foliage	Spring	Summer	Fall	Low	Medium	Tall
Ajuga	•	•				•	•	•	•	•		•		
Anemone	•	•			•	•	•		•	•	•		•	•
Artemisia	•				•			•		•	•		•	•
Aster	•	•	•			•	•			•	•	•	•	•
Astilbe	•	•	•				•		•	•		•	•	•
Baby's Breath	•	•					•			•	•	•	•	•
Balloon Flower	•	•				•				•				•
Bergenia	•	•	•				•		•				•	
Black-eyed Susan				•	•					•	•		•	•
Bleeding Heart	•	•	•						•	•		•	•	•
Boltonia	•	•					•			•	•			•
Brunnera						•			•				•	
Bugbane	•	•								•	•			•
Butterfly Weed	•	•	•	•	•		•		•	•	•		•	•
Campanula	•					•	•			•	•	•	•	•
Candytuft	•								•			•		
Cardinal Flower	•	•	•			•	•			•	•			•
Catmint	•	•				•	•		•	•		•	•	•
Chrysanthemum		•	•	•	•		•			•	•	•	•	•
Clematis	•	•	•		•	•	•			•			•	•
Columbine	•	•	•		•	•	•		•	•		•	•	•
Coneflower	•	•					•			•	•			•
Coreopsis		•		•	•					•		•	•	•
Cornflower	•	•				•	•		•	•			•	
Daylily		•	•	•	•		•			•			•	•
Delphinium	•	•			•	•	•		•	•		•	•	•
Euphorbia				•	•				•	•			•	•
Feverfew	•	•	•		•		•			•		•	•	•
Flax						•			•	•	•	•	•	

| LIGHT | | | | SOIL CONDITIONS | | | | | | USDA Zones | Page Number | SPECIES by Common Name |
Sun	Part Shade	Light Shade	Shade	Moist	Well Drained	Dry	Fertile	Average	Poor			
	•	•			•					3–8	70	Ajuga
	•	•		•			•	•		3–9	74	Anemone
•					•		•	•		3–8	78	Artemisia
•				•	•		•			3–8	82	Aster
	•	•		•	•		•			3–9	86	Astilbe
•								•		3–7	90	Baby's Breath
•	•			•	•		•	•		3–8	94	Balloon Flower
•	•			•	•		•	•		3–8	96	Bergenia
•	•				•			•		3–9	100	Black-eyed Susan
		•		•	•		•			3–9	102	Bleeding Heart
•				•	•		•			4–9	106	Boltonia
		•		•	•			•		3–8	108	Brunnera
	•	•		•			•			3–8	110	Bugbane
•				•	•		•	•	•	4–9	112	Butterfly Weed
•	•	•			•			•		3–7	114	Campanula
•				•	•			•	•	3–9	118	Candytuft
•	•	•		•			•			3–9	120	Cardinal Flower
•	•				•			•		3–8	124	Catmint
•				•	•		•			5–9	128	Chrysanthemum
•				•	•		•			3–8	132	Clematis
•	•			•	•		•			2–9	136	Columbine
	•				•		•	•		3–8	140	Coneflower
•					•			•		3–9	142	Coreopsis
•	•			•	•			•	•	3–8	146	Cornflower
•	•	•	•	•	•		•			2–9	148	Daylily
•				•	•		•			3–7	152	Delphinium
	•			•	•			•		4–9	156	Euphorbia
•					•					3–8	160	Feverfew
•	•				•			•		3–8	162	Flax

Height Legend: Low: < 12" • Medium: 12–24" • Tall: > 24"

SPECIES by Common Name	White	Pink	Red	Orange	Yellow	Blue	Purple	Foliage	Spring	Summer	Fall	Low	Medium	Tall
Foamflower	•	•							•			•		
Foxglove	•	•	•		•		•		•	•				•
Gaillardia			•		•					•	•		•	•
Gas Plant	•	•					•			•			•	•
Globe Flower				•	•				•	•			•	•
Globe Thistle						•	•			•				•
Goat's Beard	•									•		•	•	•
Goldenrod					•					•	•			•
Goutweed	•							•		•		•	•	
Hardy Geranium	•	•	•			•	•		•	•	•	•	•	•
Hens and Chicks	•		•		•	•	•	•		•		•		
Heuchera	•	•	•				•		•	•		•	•	•
Hollyhock	•	•	•		•		•			•	•			•
Hosta	•						•	•		•	•	•	•	•
Iris	•	•	•		•	•	•		•	•		•	•	•
Jacob's Ladder	•					•	•		•	•		•	•	•
Joe-Pye Weed	•	•				•	•			•	•			•
Jupiter's Beard	•	•	•							•				•
Lady's Mantle					•					•	•	•	•	
Lamb's Ears		•					•	•		•		•	•	
Lamium	•	•			•		•		•	•		•	•	
Liatris	•						•			•			•	•
Ligularia				•	•			•		•				•
Loosestrife	•				•				•	•			•	•
Lungwort	•	•	•			•	•	•	•			•	•	
Lupine	•	•	•		•	•				•			•	•
Lychnis	•		•	•						•				•
Mallow	•	•				•	•			•	•	•	•	•
Marguerite	•			•	•					•		•	•	•

LIGHT				SOIL CONDITIONS								SPECIES by Common Name
Sun	Part Shade	Light Shade	Shade	Moist	Well Drained	Dry	Fertile	Average	Poor	USDA Zones	Page Number	
	•	•	•	•				•		3–8	164	Foamflower
	•	•		•			•			3–8	166	Foxglove
•					•		•			3–10	170	Gaillardia
•					•			•	•	3–9	172	Gas Plant
	•			•			•			3–7	174	Globe Flower
•					•			•	•	3–8	176	Globe Thistle
	•	•	•	•			•			3–7	178	Goat's Beard
•					•			•	•	2–8	182	Goldenrod
•	•	•	•		•				•	3–8	184	Goutweed
•	•	•			•			•	•	3–8	186	Hardy Geranium
•	•				•			•	•	3–8	192	Hens and Chicks
	•	•		•	•		•	•		3–9	194	Heuchera
•					•			•		3–7	198	Hollyhock
	•	•		•	•		•			3–8	202	Hosta
•				•	•			•	•	3–10	208	Iris
	•	•		•	•		•			3–7	212	Jacob's Ladder
•				•			•			3–9	214	Joe-Pye Weed
•					•			•		4–8	218	Jupiter's Beard
	•	•		•	•			•		3–7	220	Lady's Mantle
•					•			•	•	3–8	224	Lamb's Ears
	•	•		•	•			•		3–8	226	Lamium
•					•			•		3–9	230	Liatris
	•	•		•				•		4–8	232	Ligularia
•	•			•	•		•			3–9	236	Loosestrife
	•	•	•	•	•		•			3–8	240	Lungwort
•				•	•			•	•	3–8	244	Lupine
•					•			•		3–8	248	Lychnis
•	•			•	•			•	•	4–9	250	Mallow
•					•			•		3–7	254	Marguerite

Height Legend: Low: < 12" • Medium: 12–24" • Tall: > 24"

SPECIES by Common Name	White	Pink	Red	Orange	Yellow	Blue	Purple	Foliage	Spring	Summer	Fall	Low	Medium	Tall
Meadow Rue	•	•			•		•			•	•			•
Meadowsweet	•	•	•						•	•	•			•
Monarda		•	•							•				•
Monkshood	•					•	•			•				•
Obedient Plant	•	•					•			•	•		•	•
Oriental Poppy	•	•	•	•					•	•		•	•	•
Ox-eye				•	•					•	•			•
Pachysandra	•							•	•			•		
Pasqueflower	•		•			•	•		•			•		
Penstemon	•	•	•				•		•	•	•	•	•	•
Peony	•	•	•		•				•	•				•
Perennial Salvia	•	•				•	•		•	•	•		•	•
Phlox	•	•	•	•		•	•		•	•	•	•	•	•
Pincushion Flower	•	•				•	•			•	•		•	
Pinks	•	•	•				•		•	•		•	•	
Rose Mallow	•	•	•							•	•		•	•
Russian Sage						•	•			•	•			•
Sea Holly	•					•	•			•	•			•
Sedum	•	•	•		•			•		•	•	•	•	
Shasta Daisy	•									•	•	•	•	•
Solomon's Seal	•								•	•			•	•
Speedwell	•	•				•	•		•	•	•	•	•	•
Spiderwort	•	•	•			•	•			•	•		•	•
Thyme	•	•					•	•	•	•		•	•	
Turtlehead	•	•					•			•	•		•	•
Vinca	•					•	•		•	•	•	•		
Wild Ginger								•		•		•		
Yarrow	•	•	•	•	•		•			•	•	•	•	•

LIGHT				SOIL CONDITIONS								SPECIES by Common Name
Sun	Part Shade	Light Shade	Shade	Moist	Well Drained	Dry	Fertile	Average	Poor	USDA Zones	Page Number	
	•	•		•	•			•		3–8	256	Meadow Rue
	•	•		•			•			3–8	260	Meadowsweet
•	•	•		•	•			•		3–9	264	Monarda
	•	•		•				•	•	3–8	268	Monkshood
•				•				•	•	2–9	272	Obedient Plant
•					•			•	•	3–7	274	Oriental Poppy
•				•	•			•	•	2–9	276	Ox-eye
		•	•	•	•			•		4–9	278	Pachysandra
•	•				•			•		3–7	280	Pasqueflower
•					•			•	•	3–8	282	Penstemon
•				•	•		•			2–7	286	Peony
•					•			•		3–9	290	Perennial Salvia
•	•	•		•	•		•			3–8	294	Phlox
•					•			•		3–7	298	Pincushion Flower
•					•					3–9	300	Pinks
•				•	•			•		4–9	304	Rose Mallow
•					•			•	•	4–9	306	Russian Sage
•					•		•	•		2–8	308	Sea Holly
•					•			•		3–8	310	Sedum
•	•			•	•		•			4–9	314	Shasta Daisy
	•	•	•	•	•		•			4–8	316	Solomon's Seal
•				•	•			•		3–8	318	Speedwell
•	•			•	•			•		3–9	322	Spiderwort
•					•			•	•	4–8	324	Thyme
•	•			•	•		•			3–7	328	Turtlehead
	•	•	•	•						4–9	330	Vinca
	•	•	•	•				•		4–8	332	Wild Ginger
•					•			•		3–9	334	Yarrow

Glossary

Acid soil: soil with a pH lower than 7.0

Alkaline soil: soil with a pH higher than 7.0

Basal leaves: leaves that form from the crown

Basal rosette: a ring or rings of leaves growing from the crown of a plant at or near ground level; flowering stems of such plants grow separately from the crown

Crown: the part of a plant where the shoots join the roots, at or just below soil level

Cultivar: a *culti*vated (bred) plant *vari*ety with one or more distinct differences from the parent species, e.g., in flower color, leaf variegation or disease resistance

Damping off: fungal disease causing seedlings to rot at soil level and topple over

Deadhead: to remove spent flowers to maintain a neat appearance and encourage a longer blooming period

'Marshall's Delight': a hybrid of *Monarda didyma*

Direct sow: to plant seeds straight into the garden, in the location you want the plants to grow

Disbud: to remove some flowerbuds to improve the size or quality of the remaining ones

Dormancy: a period of plant inactivity, usually during winter or other unfavorable climatic conditions

Double flower: a flower with an unusually large number of petals, often caused by mutation of the stamens into petals

Genus: category of biological classification between the species and family levels; the first word in a scientific name indicates the genus, e.g., *Digitalis* in *Digitalis purpurea*

Hardy: capable of surviving unfavorable conditions, such as cold weather

Humus: decomposed or decomposing organic material in the soil

Hybrid: a plant resulting from natural or human-induced crossbreeding between varieties, species or genera; the hybrid expresses features of each parent plant

Invasive: able to spread aggressively from the planting site and outcompete other plants

Knot garden: a formal design, often used for herb gardens, in which low, clipped hedges are arranged in elaborate, knot-like patterns

Neutral soil: soil with a pH of 7.0

Node: the area on a stem from which a leaf or new shoot grows

Offset: a young plantlet that naturally sprouts around the base of the parent plant in some species

pH: a measure of acidity or alkalinity (the lower the pH, the higher the acidity); the pH of soil influences availability of nutrients for plants

Rhizome: a root-like, usually swollen stem that grows horizontally underground, and from which shoots and true roots emerge

Rootball: the root mass and surrounding soil of a container-grown plant or a plant dug out of the ground

Rosette: see Basal rosette

Self-seeding: reproducing by means of seeds without human assistance, so that new plants constantly replace those that die

Semi-hardy: a plant capable of surviving the climatic conditions of a given region if protected

Semi-double flower: a flower with petals that form two or three rings

Single flower: a flower with a single ring of typically four or five petals

Species: the original plant from which cultivars are derived; the fundamental unit of biological classification, indicated by a two-part scientific name, e.g., *Digitalis purpurea* (*purpurea* is the specific epithet)

Sport: an atypical plant or part of a plant that arises through mutation; some sports are horticulturally desirable and propagated as new cultivars

Subshrub: a perennial plant that is somewhat shrubby, with a woody basal stem; its upper parts are herbaceous and die back each year

Subspecies (subsp.): a naturally occurring, regional form of a species, often isolated from other subspecies but still potentially interfertile with them

Taproot: a root system consisting of one main vertical root with smaller roots branching from it

Tender: incapable of surviving the climatic conditions of a given region; requiring protection from frost or cold

True: describes the passing of desirable characteristics from the parent plant to seed-grown offspring; also called breeding true to type

Tuber: a swollen part of a rhizome or root, containing food stores for the plant

Variegation: describes foliage that has more than one color, often patched or striped or bearing differently colored leaf margins

Variety (var.): a naturally occurring variant of a species; below the level of subspecies in biological classification

Variegated cultivar of *Brunnera macrophylla*

Index

Page numbers in **bold** indicate main flower headings.

A

Achillea, **334–37**
  'Coronation Gold,' 336
  filipendulina, 337
    'Cloth of Gold,' 337
    'Gold Plate,' 337
  Galaxy hybrids, 337
  millefolium, 337
    'Cerise Queen,' 337
    'Summer Pastels,' 337
  'Moonshine,' 337
Aconitum, **268–71**
  Cammarum hybrids. *See*
    x *cammarum*
  x *cammarum,* 270
    'Bicolor,' 270
    'Bressingham Spire,' 270
  carmichaelii, 271
    'Arendsii,' 271
  napellus, 271
Aegopodium, **184–85**
  podagraria, 185
    'Variegatum,' 185
Ageratina altissima. See
  Eupatorium rugosum
Ajuga, **70–73**
Ajuga, **70–73**
  pyramidalis, 72
    'Metallica Crispa,' 72
  reptans, 72
    'Braunhertz,' 72
    'Bronze Heart.' *See*
      'Braunhertz'
    'Burgundy Glow,' 73
    'Caitlin's Giant,' 73
    'Jungle Beauty,' 73
    'Multicolor,' 73
    'Rainbow.' *See*
      'Multicolor'
    'Tricolor.' *See*
      'Multicolor'
    'Variegata,' 73
Alcea, **198–201**
  rosea, 201
    Chater's Double
      hybrids, 201
    'Nigra,' 201
    'Summer Carnival,' 201
Alchemilla, **220–23**
  erythropoda, 223
  mollis, 223
Alum root. *See* heuchera

Anemone, **74–77**
  Japanese, 76
  meadow, 76
  snowdrop, 76
Anemone, **74–77**
  canadensis, 76
  x *hybrida,* 76
    'Honorine Jobert,' 76
    'Königin Charlotte,' 76
    'Pamina,' 76
    'Queen Charlotte.' *See*
      'Königin Charlotte'
    'Whirlwind,' 76
  pulsatilla. See *Pulsatilla*
    vulgaris
  sylvestris, 76
  tomentosa, 77
    'Robustissima,' 77
Anthemis, **254–55**
  tinctoria, 255
    'Beauty of Grallach,' 255
    'E.C. Buxton,' 255
    'Grallach Gold,' 255
    'Moonlight,' 255
Aquilegia, **136–39**
  alpina, 138
  caerulea, 138
  canadensis, 138
  chrysantha, 138
    'Yellow Queen,' 138
  x *cultorum.* See x *hybrida*
  x *hybrida,* 138
    'Double Pleat,' 138
    'Dragonfly,' 138
    'McKana Giants.' *See*
      McKana hybrids
    McKana hybrids, 139
  Songbird Series, 139
  vulgaris, 139
    'Nora Barlow,' 139
Artemisia, **78–81**
Artemisia, **78–81**
  absinthium, 80
    'Lambrook Silver,' 80
  lactiflora, 80
    'Guizhou,' 80
  ludoviciana, 80
    'Silver King,' 80
    'Silver Queen,' 80
    'Valerie Finnis,' 80
  schmidtiana, 80
    'Nana,' 81
  stelleriana, 81
    'Silver Brocade,' 81
Aruncus, **178–81**
  aethusifolius, 181

  dioicus, 181
    'Child of Two Worlds.'
      See 'Zweiweltkind'
    'Kneiffii,' 181
    'Zweiweltkind,' 181
Asarum, **332–33**
  canadense, 333
  europaeum, 333
Asclepias, **112–13**
  incarnata, 113
    'Cinderella,' 113
    'Ice Ballet,' 113
  syriaca, 113
  tuberosa, 113
    'Gay Butterflies,' 113
Aster, **82–85**
  bushy, 84
  calico, 85
  heath, 84
  New England, 85
  smooth, 85
Aster, **82–85**
  alpinus, 84
  dumosus, 84
    'Wood's Blue.' *See*
      'Wood's Light Blue'
    'Wood's Light Blue,' 84
    'Wood's Pink,' 84
    'Wood's Purple,' 84
  ericoides, 84
  x *frikartii,* 85
    'Mönch,' 85
  laevis, 85
    'Bluebird,' 85
  lateriflorus, 85
    'Lady in Black,' 85
    'Prince,' 85
  novae-angliae, 85
    'Alma Potschke,' 85
    'Hella Lacy,' 85
    'Purple Dome,' 85
Astilbe, **86–89**
  Chinese, 88
  Japanese, 89
Astilbe, **86–89**
  Arendsii Group. *See*
    x *arendsii*
  x *arendsii,* 88
    'Bressingham Beauty,' 88
    'Cattleya,' 88
    'Etna,' 88
    'Fanal,' 88
    'Weisse Gloria,' 88
  chinensis, 88
    'Pumilla,' 89
    'Veronica Klose,' 89

'Visions,' 89
japonica, 89
'Avalanche,' 89
'Deutschland,' 89
'Peach Blossom,' 89
simplicifolia, 89
'Hennie Graafland,' 89

B

Baby's breath, 90–93
Balloon flower, 94–95
Beard-tongue. See also
penstemon
large, 285
slender, 285
Bee balm. See also monarda
wild, 267
Bellflower. See also campanula
Carpathian, 116
clustered, 116
Dalmatian, 117
peach-leaved, 117
Serbian, 117
Bergamot. See monarda
Bergenia, 96–99
heart-leaved, 98
Bergenia, 96–99
'Abëndglut,' 98
'Bressingham White,' 98
cordifolia, 98
'Rotblum,' 98
'Evening Glow.' See
'Abëndglut'
'Winter Fairy Tale.' See
'Wintermärchen'
'Winter Glow.' See
'Winterglut'
'Winterglut,' 99
'Wintermärchen,' 99
Betony, woolly. See lamb's ears
Black-eyed Susan, 100–1
Blanket flower. See gaillardia
Blazing star. See also liatris
prairie. See snakeroot, button
royal. See gayfeather, rough
Bleeding heart, 102–5
common, 105
fringed, 104
Blue flag, 211
Bluet, mountain. See
cornflower
Boltonia, 106–7
Boltonia, 106–7
asteroides, 107
'Pink Beauty,' 107
'Snowbank,' 107
Boneset. See also Joe-Pye weed
common, 215
Brunnera, 108–9

Brunnera, 108–9
macrophylla, 109
'Dawson's White,' 109
'Hadspen Cream,' 109
'Langtrees,' 109
'Variegata.' See
'Dawson's White'
Bugbane, 110–11
Bugleweed. See ajuga
Bugloss, Siberian. See brunnera
Burning bush. See gas plant
Butterfly weed, 112–13

C

Campanula, 114–17
Campanula, 114–17
x 'Birch Hybrid,' 116
carpatica, 116
'Blue Clips,' 116
'Bressingham White,' 116
'Jewel,' 116
'White Clips,' 116
glomerata, 116
'Superba,' 116
persicifolia, 117
portenschlagiana, 117
poscharskyana, 117
rotundifolia, 117
Candytuft, 118–19
Cardinal flower, 120–23
blue. See lobelia, great blue
Catmint, 124–27
Centaurea, 146–47
montana, 147
'Alba,' 147
'Carnea,' 147
'Rosea.' See 'Carnea'
Centranthus, 218–19
ruber, 219
'Albus,' 219
Cheeses, 253
Chelone, 328–29
glabra. See obliqua 'Alba'
lyonii, 329
obliqua, 329
'Alba,' 329
Chrysanthemum, 128–31
Cimicifuga, 110–11
racemosa, 111
'Atropurpurea,' 111
simplex, 111
'Brunette,' 111
'White Pearl,' 111
Clematis, 132–35
ground, 134
Jackman, 134
solitary, 134
sweet autumn, 135
tube, 134

Clematis, 132–35
'Gravetye Beauty,' 134
heracleifolia, 134
var. davidiana, 134
integrifolia, 134
x jackmanii, 134
maximowicziana. See
terniflora
recta, 134
'Purpurea,' 134
tangutica, 135
terniflora, 135
Cohosh, black. See bugbane
Columbine, 136–39
Canada. See columbine, wild
common. See columbine,
European
European, 139
hybrid, 138
wild, 138
Coneflower, 140–41
cutleaf, 101
sweet, 101
Coral bells. See heuchera
Coreopsis, 142–45
lanceleaf, 144
large-flowered, 144
thread-leaf, 145
Coreopsis, 142–45
auriculata, 144
grandiflora, 144
'Early Sunrise,' 144
lanceolata, 144
rosea, 144
'American Dream,' 144
verticillata, 145
'Golden Showers,' 145
'Moonbeam,' 145
'Zagreb,' 145
Cornflower, 146–47
Cranesbill
bloodred. See cranesbill,
bloody
bloody, 191
dusky, 190
meadow, 191
scented. See geranium,
bigroot
Creeping Jenny, 239

D

Daisy, Marguerite. See
Marguerite
painted. See feverfew
Daylily, 148–51
Delphinium, 152–55
Delphinium, 152–55
x belladonna, 155
'Blue Bees,' 155

Delphinium (cont.)
  'Wendy,' 155
  grandiflorum, 155
  Pacific Giant Group, 155
Dendranthema, **128–31**
  'Mei-Kyo,' 130
  Morden Series, 130
  My Favorite Series, 130
  'Autumn Red,' 130
  Prophet Series, 130
  'Christine,' 130
  'Raquel,' 130
  'Stacy,' 130
  Rubellum Group, 131
  'Clara Curtis,' 131
  'Mary Stoker,' 131
  weyrichii, 131
  'Pink Bomb,' 131
  'White Bomb,' 131
Dianthus, **300–3**
  allwoodii, 302
  'Frosty Fire,' 302
  'Helen,' 302
  deltoides, 302
  'Brilliance.' *See* 'Brilliant'
  'Brilliancy.' *See* 'Brilliant'
  'Brilliant,' 302
  gratianopolitanus, 302
  'Bath's Pink,' 302
  'Feuerhexe,' 302
  'Firewitch.' *See*
    'Feuerhexe'
  'Mountain Mist,' 303
  'Tiny Rubies,' 303
  plumarius, 303
  'Doris,' 303
  'Sonata,' 303
  'Spring Beauty,' 303
Dicentra, **102–5**
  exima, 104
  'Snowdrift,' 104
  'King of Hearts,' 104
  'Luxuriant,' 105
  spectabilis, 105
  'Alba,' 105
Dictamnus, **172–73**
  albus, 173
  'Purpureus.' *See* var.
    purpureus
  var. *purpureus*, 173
  fraxinella. See *albus*
Digitalis, **166–69**
  grandiflora, 168
  x *mertonensis*, 168
  purpurea, 169
  'Alba,' 169
  'Apricot,' 169
  Excelsior hybrids, 169
  Foxy hybrids, 169

Dittany. *See* gas plant
Dragonhead, false. *See*
  obedient plant
Dropwort, 262

E
Echinacea. *See* coneflower
Echinacea, **140–41**
  purpurea, 141
  'Bright Star.' *See*
    'Leuchstern'
  'Leuchstern,' 141
  'Magnus,' 141
  'White Swan,' 141
Echinops, **176–77**
  ritro, 177
  'Vietch's Blue,' 177
Eryngium, **308–9**
  alpinum, 309
  amethystinum, 309
  yuccafolium, 309
Eryngo, blue-top. *See*
  sea holly, alpine
Eupatorium, **214–17**
  maculatum, 215
  'Gateway,' 215
  perfoliatum, 215
  purpureum, 216
  rugosum, 216
  'Chocolate,' 216
Euphorbia, **156–59**
Euphorbia, **156–59**
  corollata, 158
  dulcis, 159
  'Chameleon,' 159
  epithimoides. See
    polychroma
  polychroma, 159

F
Feverfew, **160–61**
Filipendula, **260–63**
  rubra, 262
  'Venusta,' 262
  ulmaria, 262
  'Aurea,' 262
  'Flore Pleno.' *See* 'Plena'
  'Plena,' 262
  vulgaris, 262
  'Flore Pleno.' *See* 'Plena'
  'Plena,' 262
Flax, **162–63**
Foamflower, **164–65**
Foxglove, **166–69**
  purple, 169
  strawberry, 168
  yellow, 168
Fraxinella. *See* gas plant

G
Gaillardia, **170–71**
Gaillardia, **170–71**
  x *grandiflora*, 171
  'Burgundy,' 171
  'Goblin.' *See* 'Kobold'
  'Kobold,' 171
Gas plant, **172–73**
Gayfeather. *See also* liatris
  Kansas. *See* snakeroot, button
  rough, 231
Geranium,
  bigroot, 190
  Cambridge, 188
  cranesbill. *See* geranium,
    hardy
  grayleaf, 188
  hardy, **186–91**
Geranium, **186–91**
  'Brookside,' 188
  cinereum, 188
  'Ballerina,' 189
  endressii, 189
  'Wargrave Pink,' 189
  himalayense, 189
  'Birch Double.' *See*
    'Plenum'
  'Plenum,' 190
  'Johnson's Blue,' 190
  macrorrhizum, 190
  'Bevan's Variety,' 190
  'Ingwersen's Variety,' 190
  x *oxonianum*, 190
  'A.T. Johnson,' 190
  'Claridge Druce,' 190
  phaeum, 190
  pratense, 191
  'Mrs. Kendall Clarke,' 191
  sanguineum, 191
  'Album,' 191
  'Alpenglow,' 191
  'John Elsley,' 191
  'Max Frei,' 191
  'New Hampshire
    Purple,' 191
  var. *striatum*, 191
Globe flower, **174–75**
  common, 175
  hybrid, 175
Globe thistle, **176–77**
Goat's beard, **178–81**
  common, 181
  dwarf Korean, 181
  giant. *See* goat's beard,
    common
Golden buttons. *See* tansy
Goldenrod, **182–83**
Goutweed, **184–85**

Groundsel, golden. *See*
   ligularia, bigleaf
Gypsophila, **90–93**
   paniculata, 92
      'Bristol Fairy,' 92
      'Fairy Perfect.' *See*
         'Perfecta'
      'Perfecta,' 92
      'Pink Fairy,' 92
      'Viette's Dwarf,' 93
   repens, 93
      'Rosea,' 93

H
Hardy geranium. *See*
   geranium, hardy
Harebell, Carpathian. *See*
   bellflower, Carpathian
Heliopsis, **276–77**
   helianthoides, 277
      'Ballerina,' 277
      'Incomparabilis,' 277
      'Sommersonne.' *See*
         'Summer Sun'
      'Summer Sun,' 277
Hemerocallis, **148–51**
   'Barbara Mitchell,' 150
   'Fairy Tale Pink,' 150
   'Happy Returns,' 151
   'Hyperion,' 151
   'Ice Carnival,' 151
   'Little Grapette,' 151
   'Pardon Me,' 151
   'Stella d'Oro,' 151
   'Strutter's Ball,' 151
Hens and chicks, **192–93**
Heuchera, **194–97**
Heuchera, **194–97**
   americana, 196
      'Ruby Veil,' 196
   Bressingham hybrids, 196
   x *brizioides*, 196
      'Coral Cloud,' 196
      'June Bride,' 196
      'Mt. St. Helens,' 196
      'Raspberry Regal,' 197
   micrantha, 197
      'Chocolate Ruffles,' 197
      var. *diversifolia* 'Palace
         Purple,' 197
      'Pewter Moon,' 197
   'Pewter Veil,' 197
   'Plum Pudding,' 197
   sanguinea, 197
      'Frosty,' 197
Hibiscus, hardy. *See*
   rose mallow
Hibiscus, **304–5**
   moscheutos, 305

'Blue River II,' 305
'Disco Belle,' 305
'Lord Baltimore,' 305
'Southern Belle,' 305
Hollyhock, **198–201**
Hosta, **202–7**
   fortune's, 205
   fragrant, 207
   Siebold's, 207
Hosta, **202–7**
   'August Moon,' 204
   'Blue Angel,' 204
   fortunei, 205
      'Aureomarginata,' 205
   'Francee,' 205
   'Golden Tiara,' 205
   'Gold Standard,' 205
   'Guacamole,' 205
   'Halcyon,' 205
   'Honeybells,' 206
   'June,' 206
   'Krossa Regal,' 206
   'Love Pat,' 206
   montana forma *aureomar-
      ginata*, 206
   'Patriot,' 206
   'Paul's Glory,' 206
   plantaginea, 207
      'Aphrodite,' 207
   'Regal Splendor,' 207
   'Royal Standard,' 207
   sieboldiana, 207
   'Sum & Substance,' 207
Houseleek
   cobweb, 193
   roof. *See* hens and chicks
Hylotelephium
   'Autumn Joy.' *See Sedum*
      'Autumn Joy'
   spectabile. See *Sedum*
      spectabile
   'Vera Jameson.' See *Sedum*
      'Vera Jameson'

I
Iberis, **118–19**
   sempervirens, 119
      'Autumn Snow,' 119
      'Little Gem,' 119
      'Snowflake,' 119
Iris, **208–11**
   bearded, 211
   Japanese, 210
   Siberian, 211
   wild. *See* blue flag
Iris, **208–11**
   ensata, 210
   germanica, 211
   Germanica Group. See

germanica
kaempferi. See *ensata*
siberica, 211
versicolor, 211

J
Jacob's ladder, **212–13**
   creeping, 213
Joe-Pye weed, **214–17**
   sweet, 216
Jupiter's beard, **218–19**

L
Lady's mantle, **220–23**
   common, 223
Lamb's ears, **224–25**
Lamiastrum galeobdolon. See
   Lamium galeobdolon
Lamium, **226–29**
Lamium, **226–29**
   galeobdolon, 228
      'Florentinum,' 228
      'Herman's Pride,' 228
      'Variegatum.' *See*
         'Florentinum'
   maculatum, 229
      'Anne Greenaway,' 229
      'Beacon Silver,' 229
      'Beedham's White,' 229
      'Chequers,' 229
      'White Nancy,' 229
Larkspur, candle. *See*
   delphinium
Leucanthemum, **314–15**
   x *superbum*, 315
      'Becky,' 315
      'Marconi,' 315
      'Snowcap,' 315
      'Thomas Killen,' 315
Liatris, **230–31**
Liatris, **230–31**
   aspera, 231
   punctata, 231
   pycnostachya, 231
      'Alba,' 231
   spicata, 231
      'Floristan Violet,' 231
      'Floristan White,' 231
      'Kobold,' 231
Ligularia, **232–35**
   bigleaf, 234
   narrow-spiked, 235
   Shevalski's, 234
Ligularia, **232–35**
   dentata, 234
      'Desdemona,' 234
      'Othello,' 234
   przewalskii, 234

Ligularia (cont.)
  stenocephala, 235
    'The Rocket,' 235
Linum, **162–63**
  perenne, 163
    'Blau Saphyr.' *See*
      'Sapphire'
    'Blue Sapphire.' *See*
      'Sapphire'
    'Diamant.' *See*
      'Diamond'
    'Diamond,' 163
    'Nanum Saphyr.' *See*
      'Nanum'
    'Nanum,' 163
    'Sapphire,' 163
    'White Diamond.' *See*
      'Diamond'
Lobelia,
  great blue, 123
Lobelia, **120–23**
  cardinalis, 122
    'Alba,' 122
    'Purple Towers,' 122
    'Ruby Slippers,' 122
  siphilitica, 123
    var. *alba*, 123
Loosestrife, **236–39**
  fringed, 238
  garden. *See* loosestrife,
    yellow
  gooseneck, 238
  Japanese. *See* loosestrife,
    gooseneck
  yellow, 239
Lungwort, **240–43**
  blue, 242
  common, 242
  long-leaved, 242
  red, 242
Lupine, **244–47**
Lupinus, **244–47**
  Gallery hybrids, 247
  Russell hybrids, 247
Lychnis, **248–49**
Lychnis, **248–49**
  chalcedonica, 249
    'Alba,' 249
  coronaria, 249
    'Alba,' 249
    'Angel's Blush,' 249
    'Atrosanguinea,' 249
Lysimachia, **236–39**
  ciliata, 238
    'Firecracker,' 238
    'Purpurea.' *See*
      'Firecracker'
  clethroides, 238
  nummularia, 239

'Aurea,' 239
punctata, 239
  'Alexander,' 239

M
Mallow, **250–53**
  hollyhock, 252
  musk, 252
Maltese cross. *See* lychnis
Malva, **250–53**
  alcea, 252
    'Fastigiata,' 252
  moschata, 252
  sylvestris, 253
    'Bibor Felho,' 253
    'Braveheart,' 253
    'Primley Blue,' 253
    'Zebrina,' 253
Marguerite, **254–55**
Meadow rue, **256–59**
  columbine, 258
  dusty, 259
  Kyushu, 259
  lavender mist, 259
  Yunnan, 259
Meadowsweet, **260–63**
Milkweed
  common, 113
  swamp, 113
Monarda, **264–67**
Monarda, **264–67**
  didyma, 266
    'Beauty of Cobham,' 266
    'Blaustrumph,' 266
    'Blue Stocking.' *See*
      'Blaustrumph'
    'Gardenview Scarlet,' 267
    'Jacob Cline,' 267
    'Jacob Kline.' *See*
      'Jacob Cline'
    'Marshall's Delight,' 267
    'Panorama Mixed,' 267
    'Panorama Red Shades,'
      267
    'Raspberry Wine,' 267
  fistulosa, 267
Moneywort. *See* creeping
  Jenny
Monkshood, **268–71**
  azure, 271
  bicolor, 270
  common, 271
Mother of thyme, 327
Mourning widow. *See*
  cranesbill, dusky
Mugwort. *See also* artemisia
  white, 80
Mum. *See* chrysanthemum
Myrtle. *See* vinca

N
Nepeta, **124–27**
  x *faassenii*, 126
    'Blue Wonder,' 126
    'Dropmore,' 126
    'Snowflake,' 126
    'Walker's Low,' 127
  grandiflora 'Dawn to
    Dusk,' 127
  sibirica 'Souvenir d'Andre
    Chaudron,' 127
  subsessilis, 127
Nettle, dead. *See* lamium

O
Obedient plant, **272–73**
Oriental poppy, **274–75**
Ox-eye, **276–77**

P
Pachysandra, **278–79**
  Allegheny. *See* spurge,
    Allegheny
Pachysandra, **278–79**
  procumbens, 279
  terminalis, 279
    'Variegata,' 279
Paeonia, **286–89**
  lactiflora, 288
    'Bowl of Cream,' 288
    'Duchess de Nemours,'
      288
    'Kansas,' 289
    'Krinkled White,' 289
    'Miss America,' 289
    'Raspberry Sundae,' 289
    'Red Charm,' 289
    'Sara Bernhardt,' 289
    'Scarlet O'Hara,' 289
    'Seashell,' 289
  officinalis, 289
Papaver, **274–75**
  orientale, 275
    'Allegro,' 275
    'Black and White,' 275
    'Pizzicato,' 275
Pasqueflower, **280–81**
Penstemon, **282–85**
Penstemon, **282–85**
  barbatus, 284
    'Elfin Pink,' 284
    'Prairie Dusk,' 284
  digitalis, 284
    'Husker Red,' 285
  gracilis, 285
  grandiflorus, 285

Peony, 286–89
  Chinese. *See* peony,
    common garden
  common, 289
  common garden, 288
Perennial salvia, 290–93
Periwinkle. *See also* vinca
  lesser, 331
Perovskia, 306–7
  atriplicifolia, 307
    'Filigran,' 307
    'Longin,' 307
Phlox, 294–97
  creeping, 297
  early, 296
  garden, 296
  moss, 297
Phlox, 294–97
  maculata, 296
    'Delta,' 296
    'Omega,' 296
    'Rosalinde,' 296
  Maculata Group. *See*
    maculata
  paniculata, 296
    'Crème de Menthe,' 296
    'David,' 296
    'Eva Cullum,' 296
    'Franz Shubert,' 296
    'Katherine,' 296
    'Laura,' 296
    'Starfire,' 296
  Paniculata Group. *See*
    paniculata
  stolonifera, 297
  subulata, 297
    'Candy Stripe,' 297
Physostegia, 272–73
  virginiana, 273
    'Bouquet Rose,' 273
    'Summer Snow,' 273
    'Variegata,' 273
    'Vivid,' 273
Pincushion flower, 298–99
Pink,
  cheddar, 302
  cottage, 303
  maiden, 302
Pinks, 300–3
  allwood, 302
  moss. *See* phlox, moss
Plantain lily. *See* hosta
Platycodon, 94–95
  grandiflorus, 95
    'Albus,' 95
    'Double Blue,' 95
    'Shell Pink,' 95
Poison flag. *See* blue flag

Polemonium, 212–13
  caeruleum, 213
    'Album,' 213
    'Apricot Delight,' 213
    'Brise d'Anjou,' 213
  reptans, 213
Polygonatum, 316–17
  biflorum, 317
  canaliculatum. *See*
    biflorum
  hirtum, 317
  odoratum, 317
    'Variegatum,' 317
Pulmonaria, 240–43
  angustifolia, 242
    'Ice Ballet,' 242
  longifolia, 242
    'Bertram Anderson.' *See*
      'E.B. Anderson'
    'Diana Clare,' 242
    'E.B. Anderson,' 242
    'Majeste,' 242
  montana, 242
    'Redstart,' 242
  officinalis, 242
    'Cambridge Blue,' 243
    'Raspberry Splash,' 243
    'Roy Davidson,' 243
  rubra. See *montana*
  saccharata, 243
    'Janet Fisk,' 243
    'Mrs. Moon,' 243
    'Pierre's Pure Pink,' 243
Pulsatilla, 280–81
  vulgaris, 281
    'Alba,' 281
    var. *alba*. See 'Alba'
    'Rubra,' 281
Pyrethrum, 161

Q
Queen-of-the-meadow, 262
Queen-of-the-prairie, 262

R
Rattlesnake master, 309
Rose campion. *See* lychnis
Rose mallow, 304–5
Rudbeckia, 100–1
  fulgida, 101
  lanciniata, 101
    'Goldquelle,' 101
  nitida, 101
    'Autumn Sun.' *See*
      'Herbstsonne'
    'Herbstsonne,' 101
  subtomentosa, 101

  var. *sullivantii*
    'Goldsturm,' 101
Russian sage, 306–7

S
Sage. *See also* artemisia;
    perennial salvia
  Bethlehem, 243
  clary, 293
  common, 292
  silver. *See* sage, white
  white, 80
Salvia, 290–93
  nemorosa, 292
    'Lubeca,' 292
  officinalis, 292
    'Aurea.' *See* 'Icterina'
    'Bergarden.' *See*
      'Berggarten'
    'Berggarten,' 292
    'Icterina,' 293
    'Purpurea,' 293
    'Tricolor,' 293
  sclarea, 293
  x *superba*. See *nemorosa*
  x *sylvestris*, 293
    'May Night,' 293
    'Rose Queen,' 293
  verticillata 'Purple Rain,'
    293
Scabiosa, 298–99
  caucasica, 299
    'Fama,' 299
    Isaac House hybrids, 299
    'Perfecta Alba,' 299
  columbaria, 299
    'Butterfly Blue,' 299
    'Pink Mist,' 299
Scabious, small, 299
Sea holly, 308–9
  alpine, 309
  amethyst, 309
Sedum, 310–13
Sedum, 310–13
  acre, 312
    'Autumn Joy,' 312
    'Bertram Anderson,' 312
    'Matrona,' 312
    'Mohrchen,' 312
  spectabile, 312
    'Brilliant,' 312
    'Meteor,' 312
  spurium, 313
    'Red Carpet,' 313
    'Vera Jameson,' 313
Sempervivum, 192–93
  arachnoideum, 193
  tectorum, 193

'Atropurpureum,' 193
'Limelight,' 193
'Pacific Hawk,' 193
Shasta daisy, 314–15
Silvermound, 80
dwarf, 81
Snakeroot, 231
black. *See* bugbane
button, 231
white, 216
Snakeroot. *See* Joe-Pye weed
Snow on the mountain. *See*
goutweed
Solidago, 182–83
'Crown of Rays,' 183
'Golden Shower,' 183
Solomon's seal, 316–17
fragrant, 317
smooth, 317
Speedwell, 318–21
prostrate, 321
spike, 321
Spiderwort, 322–23
Spirea, false, 88
Spotted dog. *See* lungwort,
common
Spurge. *See also* pachysandra
Allegheny, 279
cushion. *See* euphorbia
flowering, 158
Japanese, 279
tramp's. *See* spurge,
flowering
wild. *See* spurge, flowering
Stachys, 224–25
byzantina, 225
'Big Ears,' 225
'Helen von Stein.' *See*
'Big Ears'
'Silver Carpet,' 225
lanata. See *byzantina*
Stonecrop. *See also* sedum
autumn joy, 312
gold moss, 312
showy, 312
two-row, 313
Sunflower,
false. *See* ox-eye
orange. *See* ox-eye
Sweet William, wild. *See*
phlox, early
Symphyotrichum. See *Aster*

T
Tanacetum, 160–61
coccineum, 161
'Brenda,' 161
'James Kelway,' 161
parthenium, 161

'Gold Ball,' 161
'Snowball,' 161
vulgare, 161
'Crispum,' 161
Tansy, 161
curly, 161
Thalictrum, 256–59
aquilegifolium, 258
'Purple Cloud.' *See*
'Thundercloud'
'Thundercloud,' 258
delvayi, 259
'Hewitt's Double,' 259
flavum subsp. *glaucum*, 259
kiusianum, 259
rochebruneanum
'Lavender Mist,' 259
Thoroughwort. *See* boneset,
common
Thyme, 324–27
common, 327
creeping. *See* mother of
thyme
lemon-scented, 326
wild. *See* mother of thyme
woolly, 327
Thymus, 324–27
'Atropurpureus.' *See*
Coccineus Group
x *citriodorus*, 326
'Aureus,' 326
'Silver Queen,' 326
Coccineus Group, 327
praecox, 327
pseudolanuginosus, 327
'Purple Beaty.' *See*
Coccineus Group
'Purpurteppich.' *See*
Coccineus Group
'Red Elf.' *See* Coccineus
Group
serpyllum, 327
'Snowdrift,' 327
vulgaris, 327
'Compactus,' 327
'Silver Posie,' 327
Tiarella, 164–65
cordifolia, 165
'Oakleaf,' 165
wherryi, 165
Tickseed. *See also* coreopsis
mouse-eared, 144
pink, 144
Tradescantia, 322–23
Andersonia hybrids. *See* x
andersoniana
x *andersoniana*, 323
'Charlotte,' 323
'Isis,' 323

'Purple Dome,' 323
'Red Cloud,' 323
'Snowcap,' 323
virginiana. See
x *andersoniana*
Trollius, 174–75
x *cultorum*, 175
'Earliest of All,' 175
'Orange Princess,' 175
europaeus, 175
'Superbus,' 175
Turtlehead, 328–29
pink, 329
rose, 329

V
Valerian, red. *See* Jupiter's
beard
Veronica. *See* speedwell
Veronica, 318–21
'Giles van Hees,' 320
'Goodness Grows,' 321
incana. See *spicata* subsp.
incana
prostrata, 321
spicata, 321
'Blue Charm,' 321
subsp. *incana*, 321
'Sunny Border Blue,' 321
'Waterperry Blue,' 321
Vinca, 330–31
Vinca, 330–31
minor, 331
'Alba,' 331
'Atropurpurea,' 331
Virgin's bower, 135

W
Wild ginger, 332–33
Canadian, 333
European, 333
Windflower. *See* anemone
Wormwood. *See also* artemisia
common, 80

Y
Yarrow, 334–37
common, 337
Yellow archangel. *See* lamium